AIDS and South Africa

D0708742

AIDS and South Africa: the Social Expression of a Pandemic

Edited by
Kyle D. Kauffman and David L. Lindauer

Department of Economics
Wellesley College
Wellesley, Massachusetts
USA

© Palgrave Macmillan Ltd 2004

All rights reserved. No reproduction, copy or transmission of this publication may be made without written permission.

No paragraph of this publication may be reproduced, copied or transmitted save with written permission or in accordance with the provisions of the Copyright, Designs and Patents Act 1988, or under the terms of any licence permitting limited copying issued by the Copyright Licensing Agency, 90 Tottenham Court Road, London W1T 4LP.

Any person who does any unauthorised act in relation to this publication may be liable to criminal prosecution and civil claims for damages.

The authors have asserted their rights to be identified as the authors of this work in accordance with the Copyright, Designs and Patents Act 1988.

First published 2004 by
PALGRAVE MACMILLAN
Houndmills, Basingstoke, Hampshire RG21 6XS and
175 Fifth Avenue, New York, N. Y. 10010
Companies and representatives throughout the world

PALGRAVE MACMILLAN is the global academic imprint of the Palgrave Macmillan division of St. Martin's Press, LLC and of Palgrave Macmillan Ltd.
Macmillan® is a registered trademark in the United States, United Kingdom and other countries. Palgrave is a registered trademark in the European Union and other countries.

ISBN 1-4039-1888-0 hardback
ISBN 1-4039-3256-5 paperback

This book is printed on paper suitable for recycling and made from fully managed and sustained forest sources.

A catalogue record for this book is available from the British Library.

Library of Congress Cataloging-in-Publication Data

AIDS and South Africa: the social expression of a pandemic / edited by Kyle D. Kauffman and David L. Lindauer.

p. cm.
Includes bibliographical references and index.
ISBN 1-4039-1888-0 (cloth) – ISBN 1-4039-3256-5 (pbk.)
1. AIDS (Disease)–South Africa. I. Kauffman, Kyle D., 1966- II. Lindauer, David L., 1952-
RA643.86.S6A337 2004
362.196'9792'00968–dc22

2003053656

1.

10   9   8   7   6   5   4   3   2   1
13   12   11   10   09   08   07   06   05   04

Printed and bound in Great Britain by
Antony Rowe Ltd, Chippenham and Eastbourne

In memory of

Benjy, Onica, Sifiso and Victoria

whose images appear in this volume and who are four of the over one million South Africans who already have died of AIDS

Contents

List of figures

List of tables

List of plates

Foreword

If we go back in time, some fifteen to twenty years, the major challenge facing the people of South Africa was apartheid. All of the problems we had, whether political, social or economic, were in some way tied to apartheid. Now imagine if, back then, someone could have told us about our future. We would have been told that in 1994 Nelson Mandela would become the freely elected President of South Africa. We would have been told that South Africa had achieved a peaceful transition to democratic rule and that a process of truth and reconciliation had accompanied this transition. Had I known all this, I would have believed that much of South Africa's suffering finally would have ended.

The end of apartheid was a historic and momentous moment in the life of South Africa. But our suffering has not ended. Just as we were bringing to a close a terrible chapter in our history, another crisis was just beginning. Back in the 1980s, in the midst of our struggle against apartheid, who could have foreseen that another tragedy, that of HIV/AIDS, was just starting to unfold? In the early 1980s the international medical community was only starting to understand this dangerous new disease and here in South Africa it was something we were totally unaware of.

Today we in South Africa know a great deal about this pandemic. In some ways, South Africans may know more about this disease and its devastating consequences on individuals and society than does any other nation in the world. We have over five million citizens who are HIV positive. We already have lost well over a million of our brothers and sisters to AIDS. We have over 600 000 AIDS orphans. And the end of this plague is still not in sight; the worst still lies ahead of us.

Previously, I have called HIV/AIDS 'the new apartheid'. It is our new enemy. It is the latest threat to our society and to our humanity. To defeat HIV/AIDS requires the same spirit, the same commitment, the same passion – the same compassion – we summoned in the fight to end apartheid. And just as we realized in our battle against apartheid, we cannot do this alone. We need to summon our own will but we also need the support of the rest of the world.

In many fundamental ways this volume reflects both the approach and the spirit needed to address the challenge of HIV/AIDS in South Africa. There will not be one solution to the AIDS pandemic. We need to fight this battle on many fronts. We need to understand the politics, both nationally and internationally, that have conditioned the thus far inadequate response to HIV/AIDS. We need to anticipate the economic consequences of the epidemic and to prepare for them. We need to understand individual behaviour, especially of our youth, that puts too many at risk. We need to promote the activism required for change. This volume addresses these critical elements. By bringing together scholars from South Africa and from the United States, it also recognizes that in the fight against HIV/AIDS we in South Africa are not alone. I believe that just as happened with apartheid, this coalition between South Africans and the international community will emerge victorious. HIV/AIDS can and will be defeated.

†Desmond M. Tutu, Archbishop Emeritus
July 2003
Cape Town

Preface

Edited books, such as the one you hold in your hands, come to life for a number of reasons. Some edited books bring together academic scholars to mull over vexing, interesting, and/or tough problems. Others are concerned with addressing an issue from a number of multidisciplinary angles. Whether because of the complexity of the problem or the varied nature of the inquiry, no one scholar could write the final product alone. Thus, the expertise of the many results in an overall work which is greater than the sum of its parts. In many fundamental ways this book fits these descriptions.

We are both economists by training (one an economic historian, the other a development economist) with a deep interest in issues that affect the economic and social condition of people in developing economies, be they contemporary or historical. We both are interested in the general issue of HIV/AIDS in South Africa: why are prevalence rates so high?; what will be the long term impact?; what can be done to stem the spread of the virus? One easily could argue that the HIV/AIDS pandemic is the prime development challenge facing South Africa today.

It is clear from looking at AIDS in South Africa, however, that one cannot simply study the economy here and now, and come to any reasonable conclusion or policy implication about the incidence, impact or response to the disease. To gain an understanding of the full social expression of this pandemic requires addressing economics, politics, history, culture, and so on. Without looking at the issues from a broad, multidisciplinary approach one could not hope to: (1) explain the factors leading South Africa to being the HIV/AIDS capital of the world; (2) understand the economic costs to firms, household and society of the pandemic; (3) recommend measures to prevent the spread of the virus and to treat the millions of South Africans already infected; or (4) learn lessons to prevent other countries from facing their own AIDS tragedies. The only possible way to study HIV/AIDS and South Africa is through a broad multidisciplinary approach.

In thinking about how best to pull together experts on South Africa's AIDS crisis, we decided to hold a two-day conference at Wellesley College, just outside of Boston, in April 2002. The conference brought together scholars and practitioners from South Africa to meet and discuss HIV/AIDS issues with American counterparts. The primary audience was Wellesley College students, faculty and staff as well as others from the surrounding academic community of Boston and Cambridge.

The conference had many components including the screening of Xoliswa Sithole's AIDS documentary, *Shouting Silent*, lectures, discussions and video-conferencing between Wellesley College and the University of Cape Town. This last element of the conference allowed many more South Africans to participate, including AIDS activists, people living with HIV/AIDS, and students from the University of Cape Town.

What, perhaps, was most gratifying (and indeed surprising) was the extent to which scholars from across the disciplines were able, willing and, indeed, excited to discuss HIV/AIDS across disciplinary divides. Throughout the conference speaker after speaker would refer to an earlier talk or discussion where a colleague from another discipline had discussed a certain aspect of the AIDS epidemic and how it had made them think differently about how their own field should think about the issue. There clearly was important value added in bringing together such a diverse and interesting group of individuals.

Beyond the formal participants, the large student attendance at the conference was gratifying. Not only did the students learn a great deal from the invited speakers, the conference got them talking about AIDS in South Africa amongst themselves. This encouraged increased student activism and participation in AIDS causes. A new student AIDS group, Student Global AIDS Campaign, was formed on our campus as a result of the conference and a number of students have pursued internships in South Africa through the financial support of Wellesley College to work on HIV/AIDS issues in NGOs.

Wellesley's mission is to educate women who will make a difference in the world. When Wellesley was founded over 125 years ago the world into which our students entered was Eurocentric and vastly different from the world they enter today. Wellesley's President, Diana Chapman Walsh, enthusiastically supported this overall project from its inception and shared our vision that increasing awareness within the Wellesley community of South Africa and of the AIDS pandemic was not only important, but part of the college's mission. Her support, both moral and financial, as well as her expertise in public health, has been invaluable.

The success of the conference motivated us to expand its reach by pulling together a volume based on the presentations of the various speakers. We would not have been able to do so without the financial support of various groups within our college. We were extremely honoured to receive funding from various departments and offices at Wellesley College including the Committee on Lectures and Cultural Events; Davis Fund for World Cultures; President's Office; Departments of Anthropology, Art, Economics, Education, History, Political Science and Sociology; Davis Museum and Cultural Center; Barnette Miller Fund; Luce Program in BioEthics; Office of Equal Opportunity; and Wellesley College Information Services. We also received financial support from the Carnegie Council on Ethics and International Affairs, and from Sonia and Jeffrey Sachs.

We especially would like to single out the Multicultural Education and Research Initiative (MERI) at Wellesley College and its director Nancy Genero. Nancy was a huge supporter of this volume and deserves our utmost gratitude for ensuring its success. She is a terrific administrator for MERI with a broad vision of what multiculturalism should entail.

A large number of individuals helped at various stages of this project. We especially wish to thank Nancy Dussault, Ying Ying Hou, Anne Manning, Craig Murphy, Mae Podesta, Rick Rawlins, Sharon Wong and Li Yu. The art exhibition that was mounted in conjunction with the conference, and which is represented and discussed in Chapter 6, would not have been possible without the tireless work of Jeremy Fowler, formerly the curator of education at the Davis Museum and Cultural Center at Wellesley College. The lion's share of our thanks, however, goes to our colleague, Patricia Sjostedt, whose steady hand and eye for detail was invaluable throughout this project, and indeed in any project either of us undertakes. She keeps us in line and makes everything happen as if it were effortless.

At Palgrave Macmillan, we had the good fortune to work with an exceptional editor, Amanda Watkins, and series editor, Timothy Shaw. Thanks to both of them for all the work they put into this project.

Kyle D. Kauffman
David L. Lindauer
Wellesley, Massachusetts
June 2003

Notes on the contributors

Claudia C. Bermudes Ribiero Da Cruz is a partner at the Consumer Insight Agency, a market research firm. Her research interest in HIV/AIDS arose while completing her master's thesis on youth and condom use practice in South Africa. Ms Cruz received her degree in social anthropology from the University of Cape Town.

Kyle D. Kauffman is Jaan Walther Whitehead Associate Professor of Critical Thought and Associate Professor of Economics at Wellesley College and Research Fellow at the W. E. B. DuBois Institute at Harvard University. He has also been affiliated with the London School of Economics and the University of Cape Town. Professor Kauffman's research interests include the role of institutions in long-run economic development. He has examined such issues in Africa, Europe and the United States.

Jeffrey D. Lewis is Economic Adviser in the International Trade Department and the Prospects Group at the World Bank. He is also a member of the UNAIDS Reference Group on the Economic Impact of AIDS. Dr Lewis previously worked as the World Bank's Lead Economist for South Africa, where he analysed South African growth prospects and the macro impact of HIV/AIDS. His research interests include economic modelling, exchange rate and trade policy, and stabilization and structural adjustment policies in developing economies.

David L. Lindauer is Professor of Economics at Wellesley College. He has also served as Faculty Associate of the Harvard Institute for International Development and as Consultant to the World Bank. Professor Lindauer's research concerns labour markets in developing countries. He has worked throughout East Asia and sub-Saharan Africa.

Marilyn Martin is Director of Art Collections for Iziko Museums of Cape Town, and a board member of the National Arts Council and the Forum for African Arts. Previously, she served as director of the South African National Gallery. Ms Martin has curated exhibitions on South African art in Africa, Europe and the US, and has published widely on the subject. She is committed to working on HIV/AIDS through the visual arts.

Howard Phillips is Associate Professor in the Department of Historical Studies, Faculty of Humanities, at the University of Cape Town. He also teaches in the Faculty of Health Sciences. His teaching and research are concerned with the social history of health, disease and medicine; epidemics in history; and HIV/AIDS and society in South Africa.

Jeffrey D. Sachs is the Director of the Earth Institute, Quetelet Professor of Sustainable Development, and Professor of Health Policy and Management at Columbia University. He is also Special Adviser to United Nations Secretary General Kofi Annan. Before coming to Columbia, Professor Sachs was Director of the Center for International Development and Galen L. Stone Professor of International Trade at Harvard University. His current research interests include health and economic development, economic geography and international financial markets. Professor Sachs has served as an economic adviser to governments in Africa, Asia, Eastern Europe and Latin America.

Sonia Ehrlich Sachs is a paediatrician interested in paediatric issues in developing countries, especially childhood malaria and AIDS orphans. Dr Sachs was a paediatrician at the Harvard University Health Services from 1987 to 2000, and completed an MPH in International Health at the Harvard School of Public Health in 2003.

Virginia van der Vliet is a social anthropologist. She taught in the African Studies Department at Rhodes University and in the Social Anthropology Department at the University of Cape Town. She is the author of *The Politics of AIDS* (1996) and currently edits the fortnightly newsbrief, *AIDSAlert*.

Cal Volks is Director of the HIV/AIDS Unit at the University of Cape Town. Previously, she worked for the AIDS Law Project and for Balisa. Her main areas of interest are HIV treatment education, peer education, the role of higher education institutions in HIV and AIDS, and evaluating HIV/AIDS interventions.

Diana Chapman Walsh is the President of Wellesley College. Before assuming the Wellesley presidency, she was Florence Sprague Norman and Laura Smart Norman Professor at the Harvard School of Public Health, where she chaired the Department of Health and Social Behavior. Her research included the analysis of social and cultural determinants of health and illness. President Walsh is also a member of the American Academy of Arts and Sciences.

Acknowledgements

An earlier version of Howard Phillips' chapter, 'HIV/AIDS in the Context of South Africa's Epidemic History' appeared in the *South African Historical Journal*, 45 (November 2001). We thank the journal and its coordinating editor, Greg Cuthbertson, for permission to reproduce the article.

The figures and tables that appear in Jeffrey Lewis' chapter, 'Assessing the Demographic and Economic Impact of HIV/AIDS', were drawn from a number of sources. We wish to thank a number of individuals and organizations for their permission to reproduce these exhibits. Specifically, we wish to thank UNAIDS/WHO for permission to reproduce the figure, 'HIV prevalence in adults in sub-Saharan Africa, 1986–2001' from 'HIV/AIDS in sub-Saharan Africa'; and Sydney Rosen and her colleagues at the Center for International Health and Development, Boston University School of Public Health for 'Distribution of the cost of an incident infection' from 'Investing in the Epidemic: the Cost of Aids to Businesses in Africa'. Jeffrey Lewis' chapter reproduces a number of figures and charts that originally appeared in articles from the *South African Journal of Economics*. We thank the journal and its managing editor for permission to reproduce: Figure 1 and Table 1 from C. Arndt and J. Lewis (2000), 'The Macro Implications of the HIV/AIDS Epidemic: a Preliminary Assessment', Vol. 58: 5; Figure 4 from R. Bonnel (2000), 'HIV/AIDS and Economic Growth: a Global Perspective', Vol. 58: 5; and Figure 6 from F. Booysen (2002), 'Financial Responses of Households in the Free State Province to HIV/AIDS-Related Morbidity and Mortality', Vol. 70: 7. We thank Frikkie Booysen and his colleagues at Bloemfontein: Centre for Health Systems Research & Development, University of the Free State, for permission to reproduce material from Figures 1 and 11 in 'The Socioeconomic Impact of HIV/AIDS on Households in South Africa: Pilot Study in Welkom and Qwaqwa, Free State Province'; the Health Systems Trust for permission to reproduce Figure 9 from *South African Health Review, 2000*; and the *Harvard Business Review* for material adapted from 'The AIDS "Tax"' S. Rosen et al. (2003), 'AIDS is your Business' (February).

The artwork that appears in the volume was reproduced with the permission of David Goldblatt for his untitled digital print and of Wellesley College for all the other images.

1
Too Poor to Stay Alive

Sonia Ehrlich Sachs and Jeffrey D. Sachs

A physician's observations

My observations on health issues in poor countries are from the point of view of a mother, a paediatrician and, in mid-life, a student of public health. I accompany Jeff often and we frequently take our kids to developing countries, and did so from when they were infants. Acquaintances often question the prudence of taking our children to countries with such high prevalence of diseases and low quality of medical care. But Jeff deflects such concerns by pointing at me, saying that he travels with his kids' paediatrician. This is my first and only, albeit unofficial, role in health issues in poor countries. So before I became interested in public health, I was in charge of my family's private health.

Over the years of travelling to poor countries, I have gotten the mother/doctor bit down to a science. I mean that quite literally. I keep up with the medical literature on infectious diseases. I read the CDC advisories of latest outbreaks and latest recommendations on travel precautions. Accordingly, to keep my family safe I have, over the years, shot them up with the following immunizations:

DPT booster
Polio booster
MMR boosters
Hepatitis A series of 2 shots
Hepatitis B series of 3 shots
Yellow Fever
Meningococcal vaccine every 3 years
Typhoid vaccine every 3 years
Malaria prophylaxis for each and every trip

So far, this list, which provides short-term protection for my family, already costs over $500 per person which, my in-house economist informs me, is above the average yearly income in sub-Saharan Africa and many other places in the world.

But, being a doting mother and an obsessively compulsive doctor, I do not stop at this expense. I always travel with the following medical paraphernalia and pharmacopoeia:

Insect repellant

Fansidar – in case we get malaria in spite of prophylaxis, since in a lot of places malaria is resistant to currently used anti-malarials

Ciprofloxacin – the antibiotic that became a household name in the Anthrax scare, but we use it for traveller's diarrhoea or, frankly, when one of us gets a fever and I do not know the cause (misusing the antibiotic in this case is better than going to some clinic, usually woefully understocked and understaffed)

Syringes and IV antibiotic in powder form

Lomotil

Antiseptic ointment

Antiseptic solutions – for hand cleansing since most bathrooms consist of a partitioned hole in the floor without plumbing and without hand-washing facilities.

When we stay in Africa, we drink only bottled or boiled water; we eat only cooked food. We adhere to the dictum: 'boil it, peel it or forget it'. Whenever we deviate from this mantra, we pay dearly for it, for about two days. Whenever one of us gets sick, I triage. Sometimes I take care of it; sometimes, as when it was an eye emergency, I made an international phone call to my colleague at a hospital in Boston; and when one of our children needed surgery, I practically had the surgery done via an international phone call.

So now, juxtapose this scenario of maternal care with that of my counterpart: a mother in Africa. My most recent experience in Africa was in January 2002. We went to a small village in Malawi, near Lilongwe. We sat on mats in the dusty centre of the village watching the village women give us a warm welcome consisting of singing while performing a dance, miming their chores in the fields. The villagers were mostly older women and their grandchildren. We became painfully aware of the missing generation. Each woman had a story about her dead husband, dead sons and dead daughters lost to AIDS. The grandmothers frequently had seven to nine children to take care of, feeding them millet picked up from the ground after the harvest, putting them to sleep on a dirt floor of a tiny hut. The women knew perfectly well what AIDS is and how you get it and yet, they told us, they were not in a position to prevent themselves from getting infected.

Among these women was a young mother with very few teeth who was cradling a limp, listless little boy in her lap. He seemed about one year old and felt hot to the touch when I stroked his cheek. By touching him I happened to put my finger on one of the most common scenarios in this part of the world. The interpreter told me the child had malaria. The previous day, the mother carried him for three hours to the government clinic, and waited for another three hours before she was seen for a few minutes by a nurse. The mother was told the child had malaria, but the clinic had run out of medicines so she was instructed to return in a few days to see whether they had been restocked. For all I know this little boy became one of the two million children under the age of five who die each year of this very treatable disease that burdens so disproportionately the families living in the tropics.

The households in these villages were too poor to buy the $6 insecticide-impregnated bed net which has been shown to reduce significantly the chances of getting malaria. The nets keep mosquitoes, which are the vectors of the malaria parasite, from biting people when they are asleep, and cause the mosquitoes to come into contact with insecticide so that they die before biting others. These mosquitoes bite mostly at night.

When I asked about the rusty pipe in the centre of the village, an older woman explained that the government had installed the water pipe, but as the village could not afford the service fees, the water has been shut off and the women and children walk two miles to fetch water in large plastic containers. She did not mention, but we knew, that the river is polluted with human and industrial waste.

While in Blantyre, we asked to be taken on medical rounds on the paediatric ward of the main hospital in Malawi. The pediatrician was in charge of 250 very sick children, usually filled three to a crib or a bed, with one nurse for 80 patients. They were all experienced health practitioners, but burdened by huge numbers of patients and deprived of any instruments of healing. More than half of the paediatric admissions to this hospital are children with severe malaria, and yet the day we were there the central pharmacy ran out of quinine, which is the main medication for malaria. A few of the children on this ward had cerebral malaria and were surely going to die. We walked past an infant dying of meningitis, dying only because the hospital pharmacy did not have the IV antibiotic necessary. Twenty per cent of the children were there to die of AIDS (and, by the way, 70 per cent of the in-patients on the adult ward were young men and women dying of AIDS, dying because they could not afford to pay the one dollar a day that would keep them alive with antiretroviral medicines).

This hospital, being the major hospital for the entire country, cannot afford screens on doors and windows to keep out mosquitoes, so many children get malaria while they are hospitalized for something else like diarrhoea, dehydration, malnutrition, surgery or AIDS. The TB wards, which are always full since it is an opportunistic disease to AIDS, usually have no real quarantine arrangement or UV lights so the disease can and does spread through the hospital.

We have been to hospitals without any running water. We have been to hospitals where they can afford electricity for only a few hours a day. We have been to hospitals that *can* afford electricity but the provision is so erratic that the inconsistent refrigeration leads to decreased efficacy of some drugs and decreased efficacy of childhood immunizations such as polio, which need consistently cold storage. We have been to hospitals where due to the lack of a respirator, surgery and recovery of a patient are done under laborious manual ventilation performed by a rotating crew of nurses and family members. We have been to a clinic in Tanzania that used biogas as the only source of power to boil water in order to wash medical paraphernalia and to sterilize instruments. The biogas was made by mixing human excrement and/or cow manure with water, collecting the methane that was emitted, and conducting it to a Bunsen burner. In all the clinics and hospitals we have been to in Africa, we see disposable syringes being routinely reused over and over again. And, by the way, I have never seen sheets on the wooden hospital beds.

I grew up in Czechoslovakia, in the beautiful capital city of Prague. As a child I vividly remember feeling sorry for the people living in the Czech countryside, in small rural villages, feeling very lucky and a bit superior that I was living in Prague, obviously the centre of the world. When I came to the US, I was shocked, offended and eventually humbled by the fact that most of my new American friends did not know where Prague is, or for that matter, where Czechoslovakia is. Now that I know that Boston is the center of the world, I wish that we would all be more aware of parts of the world that are not so fortunate as we are. I wish that we would be aware that there are parts of the world where a mother cannot spend $500 like I do to keep her child safe. We, those of us living in rich countries, have the means to help the poor get better education, better health and therefore better economic well-being. Personally, I would not blame people in developing countries for despising us for casually tolerating the huge disparity between the rich and the poor, a gap so large that the poor die of their poverty. That is why I am grateful that Jeff spends twenty-one hours a day advocating for this huge but voiceless mass of humanity, trying to get the poor out of the poverty trap and us into a more equitable and safe world.

An economist's observations

Sonia tells it straight and very accurately. She has been my teacher through all of this – of how to see and understand these very grim realities. Actually, it is enough to go once to a rural health post or to a hospital in Blantyre or, for that matter, to hospitals in dozens of countries around the world to understand how weird the world is right now. We live in a world where the rich are overflowing with money they don't know how to use, while the poor die by the millions each year of their poverty.

Every time that I have testified in Congress in the last few years, a Senator or Congressman has preceded me saying, 'Colleagues, I just took the first trip of my life to Africa and now I understand.' Actually, the problems are not subtle. One stares the fact of mass death in the eye if you open your eyes to see it. And it is not just mass death and suffering: it is also easily and readily preventable death and suffering if we simply cared to do something about it. And that is the very strange reality. The question for me for many years has been, 'How long can we obfuscate before we get to the straightforward facts?'

For years and years, the argument has been, 'It is not the money', as if the immunizations are free, as if the refrigerators are free, as if poor people cannot be saved with the same drugs and procedures that routinely save rich people. We are living with an iron law of economic arithmetic right now – of life and death in the world. Large parts of the impoverished world, as Sonia was describing, are simply too poor to stay alive.

Why they are so poor is because of many complex reasons. In some places, it is probably the simple fact of living in an environment in which one gets an average of 300 infective bites of malaria every year – causing children to die in vast numbers and their parents to compensate by having large numbers of children, creating a cycle of impoverishment, rapid rural population growth, and untreated disease. In other places, people are impoverished because they live in highland regions hundreds of miles from even regional markets, and perhaps thousands of miles from large international markets, so that no business would think to invest there. Elsewhere, there is too little education for long and sad historical as well as geographical reasons. And when the few people who are able to get an education leave, they leave behind large numbers of peasants living at subsistence, with soils that are increasingly fragile, with landscapes that are increasingly degraded and deforested, and with watershed areas that are increasingly vulnerable to flooding or soil nutrient loss, or landslides, or all of the above.

Or poverty can result from the terrible governance that often accompanies all of these other factors. But whatever it is that brought people to this miserable state – whether it is nature or nurture or politics or often some combination of those – a significant part of the world's population, perhaps 1–1.5 billion people, are in a state of absolute poverty in which the poor are too poor to stay alive. Moreover, they are too poor to achieve economic development, falling into what economists, in their formal models, call a poverty trap.

Absolute poverty is so extreme that there is no material surplus above the bare needs of survival. Saving is essentially impossible, because the meagre incomes have to be used entirely on simply staying alive. Governments do not function and do not provide 'public goods' such as education, health care, roads, public safety and the like. Public management does not work. The margin above subsistence often does not exist at all because hundreds of millions of people are physically degraded every day by undernourishment and by the immuno-suppression that comes with undernourishment. Diseases such as measles that would normally pass with a few days of illness become killer diseases instead.

So many countries, especially in sub-Saharan Africa, have fallen into a poverty trap. And despite all of the best hopes in those places, which I think are really there, the very poorest places in the world have gotten still poorer in the last generation. The approach of the rich countries, operating through multilateral institutions such as the International Monetary Fund, has been completely inadequate. If you need a vial of vaccine or you need that intravenous drug to stay alive, probably best to call for a doctor, not to call for the IMF! In many ways neither the multilateral agencies nor the donor community has even conceived, in the right way, what the real problems are, much less provided real solutions – especially since those solutions would require more money from the rich countries.

When I got into this business, I was told that many people are 'living on the edge of subsistence'. And what Sonia and I have seen now repeatedly is that the cliché is a myth. It is not that people are living on the edge of subsistence. They are dying in mass numbers, falling right over the edge by the millions, and they are not dying of greatly complicated conditions. They are dying because they are too poor to see a doctor or nurse who can provide them with a dose of quinine, at a few cents per dose, to treat them or their children of malaria. And thus, a mosquito bite becomes a killer of millions each year – estimated to be up to three million deaths – when virtually all of those deaths could be averted by straightforward treatments. And yet we have not faced up to these realities in the world. We have obfuscated them for years.

When the head of USAID for the Bush Administration came into office – he has done a little better now – he made some astounding opening comments about AIDS. He said, and I paraphrase, but accurately, that one cannot treat AIDS in Africa because people do not know how to tell time in Africa. He said something to the effect that, 'They know morning. They know afternoon. They know night. But they do not know Western time.'

In the hospital that Sonia and I went to in Blantyre, I will tell you about knowing the time. Sonia described it. It was probably the most horrendous site I have ever seen in my life, and the most shocking from the point of view of the simplicity of the issue that we are confronting.

On one side of the hall, across from the adult medical ward, was the outpatient clinic. There the antiretrovirals were being sold for one dollar a day. The doctors there were treating the patients with the triple combination coming from Cipla, the Indian generic drug producer, and the drugs were working fine. That is, of course, not a shock. We are all humans. We have the same biology. The drugs work in poor people as they work in rich people. The drugs work in Haiti where Sonia and I visited our astounding colleague Paul Farmer, who for eighteen years has been running a clinic in one of the poorest places in the world treating AIDS patients and keeping them alive. The drugs were working in Haiti, and they were working in Malawi.

Literally across the hall from the outpatient clinic and the drugs, was the medical ward. Virtually every medical ward in Africa is overrun with people dying from the AIDS pandemic. About 70 per cent of this hospital's admissions were HIV-related. The hospital ward that we saw had 160 beds. Yet on that day there were 450 patients.

What Sonia described in the paediatric ward was replicated in the adult ward – three adults to a bed. I had never seen anything like it. There were literally two people lying head to foot in the bed, and then a person lying on the ground underneath the bed – maybe on a piece of carboard, maybe not. And the room was filled with dying people. The doctors were there but they were not giving any drugs to these people. The drugs were across the hall. The people were dying in the medical ward on one side of the hall because they could not pay the one dollar a day on the other side of the hall. And this is the main hospital of the country.

Until about a decade ago, I somehow imagined that life-and-death issues like AIDS were really so serious that, of course, people in authority in our country and in the international agencies were looking after these great calamities. I kind of knew they were not looking after the exchange rates the right way, but I supposed that AIDS was another matter entirely. I thought that AIDS is something one does not fool around with. And, in truth, I did not think too much about the AIDS pandemic in Africa, especially when I was working in Central Europe and Latin America. I did not think too much about it at all because I was confident that it was being addressed with urgency. I heard all of the big speeches by presidents and heads of international agencies, saying that AIDS is the most important pandemic of modern history, and how we are doing this and that in response.

Then I started visiting Africa in the 1990s for the first time on a frequent, professional basis. In a project in Zambia, about eight of thirty counterparts died during three years of the project. These were central bank and finance ministry professionals. Of course I had to ask with rising urgency, 'What's really going on here?' I started to ask a few questions. Then I started to become a bit disturbed, because, I realized for the first time how systematically the rich world had been avoiding rather than addressing the real issues.

I would not have realized – I could not have imagined – that for five years, from 1996–2000, the World Bank did not manage to have one loan programme dedicated fully to AIDS in Africa. I just could not have even conceived that the World Bank would be unable to get itself organized to launch even one AIDS programme in the second half of the 1990s. Yes, it had little scraps here and there embedded in 'health sector loans', but no programmes in Africa dedicated to AIDS, and none even remotely at a scale that would be needed.

I increasingly started to dig deeper into the data about what the donors were really doing. It turned out they were not doing anything at all. It is just about fair to say – with only the tiniest of exaggeration – that the rich world was allowing this pandemic to run its 'natural course' in Africa during the first twenty years (1981 to the beginning of the new century), almost without any intervention at all. In the second half of the 1990s, the rich countries were spending about $70 million a year in Africa for a continent already with 20 million HIV-positive people at that point and millions more that had already died without any real help from anybody.

We have until today had around 65 million people infected, 25 million of whom have already died, and 40 million living with the virus, of whom 30 million are in Africa. Incredibly, there is not one single human being in Africa that has been put on antiretroviral drug therapy thanks to an official donor programme. Sixty-five million people need to depend on these antiretrovirals, yet until this year, neither the World Bank nor USAID nor other donor agencies had even sponsored one trial programme to see whether antiretrovirals would work in these settings. Not a single individual in the world was kept alive on these drugs as the result of a US foreign assistance programme. So this is a pandemic that has been almost running its natural course.

I thought for a while that maybe this is just the case with AIDS. But I discovered to my utter astonishment that life and death in poor countries was not so important as to be treated as a life-and-death issue by rich countries. Quite the contrary, I could not have imagined how incredibly cheap life was from the point of view of the rich countries. It is not just AIDS. It is malaria. It is tuberculosis. It is millions of people dying each year from conditions that are either easily preventable or readily treatable.

At the end of 1999, the head of the World Health Organization, Dr Gro Harlem Brundtland, one of the really magnificent leaders in this world, honoured me with an invitation to head a study of health and development issues, called the WHO Commission on Macroeconomics and Health. It was a remarkably eye-opening experience, not only for me, but for the more than 100 professionals that became involved. We met first and we had the typical argument. A lot of the official agencies said, 'Yeah, it is a terrible problem. If those countries would only take care of themselves better! Look at all that waste and corruption and misallocation of resources! Those countries are just not serious!'

There is indeed a lot of waste and corruption, so the hypothesis that the death and dying could be blamed on poor governance had at least a ring of truth to it. But we worked together for two years to actually look at the evidence. And the evidence really, overwhelmingly, is something very different. The evidence is that these people are too poor to stay alive, and that their governments are too poor to keep them alive. It is not primarily a matter of resource misallocation. It is not a matter of too much spending for the 'tertiary sector' (big hospitals) rather than the primary clinics. It is a matter of too little spending overall. The problem is not too many hospitals, but too few clinics.

The overwhelming lessons of our study were three things. First, if we do not take care of these pandemic diseases, economic development is not going to take place in these countries. The pervasive, pernicious economic effects of endemic malaria, TB, AIDS and the extraordinary levels of the other killer diseases do much damage to demographics, foreign investment, trade, migration and the like. Regions living under this incredible burden of disease can neither solve it by themselves nor expect that the natural process of economic growth will solve it because economic growth is not working. The economic engine is simply not turning.

Second, we confirmed something which is very well known, but important to reiterate. The reasons poor people die are not mysterious. There are a set number of specific conditions – identifiable, quantifiable and, in general, preventable and treatable. Sonia has already mentioned many of them: HIV/AIDS, malaria, tuberculosis and diarrhoeal disease, the last of which kills more than two million children every year. Two million children die of diarrhoea for lack of access to the right antibiotics or oral rehydration therapy. Three to four million die of acute respiratory infection for lack of antibiotics or other simple precautions.

Now, how about this? It is estimated that perhaps 2.9 million people in the world die each year from vaccine-preventable diseases. Vaccines often cost only a few cents a dose. As an amazing example, there are an estimated 900,000 deaths each year from measles in poor countries. This is incredible because almost no children die of measles in the rich countries anymore. Yet in the poor countries there are almost one million deaths from measles, another 400,000 or so from perinatal tetanus, and hundreds of thousands of deaths that could be averted by the Hep-B vaccine – standard fare in the rich countries and not even given in most poor countries. There are hundreds of thousands of deaths from hepatitis B, and many millions more to come since children in many poor countries are still not receiving the Hep-B vaccine. In this downward spiral of impoverishment and disease over the last twenty years, even the most basic immunization coverage for the standard package of diphtheria, pertussus, tetanus and the like, has gone down from highs of 80–90 per cent coverage to 50 per cent or lower coverage in many very poor countries.

And then there are the half a million mothers dying in childbirth every year because they do not have a skilled birth attendant with them, and especially because they lack access to emergency obstetrical care such as a C-section. The maternal mortality rate in the poorest countries is estimated to be around one thousand times the rate of the rich countries – a thousand times!

The third finding of our study was a big one. The average cost, pretty realistically estimated, of providing the essential health interventions to keep people alive would be about $40 per person in Africa. That is all. I shudder. It sounds a little too low. We spend around $4000 per capita in the United States for health. We know that a lot of that is end-of-life treatment. Basic health interventions are, fortunately, much cheaper.

But then comes the shocking paradox. The poorest countries cannot afford even $40 per capita. That is the iron law of economic arithmetic that I spoke of earlier. $40 per capita in Malawi is 20 per cent of the gross national product per capita, which is $200 per person per year. And part of that $200 is not even monetized because it includes the farm output in peasant households that is used for subsistence, rather than being sold in the market. So Malawi cannot afford $40 a year for health for each person.

The solution, therefore, is not what the World Bank tried for twenty years, when it advised poor countries to put on 'user fees' and other 'cost recovery' methods to fund the health sector. When a country is dying of poverty, it is possible to categorize things in different ways. You can impose user fees and then see the poor excluded because they cannot pay the user fees. You can make health care 'universally available' and then see the poor dying because the government cannot provide the services. You can cut the issue lots of different ways, but the iron law of poverty applies: $40 is too much for Malawi.

Lo and behold, when we looked at that together, including representatives of the IMF, the World Bank, donor countries and academia, and we argued and debated for two years, we finally reached a consensus. And the consensus was a little bit of a breakthrough, an epiphany. The consensus holds, 'We cannot blame the poorest countries for their deaths. We have to help with adequate levels of funding.'

We did a simple calculation. We started by assuming a need of around $40 per capita per year, adjusted slightly on a country-by-country basis. I say 'we', but the hard work was done at the London School of Hygiene and Tropical Medicine by a team led by Professor Anne Mills, a leading health economist. She and her team did a wonderful job.

We then got an understanding with the IMF and others. What could poor countries really afford? We agreed that what Malawi could afford was to invest an additional 1–2 per cent of its GNP in the health sector, but not more out of its own meagre resources (which need to be used also for food, clothing, shelter, roads, water and sanitation, education, and other basic needs). But if you are at $200 per capita, 1 per cent of your GNP is only another two dollars per person per year. Two per cent of GNP adds only four dollars per person per year. For Malawi to achieve $40 per person, starting at around $6 per person, and adding perhaps $4 per person out of its own revenues, would leave a gap of say $30 per person per year. And that gap could only be filled by the rich countries.

We added up the gaps across all of the poor countries and said, 'No more excuses.' That is the financing that needs to be mobilized to save millions of lives each year. That gap includes funding for antiretroviral therapy. It includes several billion dollars a year for prevention of AIDS transmission. It includes several billion dollars for treatment of the opportunistic infections that accompany HIV infection. And of course it includes funding for malaria, TB, immunizations, and other killer conditions mentioned earlier.

When we added it up, we found that the gap was about $25 billion a year. And while people might gasp at that amount, macroeconomists are very good at coming up with the right denominator. The right measure of our capacity to provide $25 billion per year in help for poor people to stay alive is our own income every year. The rich countries are now at $25 trillion per year of income. $25 trillion! So $25 billion is one-thousandth of the combined GNPs of the donor countries. What is a thousandth of an income? It means for every hundred dollars you earn, put aside a dime. One dime for every hundred dollars. If the whole rich world did it, this would yield the $25 billion. And that, according to our estimates, would translate into approximately eight million deaths averted each year.

With $25 billion dollars, you could have millions of people in poor countries on antiretroviral therapy. You could have insecticide-impregnated bed nets in the villages given away for free so that poor people would have them. You could get immunization coverage back up above the 80 per cent threshold which really gives a so-called population immunity (or 'herd immunity') needed to break the transmission of these epidemics. You could get oral rehydration therapy to local clinics. You could keep children alive from respiratory infections. You could have attended childbirths. That is what would be possible for one dime out of every hundred dollars of rich-country GNP.

I actually refuse to believe it is much more complicated than that. I know it is a little bit more complicated. I know well that we have to get the money effectively into use. We have to make sure that it reaches the wards, not just the paying side of the hospital but the other side as well. I know we have to find a way to give some of the money to the Christian mission hospitals, which in many rural areas in Africa treat perhaps one-third of the rural population. These mission hospitals often have excellent management. They just do not have money, so they use biogas rather than electricity. Without our help they are so impoverished that even the most basic things look impossibly distant to them. But a dime out of every hundred dollars would make a huge difference.

So, where are we on this? We need a few things to come together. We need the public to understand the basic arithmetic. I have yet to find in any place that I have spoken in this country or in Europe or in Japan, where someone has objected by saying 'You keep your hands off of my one dime per hundred dollars.' It just has not happened. It is not going to happen because there are such overwhelming reasons for us to help, from the point of view of our own humanity; our own international foreign policy needs; our concerns about the implications of fulminant diseases spreading across national borders; terrorism spreading into collapsed states; and the like. These parts of the calculations make sense to everybody when the facts are made clear.

We need an equal political commitment, of course, in the poor countries. Some people treat African governance as an undifferentiated disaster. Yes, there are terrible leaders, like Mr Mugabe in Zimbabwe, who are bringing their country to its knees. And yet, there are also many dedicated governments, which simply lack the financing that they need to solve urgent problems. Sub-Saharan Africa has forty-nine governments. Many of these forty-nine countries are already democratic, with committed though impoverished governments.

Leaders from these well-governed countries call me to tell me that their children or their foster children have died of AIDS. They are not blind to the reality that is engulfing their continent. There are many highly capable leaders of impoverished countries desperate for help, not in all poor countries, but certainly in many. Even in South Africa, where the national leadership has been extraordinarily harmful and obtuse on AIDS, regional governments and civil society have been in action and can be helped.

So, the will must be found in the rich countries. What about the way? The way involves two things: the money and the strategy. Kofi Annan, the United Nation's Secretary General, put it together brilliantly last year when he dazzled the world with an idea, a very good one. He said, 'Why don't we have a Global Fund to do this?' The beauty of this idea is twofold. First, the Global Fund allows us to watch who is putting money into the effort, and how much. Second, the Global Fund gives a post-office box, for the first time, for poor countries to submit their proposals. For the first time, these impoverished countries have a way to say to the world, 'We are ready to act. We need your help.'

So Kofi Annan launched the Global Fund. The United States was the first to sign on. President Bush took Kofi Annan and President Obasanjo of Nigeria to the Rose Garden and announced the United States would participate. He called on Americans to give 74 cents per American for the cause – in other words $200 million, roughly about a tenth of what we ought to be doing – but at least he got it started.

The Global Fund had its first meeting in January 2002. On 28 January the Global Fund invited proposals. They did a funny thing. It was like springing a surprise term paper: 'Due next week: forty pages.' They did not quite say that. What they said was, 'Your proposal has to be in by 10 March.' Poor countries asked, 'Can we have an extension, please?' The Global Fund said, 'No. First proposals: 10 March.'

So the poor countries had six weeks to prepare proposals. So desperate was the desire of these countries to get funding that 316 proposals went in from 50 countries. That is the good news. The bad news is there is not yet enough money to fund those proposals, and certainly not enough to fund them at the scale that they need. The Global Fund is going to have subsequent meetings. It is going to be a little bittersweet because, on the one side, a breakthrough may be underway. But, on the other side, many worthy proposals will be turned down or scaled back. We saw this close-up in the case of Malawi, where the donors told the government, 'Don't you dare ask for that much money.' The Malawians said, 'But we can do this.' The response, 'Don't you dare ask for that much money. We are not giving that much money away.'

So we are still in a transition between the falsehoods of high-flown rhetoric which leaves millions to die and the prospect for the first time in the twenty-one-year course of this pandemic that official money might start flowing at a scale needed to keep people alive. This is of great significance and tremendous promise.

Where will we go from here? As the cliché says, 'We are at a critical moment.' We really are. Can we find our voice, our strategy and, of course, our wallets to get the job done? Over twenty years of slumber we ignored AIDS among the poorest of the poor and the most voiceless of the voiceless in the world. When you are dying of your poverty, nobody can hear you at all. After twenty years of letting this mass death occur, we may be finding a new way.

The world's most important political leader, Bono, met with the second most important political leader, George Bush, at the White House and President Bush promised Bono that money would not stand in the way. If we who care, and those who have the expertise to point the way, can demonstrate what will work, can demonstrate the commitment, and the mechanisms and the seriousness, the President personally pledged that money will not be the obstacle to keeping people alive. I believe it is our urgent work ahead to hold him to his word, to get other political leaders to make the same commitment, and for us to get the job done.

Editor's postscript

The Global Fund to Fight AIDS, TB and Malaria was formally launched in January 2002. By May 2003 the Global Fund had completed two rounds of proposals and approved grants to 92 nations. Two years of initial financing for 153 proposals totalled $1.5 billion. Disbursements of $20 million had been made to 25 countries. Approximately 60 per cent of all approved grant dollars were directed at AIDS; 61 per cent of all grant dollars went to sub-Saharan Africa.

According to the Global Fund, 'local programs approved in Rounds 1 and 2 will support an unprecedented scale-up of HIV treatment. Over five years, an estimated 500,000 people will begin receiving antiretroviral treatment, representing a tripling of current coverage in poor countries (including a six-fold increase in Africa.) In Round 2 alone, an expected 500,000 children orphaned by AIDS will also receive support' (Global Fund, 2003).

Despite the successful launching of the Global Fund, money remains a problem. According to the United States Government Accounting Office, 'The Fund's ability to approve and finance additional grants is threatened by a lack of sufficient resources. The Fund currently does not have enough pledges to allow it to approve more than a small number of additional proposals in 2003. In addition, without significant new pledges, the Fund will be unable to support all of the already approved grants beyond their initial 2-year agreements' (Government Accounting Office, 2003, p. 32). Immediate financial constraints are the result, in part, of a gap between pledges and actual contributions.

On 27 May 2003 President Bush signed into law a $15 billion programme that he lauded as 'a great mission of rescue', intended to help prevent and treat AIDS in poor countries of Africa and the Caribbean that have been devastated by the pandemic. Although the law envisions $3 billion a year in subsidies through 2008, it remains uncertain how much actually will be spent because the programme will have to win new congressional budget approval each year. The package recommends that approximately 55 per cent of direct aid go to treatment programmes, 20 per cent to prevention, 15 per cent to palliative care and 10 per cent to children orphanned by the disease. It would also allow, but *not require, the administration to contribute up to $1 billion in 2004 to the Global Fund.*

In the case of South Africa, money is not the only constraint on the success of the Global Fund to help those with HIV/AIDS. South Africa submitted two first-round proposals to the Global Fund, one from the KwaZulu-Natal Provincial Coordinating Mechanism and the other from the South African National AIDS Council. The two proposals called for $50 million in grants. Over one year has passed since the proposals were approved by the Global Fund, yet a grant agreement remains unsigned and no disbursements have occurred. Most of the delay appears due to the inaction of the South African government and not the Global Fund. (Chapter 4 below explores the controversy over South Africa's Global Fund proposals in more detail.)

References

Global Fund to Fight AIDS, Tuberculosis and Malaria (2003), *Questions and Answers: A Partnership to Prevent and Treat AIDS, Tuberculosis and Malaria*, www. globalfundatm.org/qa.html

Government Accounting Office (2003), '*GLOBAL HEALTH: Global Fund to Fight AIDS, TB and Malaria has Advanced in Key Areas, but Difficult Challenges Remain*', Report GAO-03-601 (May).

2
Why is South Africa the HIV Capital of the World? An Institutional Analysis of the Spread of a Virus

Kyle D. Kauffman

Introduction

Africa, the poorest region of the world, has the highest HIV/AIDS rate. The puzzling question is why? And even more puzzling, within Africa, why does Southern Africa have the highest HIV rates? Indeed, South Africa has the largest absolute number of people living with HIV of any nation. Was the spread of this virus inevitable in Southern Africa? Or could a firewall have been built by governments and by civil society? This chapter takes a preliminary look at both the formal and the informal institutions in place in South Africa, and by extension in most of Southern Africa, and how they provided the dry underbrush necessary for the rapid spread of HIV in the region.

It is hard to overstate the economic and social impact that AIDS has had on Southern Africa. The diseases associated with the millions of compromised immune systems have wiped out much of the modest demographic, economic and social gains of the last thirty years. As noted in Chapter 5, Figure 5.4, many countries in Southern Africa were experiencing modest growth in life expectancy until the AIDS crisis hit. AIDS has effectively knocked many of these countries off their modest development path and set them back twenty years (perhaps many more). Debt repayments, weak currencies, low levels of education are all serious development issues facing Southern African countries. But AIDS, arguably, has become the prime obstacle that must be overcome before these countries can hope even to return to the levels achieved by the early 1990s.

In thinking about why Southern Africa in general, and South Africa in particular, has been hit so hard by HIV/AIDS many reasons come to mind. However, is it possible to bundle the many and varying explanations into one coherent theory? This essay makes a preliminary attempt at framing the causes of the spread of the virus in terms of what has become known as the 'new institutional' analysis. This framework, used by many social scientists, has been helpful in contextualizing many social and economic issues in Africa and around the world.[1] Anthropologists, economists, political scientists and sociologists have all adopted new institutional analysis as a way of understanding broad trends in social phenomenon as well as a way to better understand individual behaviour. New institutional analysis could provide insights into why the epicentre of the worldwide AIDS pandemic is South Africa and why regional patterns in HIV rates vary so much even within sub-Saharan Africa.

New institutional analysis

Institutions affect all aspects of human interaction. We use them to define our dealings with others. Often they are meant to give clarity and to reduce uncertainty in our lives, but sometimes they have the unintended effect of doing harm. We define institutions as the humanly devised constraints that we place (or are placed by others) on our lives. There can be both formal and informal constraints. The formal constraints include national constitutions and laws. For instance, the new South African constitution has enshrined a large number of rights, including the right not to be discriminated against in terms of race or gender. Under the former apartheid regime, many laws not only were discriminatory against non-whites, but went so far as to categorize certain occupations based on race, to disallow interracial marriages, etc. These formal institutions affected the lives of the South African citizenry enormously. The constraints placed on non-whites were clear. The laws and rules under which they were obliged to function reduced their incomes, reduced their standard of living, and reduced their life expectancy.

There was a seismic institutional change in 1994 as witnessed by the election of Nelson Mandela. The formal institutions changed. The overarching sets of rules and laws known as apartheid were dismantled and replaced with a different set of rules. Now, non-whites could be elected to the government and could begin to affect policy so as to redress issues of inequity developed over the previous decades. Political parties (such as the African National Congress, the Pan African Congress, and the New National Party), government ministries and agencies (such as the Department of Home Affairs, and the Department of Education), schools and universities, and churches, mosques and synagogues, who in one way or another helped to effect the change, are *not* institutions in this context. These are all referred to as organizations in the parlance of new institutional analysis. The *institutions* are the 'rules of the game' and the *organizations* are groups of individuals, who are affected by and consequently try themselves to affect the institutions, but are viewed as separate entities.

Organizations have incentives to change and to affect the rules by which society is governed. A prime example is the Catholic Church (an organization in this framework) when it lobbies governments around the world to outlaw abortions (an institution in this framework). The Church tries to change the rules regarding the legalization of abortion and by doing so redefines how a country is organized that subsequently adopts such rules. The effect is clear. Individuals in that society would then have different constraints placed on them and would therefore have their behaviour altered. If a woman wanted to get an abortion she would either have to travel to another country, have an illegal abortion (and bear any possible consequences), or have the child. The effect of this institutional change also could spill over into other areas such as increased use of birth control, which may subsequently affect the number of sexually transmitted infections, gender dynamics between men and women, and so on.

Not only do formal institutions have an effect on a society, but informal institutions have an important, sometimes greater, impact. Informal institutions are not those coming from a constitution or from government legislation, but rather are the codes of behaviour that individuals live their lives by. These are norms, customs, traditions and personal ethics. Informal institutions often are more influential in dictating behaviour than formal institutions. Going back to the abortion example, even in places where abortion is legal many individuals do not get abortions because of personal beliefs based on religion, local customs, or other reasons. Even though the formal institution allows for a particular type of behaviour, an informal institution could prevent it.

Informal institutions abound in South Africa. The tradition of paying *lobola* (a bride price) among many in traditional societies is an example of an informal institution. The Zulu people have over the course of many decades decided that when a man and a woman marry, the husband's family pays the bride's family a certain number of cattle and other gifts. This is a humanly constructed, locally dictated interaction. There is no biological, constitutional or legal mandate for *lobola* to be paid when a man and woman marry. In other parts of the world the informal institution is reversed; the woman's family provides the gifts in the form of a dowry. Living arrangements, labour markets, and a myriad of other factors determine the local custom of whether a bride price or a dowry is offered at the time of marriage. Many 'Western' marriage traditions mirror these practices, such as the custom of the wife's family paying for most of the wedding costs.

Informal institutions dictate much of our interactions with others. How we greet others is dictated by custom – sometime with a handshake, sometimes with a kiss, sometimes it is just verbal. How men and women are allowed to interact and to function in society primarily is determined by local custom. Such things as: what is considered acceptable clothing for a woman?; what types of jobs are deemed 'women's work'?; can a woman make eye contact with a man? all illustrate norms and customs and are examples of informal institutions that affect our behaviour.

Just as there are punishments for those who contravene formal institutions (such as jail or monetary fines) there are also punishments for those who ignore or choose to flout informal institutions (such as shunning or mocking or otherwise treating the person as an outcast). The intent of the punishment in both cases is the same: increase the cost of contravening an institution. These costs (be they jail or shunning) are meant to affect behaviour and to force individuals to abide by the formal and informal institutions.

Institutions and the rise of HIV/AIDS

Institutions can arise for a number of reasons. They may make perfect sense in terms of trying to elicit a particular behaviour. But institutions can also have unintended consequences. Because institutions are difficult to amend or to change, the negative consequences can be hard to suppress.

If we look at the formal institutions of South Africa, the government's laws and regulations, there are many provisions that have an affect on those living with HIV as well as on the spread of the virus. Some of these probably were not intended when the formal institutions were developed. For instance, it is illegal to discriminate in South Africa on the basis of someone's health status, which today would include a person's HIV status. Most would agree that this is a humane policy. There is, however, an economic cost to such a law. As noted in Chapter 5, Figure 5.2, the costs of hiring an HIV-infected worker are higher than the costs of hiring an HIV-negative worker. Thus, this policy increases hiring costs for employers and may encourage the substitution of capital for workers, hardly a desirable outcome in an economy plagued by extraordinary levels of unemployment.

Policies from government ministries can also be thought of as formal institutions. Most government policy that directly affects HIV/AIDS issues in South Africa comes from the Department of Health. Virginia van der Vliet spells out in Chapter 4 how the policies pursued by the last two Ministers of Health, as well as by other government officials, have stymied efforts to make antiretroviral drugs available to AIDS patients, blocked the distribution of Navirapine (a drug which significantly reduces mother-to-child transmission of HIV) to pregnant mothers who are HIV positive, and delayed the disbursement of millions of Rands meant to pay for prevention, education and treatment programmes. In addition, many of their policies have sown confusion among the general population as to the medical link between HIV and AIDS. These policies have served as a roadblock to both prevention and treatment efforts. On the whole, formal institutions in South Africa have done little to prevent the rapid spread of the virus; indeed, they are likely to have accelerated it.

Informal institutions, as noted earlier, can have an even greater influence on behaviour than formal institutions. There are a number of social norms and customs that directly or indirectly affect HIV transmission. Two examples that illustrate this point are male circumcision practices and the role and treatment of women in South African society.

Male circumcision rates vary widely across the world. Followers of certain religions, such as Jews and Muslims, for centuries have circumcised baby boys within days of birth. There are, however, other societies such as the Zulu in South Africa who do not circumcise at all. Others, such as the Xhosa, circumcise men as part of a manhood ceremony when the individual is in his teens. Still others leave the decision up to the household (Murdock, 1967, p. 53). The societal decision whether or not to circumcise baby boys is an informal institution. It is a social norm developed over centuries that has associated with it extremely high costs of contravention, such as stigma and shunning.

The medical literature identifies a strong causal link between male circumcision and the likelihood of contracting and spreading HIV. The findings, which show as much as an eight-fold increase in the risk of contracting and spreading HIV among *non-circumcised* men, are less well known in the social science literature (Cameron et al., 1989).[2] This socially constructed informal institution, which has dictated human behaviour for centuries, is now inadvertently affecting the transmission of HIV.

This one informal institution may go some way in explaining the path of infection and may help to predict regions of the world where the virus could spread. Across Africa male circumcision practices vary widely by region and even within countries (Murdock, 1967 and Marck, 1997). As a general rule we tend to see the societies in Africa that practise male circumcision to be the ones with lower rates of HIV infection. The Luo people of western Kenya, situated primarily in the district of Nyanza, are the only major ethnic group in Kenya who do not practise male circumcision (about 90 per cent are not circumcised). Data from the UNAIDS sentinel site in Kisumu, Nyanza, report that in 1999 (the latest year in which a survey was done in Kisumu) the HIV rate was 27.2 percent among women attending antenatal clinics. This compares to an overall HIV rate among adult Kenyans of 15.0 per cent (http://www. unaids.org). While this is in no way proof that lack of male circumcision is the driving force behind the spread of HIV, it is suggestive that this informal institution may be a significant factor.

In South Africa, the major ethnic group that does not practise male circumcision is the Zulu (Murdock, 1967). One would then expect that the province (and the neighbouring provinces) where the majority of the Zulu people reside would also have high HIV rates. As it turns out, the epicentre of the AIDS crisis is indeed the province of KwaZulu-Natal (Table 2.1). In every year since 1998, the extremely high rate of HIV in KwaZulu-Natal is starkly contrasted with that of the Western Cape where the primary ethnic group, the Xhosa, practise male circumcision.

A second informal institution involves the norms and traditions surrounding the treatment and the role of women in society, in general, and the ability to negotiate safe sex and control over their own bodies, in particular. As Claudia Cruz argues in Chapter 7, women have much less bargaining power than men in the negotiation surrounding safe sex. Even when women would like to use condoms, male South Africans traditionally have the 'power' to say no. One question many might ask is: why would the woman then go ahead with sex if she wants to use a condom, but is told by the man that he is unwilling to use one? The answer rests with the informal institutions governing male–female relations. If a woman does not want to be stigmatized or shunned by the

Table 2.1 Antenatal clinic HIV prevalence in South Africa by province

Province	1998	1999	2000	2001
KwaZulu-Natal	32.5	32.5	36.2	33.5
Mpumalanga	30.0	27.3	29.7	29.2
Gauteng	22.5	23.9	29.4	29.8
Free State	22.8	27.9	27.9	30.1
North West	21.3	23.0	22.9	25.2
Eastern Cape	15.9	18.0	20.2	21.7
Limpopo	11.5	11.4	13.2	14.5
Northern Cape	9.9	10.1	11.2	15.9
Western Cape	5.2	7.1	8.7	8.6
National	22.8	22.4	24.5	24.8

Source: South African Department of Health: http://www.doh.gov.za/facts/index.html

community, and if she wants to continue to see her partner, she will abide by the local norms which dictate the subservient role of women. While a woman may know that there is some probability that she would contract HIV from a man who demands they have sex without a condom, she also knows that there is a cost to be paid for not agreeing to his wishes which may include abuse, loss of financial support, and so on. In many cases when the woman weighs the costs and benefits of her actions, she will choose not to break the local norms of subservience to men. The perceived social, physical and economic costs are simply too high.

Extremely high rates of rape in South Africa also are an indication of the way South African men view their relations with women. South Africa has one of the highest rates of reported rapes against women in the world. According to Interpol statistics, South Africa reported 12.5 rapes per 10 000 people in 2001 compared to 3.2 rapes per 10 000 people in the United States.[3] While there are many underlying reasons for these statistics, it is emblematic in some measure of the social institutions between the genders in South Africa.

Besides male circumcision and the treatment of women, there are a number of other informal institutions that one can point to in South Africa that affect HIV rates. In a number of high-profile cases where HIV-positive individuals have publicly revealed their HIV status, individuals have been stigmatized, shunned by their community, and in some cases even killed. (One such person, Gugu Dlamini, is memorialized in one of the works of art by Senzeni Marasela included in this volume (Figure 6.9).) This very visible social punishment serves only to raise the cost of being tested and of revealing one's status. The upshot is that fewer people will know they are HIV positive and they may continue to spread the virus to others.

What can be done to change these formal and informal institutions in such a way as to *prevent* the spread of HIV rather than to *promote* it? Institutional change is extremely difficult to effect, is often very costly, and generally occurs slowly (North, 1990 and Alston, Eggertsson and North, 1996). In the case of formal institutions, laws and government regulations need to be changed and that sort of political change comes only when there is sufficient political will or sufficient political pressure.

As noted in Chapter 4, there has been little political leadership on HIV/AIDS prevention among those at the top of the ruling party, the African National Congress (ANC). Indeed, the leadership of the ANC probably has done more to confuse the public by its inaction. It would seem that the South African electorate would want to vote the ANC out of power if it is failing in its role of protecting the people. While the AIDS issue is extremely important, there are a number of other factors that determine whether or not a political party is re-elected. By all accounts the ANC is extremely popular, winning nearly two-thirds of the vote in the 1999 national election. The government apparently can afford to lose votes due to its AIDS policy and still command a large majority in parliament. There is little incentive for the formal institutions in South Africa to change unless and until the electorate is willing to change either the ANC party leadership or to vote the ANC out of office.

Informal institutions, perhaps, are even harder to change than formal institutions. Norms and traditions are often developed over centuries. They can develop for many reasons, but once set on a particular path, they are difficult to change. Take male circumcision. Some lives would be saved if all South African men were circumcised at birth. However, even when presented with the medical data showing the link between circumcision and reduced rates of HIV transmission, most members of ethnic groups would reply that it is part of their culture to only circumcise men during initiation ceremonies (or not at all, depending on the group) and that any change would be anathema to their cultural traditions. Imagine if the tables were turned and that instead it was safer *not* to circumcise. Would Jews and Muslims instantly change their centuries-old traditions? It is doubtful. This is not to say that traditions and norms cannot change; it simply takes a long time. Look for instance at the traditional role of women in certain societies. We see that in some Muslim societies women recently have been allowed to drive cars, to vote, and to dress less formally. These are changes in the informal institutions that govern the role of women in society. Generally, the more ingrained, the more deeply held, and the more central the institution is to a society, the harder it is to change.

Two African cases where institutions affected HIV rates

If formal and informal institutions in South Africa have contributed to the spread of HIV and AIDS then it should also be the case that there are examples of countries where different institutions were in place that thwarted the spread of the virus. Two African examples suggest how formal and informal institutions (1) can exist so as to prevent the virus from spreading and (2) can change so as to reduce high HIV rates. In Senegal, institutions were in place in the early days of the appearance of the virus and helped to prevent high infection rates. In Uganda, infection rates soared early, but institutions changed to reduce dramatically reported HIV rates.

According to UNAIDS data, Senegal has been able to keep HIV infection rates below 2 per cent. At the same time UNAIDS data suggests that Uganda was able to reverse a double digit infection rate during the 1990s and has seen a steady fall in new infections. Figure 2.1 and Figure 2.2 show the radically different path of HIV infections in South Africa, Senegal and Uganda. It is clear from these figures that there must be different underlying factors at work in the three countries to account for the dramatically different patterns of HIV infection.

President Abdou Diouf of Senegal was an early advocate of marshalling government resources, religious organizations and civil society to effect a change in behavior. One of the most dramatic steps taken by President Diouf was to enlist the support of religious groups in Senegal to help promote practices that would reduce the spread of the virus. This is in stark contrast to the response of religious leaders in other African countries who continue to preach that using birth control, including condoms, is a sin.

What had to change in Senegal in order to contain the spread of the virus was the informal institutions that governed sexual practices. From the first detected cases of HIV in the mid-1980s, Senegal mounted a dramatic and bold campaign to change the norms surrounding sexual practices. Among the predominately Muslim community in Senegal, Friday prayers often carried HIV/AIDS and safe sex messages. This message was also carried in Sunday Christian services, even in the Catholic churches. Beyond the religious sector, the prevention message was reinforced in

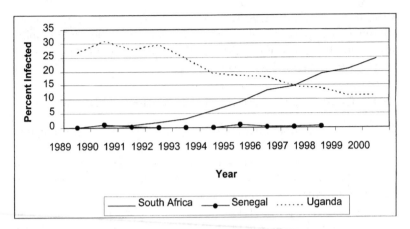

Figure 2.1   HIV infection rates among pregnant women (urban)
Source: http://www.unaids.org

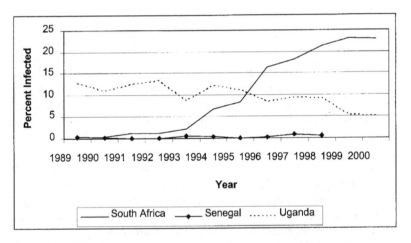

Figure 2.2   HIV infection rates among pregnant women (rural)
Source: http://www.unaids.org

schools and in the media. As a result of the many organizations attempting to influence sexual behaviour among the Senegalese, norms began to change. Condom use increased dramatically. From 1988 to 1997 condom sales increased almost tenfold (http://www.allafrica.com/stories/2003302260261.html).

On the formal institutional side, Senegalese law required that sex workers be registered and undergo regular health checks. With this law in place, the government could monitor the spread of HIV among one of the highest risk groups as well as counsel against unsafe sexual practices. By 1998 a study of condom use by sex workers in Senegal reported that 99 per cent used condoms with their most recent *new* client and 97 per cent used condoms with their most recent *regular* client. Institutional change took place in Senegal early so that by 1990 institutions were in place to thwart the spread of the virus.[4]

Uganda often is viewed as the shining example of a country that was able to dramatically reverse the trend in HIV infection rates. There are those who believe that the reversal simply is an artefact of the data (or of bad data collection), but even if the numbers are off by an order of magnitude, which is doubtful, the underlying results and trends still are impressive.

As was the case in Senegal, Uganda's success is often attributed to strong leadership by the president, in Uganda's case by President Yoweri Museveni. Much of the Uganda story mirrors that of Senegal, except that Uganda's institutional change was in response to high HIV rates whereas Senegal's was to prevent high HIV rates from occurring. President Museveni was able to engage many sectors of society to effect change in the informal institutions surrounding sexual relations between men and women. Condom use increased, but only as part of a wider campaign known as the 'ABC' programmes, which encompassed *A*bstinence, *B*eing faithful and *C*ondom use. This and other programmes contributed to changing the norms of sexual behaviour among Ugandans. Condom use, which was only 7 per cent before the program began, jumped to 50 per cent in rural areas and 85 per cent in urban areas. In terms of formal institutions, the Ugandan government changed regulations and laws surrounding the sale of medications to treat sexually transmitted infections (STIs). Not only licensed pharmacies, but also small local shops, could now sell medications to ensure the widest possible distribution. This law has contributed to increased cure rates for STIs, such as urethritis, from 46 per cent to 87 per cent. It is well documented that the existence of an STI greatly adds to the risk of transmission of HIV, so any reduction in STIs will also reduce the likelihood of transmission of HIV. In Uganda, changing formal and informal institutions, however difficult and costly, had an effect on the spread of HIV.[5]

Conclusions and lessons

Let us return to the question: Why is South Africa the AIDS capital of the world? It is impossible to point to one specific cause. In the institutional framework described above it becomes clear that both the formal and the informal institutions in South Africa were well placed to allow the virus to spread almost unabated.

Once South African society opened up in 1990, the effective insulation provided by the social, cultural and economic boycott of the apartheid regime was gone. Oddly, the isolation of South Africa allowed it to remain relatively immune to the spread of the virus from other parts of Africa. However, the dry kindling was in place. Both the formal and informal institutions were exactly right in South Africa for the virus to spread rapidly and virtually unchecked. The first democratically elected government in 1994 headed by Nelson Mandela had many other issues that it (perhaps rightly) thought were more pressing. The next government elected in 1999 sent mixed signals as to the cause of AIDS. It also failed to enact legislation and policies to stem the spread of the virus and to provide treatment for those already infected.

In terms of informal institutions, South African society treated women as subservient to men. Many local customs, such as not circumcising men, meant that the virus could spread more rapidly than in parts of Africa where male circumcision is practised. When these institutional factors are laid on top of a society, as Howard Phillips points out in Chapter 3, with a history of migratory labour and all-male hostels, and with a relatively poor healthcare and educational system for the majority of the population, it is not surprising that South Africa became the HIV capital of the world. It would have been difficult to create circumstances more favourable for spreading the virus.

Some might say that lessons learned in South Africa may not be applicable to other places such as China, India or Russia. All three of these countries on the face of it seem quite different from South Africa. However, from a broad institutional perspective, they may be similar. Formal institutions, including government policy and laws, have had an impact on the spread of the virus in South Africa. Informal institutions also show a link with the spread of the virus. So rather than conclude that the Chinese culture, the Chinese economy, and the Chinese AIDS situation are simply very different from those in South Africa and that there is nothing that can be learned by the Chinese, we should instead look at what similar institutional patterns suggest about how and where the virus might spread. Just as in South Africa, Chinese government policy regarding the movement of individuals (a formal institution) could affect the direction and pattern of infection rates. And traditions regarding such things as male circumcision rates may vary (even if only marginally) by region or ethnic group in China.

The same can be said for other countries where the possibility exists for rapid rates of increase in HIV, such as in India and Russia. Even in the United States, a country with HIV rates below 1 per cent, there are lessons to be learned. One major informal institutional change that could be a ticking time bomb is the change in the tradition of male circumcision over the past two decades. From 1979 to 1999 the overall rate of male circumcision in the United States has remained fairly constant at about two-thirds of the male population. However, over that same period the rate for blacks has been lower than the rate for whites for each year except 1997. Most striking is the regional pattern where we see a dramatic shift in the West where the male circumcision rate went from 64 percent to 37 per cent by 1999, compared to a rate of 81 per cent in the Midwest in 1999 (US Department of Health and Human Services, 2003). With the dramatic decline in the West and widening regional difference in circumcision rates, we might see a resultant shift in HIV infection patterns in the United States.

Customs, laws, norms and regulations differ widely around the world. The differences matter. They affect our actions and constrain our behaviour. The institutions cause us to act and to react in certain ways. Certain types of institutions can lead to the more rapid spread of the virus that causes AIDS. This broad-based approach to looking at how the virus was allowed to spread helps us to understand not only why HIV levels are the highest in South Africa, but also where the virus is likely to continue to spread. Much more needs to be done to identify the institutions, both formal and informal, that affect the transmission of HIV. Even though institutional change is difficult and slow, it is imperative to develop institutions that will contain the spread of the virus.

Notes

1 For an excellent introduction to new institutional analysis see North (1990), North (1991), and Alston, Eggertsson and North (1996). For how this methodology has been applied in Africa see Bates (1989), Ensminger (1992), Firmin-Sellers (1996) and Nkurunziza and Bates (2003).

2 For a discussion of the emerging medical literature on the causal link between the lack of male circumcision and contracting HIV see Marck (1997), Halperin and Bailey (1999), Szabo and Short (2000) and Bailey et al. (2001).

3 Rates based on INTERPOL crime statistics (http://www.interpol.int/Public/Statistics/ICS/Default.asp), and World Bank population statistics (http://www.worldbank.org/data/databytopic/POP.pdf).

4 The World Health Organization has compiled an excellent description of the chronology of events in Senegal, which is where much of the material for this section is derived from. See http://www.who.int/inf-new/aids3.htm.
5 The World Health Organization has well-documented evidence on the institutional change that took place in Uganda during the 1990s. The facts described in this section regarding the Uganda HIV/AIDS programmes were largely adapted from their description of the events. See: http://www.who.int/inf-new/aids2.htm.

References

Alston, Lee J., Thrainn Eggertson and Douglass C. North (eds) (1996), *Empirical Studies in Institutional Change* (New York: Cambridge University Press).

Bailey, Robert C., Francis A. Plummer and Stephen Moses (2001), 'Male Circumcision and HIV Prevention: Current Knowledge and Future Research Directions', *The Lancet Infectious Diseases*, 1 (4): 223–31.

Bates, Robert H. (1989), *Beyond the Miracle of the Market: the Political Economy of Agrarian Development in Kenya* (New York: Cambridge University Press).

Cameron, D. William, et al. (1989), 'Female to Male Transmission of Human Immunodeficiency Virus Type 1: Risk Factors for Seroconversion in Men', *The Lancet*, 2: 403–7.

Ensminger, Jean (1992), *Making a Market: the Institutional Transformation of an African Society* (New York: Cambridge University Press).

Firmin-Sellers, Kathryn (1996), *The Transformation of Property Rights in the Gold Coast: an Empirical Study Applying Rational Choice* (New York: Cambridge University Press).

Halperin, Daniel T. and Robert C. Bailey (1999), 'Male Circumcision and HIV Infection: 10 Years and Counting', *The Lancet*, 354: 1813–15.

Marck, Jeff (1997), 'Aspects of Male Circumcision in Sub-Equatorial African Cultural History', *Health Transition Review*, 7: 37–359.

Murdock, George Peter (1967), *Ethnographic Atlas* (Pittsburgh: University of Pittsburgh Press).

Nkurunziza, Janvier D. and Robert H. Bates (2003), 'Political Institutions and Economic Growth in Africa', Center for International Development, Harvard University, Working Paper 98, March.

North, Douglass C. (1990), *Institutions, Institutional Change and Economic Performance* (New York: Cambridge University Press).

North, Douglass C. (1991), 'Institutions', *Journal of Economic Perspectives*, 5 (1): 97–112.

Szabo, Robert, and R. V. Short (2000), 'How Does Male Circumcision Protect Against HIV Infection?', *British Medical Journal*, 320: 1592–4.

United States Department of Health and Human Services (2003), http://www.cdc.gov/nchs/products/pubs/pubd/ hestats/circumcisions/circumcisions.htm

3
HIV/AIDS in the Context of South Africa's Epidemic History

Howard Phillips

Introduction

In the reams of writing on AIDS in South Africa, both scholarly and popular, there runs a strong sense that this is an unspeakable epidemic, without precedent in the country's history. It 'defies description', remarked a leading AIDS scholar (Crewe, 2000, p. 23), while the South African chair of the AIDS 2000 Conference in Durban said he 'could find no parallel in history for AIDS' – it was an epidemic 'the likes of which we have never seen' (Coovadia, 2001). South Africa's official HIV/AIDS/STD Strategic Plan 2000–5 described it as 'an incomprehensible calamity' (Department of Health, 2000). Not surprisingly, at a popular level this perception has been even more marked. In 2000, *Time International* (p. 31) referred to AIDS in South Africa as being 'worse than a disaster' and of rural Kwazulu-Natal as being 'the cutting edge of a continental apocalypse'. More recently *Time* (2001, p. 47) followed up these dire descriptions of an entirely unparalled disaster by labelling AIDS 'humanity's deadliest cataclysm'.

The lack of a comparative perspective which such views suggest is a reflection not only of the authors' short historical memory, but also of the relative failure of South African historiography to make past epidemic experiences part of the mainstream narrative of the country's history. Recent general histories of South Africa make but passing reference to epidemics, and generally give greater prominence to epizootics like rinderpest and East Coast fever than to smallpox, bubonic plague and influenza. In this regard, AIDS has shown up sharply this failure of historians of South Africa to fulfil one of the basic tasks of history as a discipline, that is, what the American historian Joseph Strayer called the ability to help in 'meeting new situations, not because it provides a basis for prediction, but because a full understanding of human behavior in the past makes it possible to find familiar elements in present problems and thus makes it possible to solve them more intelligently' (Marwick, 1970, p. 18).

If HIV/AIDS in South Africa is set comparatively against South Africa's historical experience of epidemics, our ability to comprehend it (and, perhaps, to deal with it) is expanded significantly. Such comparisons help to highlight both continuities with past epidemics and discontinuities. As a result, HIV/AIDS' true character and contours become easier to discern. This attempt to provide historical perspective focuses on the main features of the AIDS epidemic in South Africa, and investigates why they are indeed without precedent in the country's epidemic history.

Arrival, transmission and dispersion

The dominant mode of transmission of HIV from person to person via sexual intercourse is well established, and in this regard HIV/AIDS has much in common with other sexually transmitted infections with a long history in South Africa. Like them, it found in the country's well-developed system of migrant labour a facilitating environment and means for entrenchment in the African population at large. This system produced a concentration of young men in cities (many in single-sex hostels) far from their wives or families for months on end, and then, after several months, dispersed them (many now unwittingly HIV positive) back to their families in rural areas during holidays or at the end of their contracts. As the director of the Medical Research Council's HIVNET put it succinctly, '[T]he social dislocation and family disruption induced by the migrant labor system . . . create the right conditions for rapid transmission of sexually transmitted infections (including HIV)' (Karim, 2000, p. 15).

Like syphillis, the dominant heterosexual clade of HIV-1 in South Africa appears to have been introduced into the country's interior via a similar men-to-the-mines route. Just as it is believed that the diamond and gold rushes of the late nineteenth century 'heralded the spread of STDs and endemic syphilis . . . into the interior from the coast' (Jochelson, 1999, p. 219), a century later it was probably migrant mineworkers primarily from Malawi who brought HIV to the Witwatersrand. In 1986, 130 Malawian miners on Rand gold mines were publicly reported as the first heterosexual HIV-positive cases in South Africa (SAIRR, 1986, p. 759). The movement of young men to and within South Africa (most obviously migrant workers, but also at certain times sailors and active or demobilized soldiers) has long been a key mode of transmission of epidemic diseases in modern South African history. Be it smallpox via sailors and migrant labourers in the eighteenth and nineteenth centuries, 'Spanish' flu via discharged Union Defence Force soldiers and homeward-fleeing mineworkers in 1918, typhus and 'Asian' flu via newly recruited mineworkers in the 1920s, 1930s and 1957 or HIV/AIDS via mineworkers, discharged South African Defence Force soldiers and returned ANC cadres in the 1980s and early 1990s, all share the young-man-as-vector characteristic.

The migrant labour system, as the most enduring and wide-ranging example of movement of millions of young men via South Africa's well-developed transport network, has been critical to the introduction and spread of communicable disease to and in the country. In this regard, HIV/AIDS fits into a very well-established pattern.

Responses

South African society's responses to the appearance of HIV/AIDS in the country also display many parallels with responses to earlier epidemics. The earliest identification of HIV-positive people in the population – cases of HIV-1 Clade B among male homosexuals in 1982 – evoked a cascade of finger-pointing along the fissures of existing prejudices. This same process turned into a veritable avalanche from the late 1980s as HIV-1 Clade C appeared in South Africa among heterosexuals, especially Africans. This comes as no surprise, for 'blaming the victim' has a long pedigree in South Africa's epidemic history. The spread of smallpox in Cape Town in 1840, 1858 and 1882 was blamed on 'dirty Malays' by the white establishment – even to the point of rumours that Muslims were deliberately infecting whites' clothing so as to wipe them out (Davids, 1983, p. 66). The bubonic plague in 1901 was attributed by many whites to 'unhygienic' Africans (van Heyningen, 1981, pp. 94–5). 'Spanish' flu in 1918 was ascribed to, inter alia, devilish German gas warfare, irresponsible members of the Native Labour Corps or malevolent whites wanting to exterminate Africans by, respectively, superpatriotic English-speaking South Africans, Afrikaners hostile to the very idea of Africans in uniform and rural Africans leery of white behaviour towards them in general (Phillips, 1990, pp. 10, 147–8). When HIV/AIDS appeared in the 1980s, various sectors of the deeply prejudiced South African population similarly explained it in terms of their pet aversions.

Nor is there anything peculiarly South African in such a response. In the face of a life-threatening epidemic, blaming others (especially 'outsiders') for bringing it in has been a standard human response throughout recorded history. In 429 BC some Athenians blamed the Peloponnesians for the plague which decimated the city (Thucydides, 1974); in 1349 Jews in Germany were blamed for the Black Death (Ziegler, 1982, pp. 98–111) and in 1830 Russians identified Polish agents as the bringers of cholera to their country (McGrew, 1965, p. 161). 'To be able to blame others is psychologically reassuring,' writes Mary Crewe (1992, p. 14). '[T]he fact that it is their fault divides "us" from them. We are innocent, at the mercy of fate; they are guilty and have behaved in such a way as to put us all at risk. We have been invaded from without, polluted by some external agent.'

Initially in South Africa, gay white men were blamed by the hetero-sexual establishment for introducing HIV into South Africa and spreading it through what one Dutch Reformed Church minister labelled their 'devious form of sexuality' and what one Groote Schuur Hospital specialist called 'the perverted practices of promiscuous homosexuality' (Grundlingh, 1999, pp. 61, 66). From the late 1980s, as the disease became more common among heterosexuals, especially Africans from without and within the country, racist white accusations turned indiscriminately in their direction too. An anonymous right-wing pamphlet circulating in 1989 urged whites to have their black domestic workers regularly tested for HIV 'to safeguard your family' (Jochelson, 1999, p. 235), while a year later another called for whites to be insulated against Africans so they could 'survive in an AIDS sea' (van der Vliet, 2001, p. 157). Acting on these stereotypes, in 1990 the director of the Highveld Blood Transfusion Service decided that blood would no longer be taken from Africans and Coloureds since, he asserted, they were likely to be HIV positive (SAIRR, 1991/2, pp. 132–3).

Among Africans, stereotypes and suspicions were equally widespread about the origin of the disease. In 1991, *Drum* carried without comment an article taken over from an African-American journal, entitled 'Is AIDS a conspiracy against Blacks' (February, p. 16), giving credence to stories that it was deliberately introduced by the government in the last days of apartheid to try and check the advance of African liberation. In the early 1990s, young activists, believing that AIDS was 'a plot devised by the government . . . to convince black people to have less sex, and therefore fewer babies, lampooned the acronym AIDS as really meaning "Afrikaner Invention to Deprive us of Sex"' (van der Vliet, 2001, p. 155). More traditionally, other Africans have interpreted this epidemic, like many others before it, as the product of malevolent individuals employing witchcraft (Ashforth, 2001, pp. 8–11).

As is usual with finger pointing, in all of these instances the action commonly reveals as much about the pointer's perceptions as about those of the individual or group pointed to. Given the marginalized status, in the eyes of South Africa's National Party government, of the majority of those who were HIV positive, it is not surprising to find government's official response as draconian as that of earlier minority regimes in the face of epidemics among their 'out' groups. Although ultimately not carried out, the National Party's decision in 1987 to deport all HIV-positive foreign migrant labourers and to bar entry to South Africa to any HIV-positive new arrivals had many precedents. It recalls the Cape government's forcible quarantining of cases of smallpox in 1892, especially those found in the Muslim community. It echoes the Natal government's wish to bar shipborne Indians arriving during the cholera scares of the 1880s and 1890s. It has parallels, too, with the attempt by the magistrate of Lydenburg in 1883 to organize patrols along the nearby border with Mozambique to keep out smallpox from Lourenco Marques, and the Transvaal government's restrictions on the movement of Indians in 1899 because they were seen as vectors of bubonic plague (Davids, 1983, p. 62; Swanson, 1983, pp. 413, 416; Viljoen, 1999, pp. 5–6; van Heyningen, 1981, p. 72).

The heavy-handed and discriminatory South African decision in 1987 was clearly prompted by a mind-set akin to that which had seen the Cape government, in the midst of the bubonic plague epidemic of 1901–3, seeking to evict all Africans from central Cape Town and Port Elizabeth to locations on the margins of those cities. Underlying the 1987 decision, too, were motives similar to those which had prompted efforts to prevent only Africans with symptoms of 'Spanish' flu from travelling by train in 1918 or those which had produced the compulsory de-verminization of all third-class African passengers on trains from the Transkei during the typhus epidemics of 1917–24 and 1933–5 (Swanson, 1977; Phillips, 1990, p. 80; Marks and Andersson, 1988, p. 271). The appeal of vigorous official action against stigmatized, politically voiceless or socially weak 'out' groups or individuals during times of epidemic fear and panic has, for most of South African history, proved irresistible to governments. And not only to governments, as the murder in 1998 of Gugu Dlamini by some in her community vividly demonstrated. Her crime, they claimed, was 'degrading her neighbourhood' by announcing her HIV-positive status on local radio (*Sunday Times*, 1998).

It is also not without precedent in South Africa's epidemic history for those in authority or their agents to adopt a position of denial, at odds with mainstream medical opinion, for reasons more political, economic or ideological than medical and scientific. Most notoriously, in 1883–4 a vehement war of words raged in Kimberley as a band of doctors, led by Dr L. S. Jameson, with close links to the mining industry, challenged the official diagnosis of the prevailing epidemic as smallpox – a dreaded designation which carried with it a statutory quarantine and the disruption of the flow of labour to the diamond fields (Viljoen, 1999). One hundred years later, South Africa's Department of Health and Welfare was equally keen to deny that fearsome cholera was rampant in its bantustans lest doing so meant that it had to accept responsibility for counter-measures. At first it attributed the rising tide of deaths to gastroenteritis, and when this fiction could not be sustained, it tried to suppress the mortality figures (Marks and Andersson, 1988, pp. 257–8).

President Mbeki's querying of the connection between HIV and AIDS or the magnitude of AIDS mortality thus needs to be problematized as far more than just the product of personal fancy or intellectual contrariness. Nor should he be puzzled as to why, as he lamented during the Virodene outcry, 'those who seek the good for all humanity have become the villains of our time' (Epstein, 2000, p. 54). Epidemics pose too elemental a threat to society for government responses to them not to attract vigorous (and often critical) debate or to become the object of political point-scoring, especially in a racially, culturally and ideologically divided society like South Africa. Whether it was a local councillor berating the Cape government for its supineness during the 1882 smallpox epidemic (Lombaard, 1981, p. 75), the opposition South African News protesting sharply at the same government's forced removal of Africans from District Six in response to the bubonic plague nineteen years later (van Heyningen, 1981, p. 87), or newspapers as diverse as *Ons Vaderland* and *The International* lambasting the Union Government's ineptitude during the 'Spanish' flu epidemic (Phillips, 1990, pp. 202, 216), they all exemplified the same sharp attacks on official conduct commonly evoked by frightening epidemics. In the anxious midst of these, governments are hard put to win across-the-board approval.

Nor is the limited support that Mbeki's dissidence has elicited in biomedical circles unanticipated. Within the South African biomedical profession dissidence has not been the norm in the face of modern epidemics. Increasingly uniform in their training, intellectual framework, agreement on the ground rules on what constitutes valid evidence and trials, and their professional code of conduct and discourse, since the 1920s South African doctors have usually been *ad idem* on the fundamentals of epidemics. As the biomedical means for accurately identifying and effectively treating epidemic diseases became hegemonic in the twentieth century, so disagreement on these became less likely (and less tolerated) within the ranks of the biomedical profession. On the few occasions that a nonconformist medical voice was raised within that community – as in the case of Dr Purvis Beattie during the 'Spanish' flu epidemic (Phillips, 1990, p. 130) or Dr de Jager during the 1948 polio epidemic (Bettzieche, 1998, p. 43) – the medical profession usually acted vigorously to deny legitimacy to such opinions.

This increasingly standard approach to epidemic diseases by the South African medical profession clearly prefigures key features of its professional stance in the midst of the HIV/AIDS epidemic, most obviously in the Medical Association of South Africa's delineation of an appropriate AIDS code of conduct for doctors and in the controversy around the anti-HIV 'wonder' drug, Virodene. As the president of the Medical Research Council summarily concluded with regard to the latter in 1999, Virodene is 'nonsense', with no scientific integrity (SAIRR, 1999/200, p. 236).

Yet, as the Virodene case also makes abundantly clear, during epidemics the premium on finding an antidote rises very dramatically, for obvious life-and-death reasons. Driven by humanitarian and economic motives and heavy pressure from government, laboratories in South Africa hurriedly produced vaccines or drugs against bubonic plague in 1901, against 'Spanish' flu in 1918, against polio in 1955 and against HIV (in the form of Virodene) in 1997. As might be expected, vaccines prepared under such precipitate circumstances, in response to pressing crises, were (with but one exception – the anti-polio vaccine) rarely effective, save as placebos.

This same urgent demand for an antidote to an epidemic has drawn, of course, even more wide-ranging responses from outside of biomedicine all through modern South African history, and in this regard HIV/AIDS is no different. Especially in South Africa, traditional healers, homeopaths, spiritual healers and even outright quacks intent on cashing in on popular panic have all plied their trades and offered their distinctive cures with hyperbolic promises of guaranteed success during epidemics. As long as there is no single sure cure, some part of the public will be attracted by promises of alternative medicine.

Another sector of the economy with a long professional interest in epidemic life and death has been the life insurance industry. In examining its response to epidemics, only the 'Spanish' flu is comparable with AIDS, for only these two epidemics claimed (or threatened to claim) a significant number of lives from among the insuring classes. In both situations the industry sought to safeguard its reserves. In the wake of paying out 1.3 million pounds to the beneficiaries of 'Spanish' flu victims in 1919, the insurance industry undertook a vigorous advertising campaign to rebuild its depleted reserves by selling new policies. Using the threat of a return of the epidemic to good effect, it wrote 20 million pounds worth of new business within a year, an unequalled South African record (Phillips, 1990, pp. 195, 213). Two generations later, in response to HIV/AIDS, some equally reserve-conscious companies laid down that in the future all applicants for life insurance must take an HIV test first. If the result proved positive, their applications would be rejected (SAIRR, 1994/5, p. 308). Others responded more flexibly, introducing new products, which accepted HIV-positive applicants for life cover, but loaded their premiums correspondingly. COSATU commented that such approaches clearly showed that maximizing profits was what the industry thought about first (SAIRR, 1995/6, p. 464; SAIRR 1996/7, p. 462).

Consequences

In the magnitude of their demographic and socio-economic impact, the 'Spanish' flu and HIV/AIDS also have much in common (Phillips, 1990). For reasons still not adequately explained, 'Spanish' flu, like AIDS, was particularly lethal to young adults, claiming perhaps 300,000 lives in its six-week rampage through South Africa in October–November 1918. At a stroke, South Africa's population lost some 9 per cent of its prime workforce, its parents and its potential child-bearers.

The consequences of this disaster were both immediate and long-lasting, and continued to echo through South Africa's subsequent demographic and social history for two generations. The almost overnight creation of over half a million orphans pushed the state, parastatal bodies like the Post Office, police and railways, and organized religion into a massive orphanage building programme, primarily for those orphans who were white. The government supplemented this programme by introducing special grants for flu widows with children. For the majority of black orphans it did little, leaving them to be indentured, incorporated into extended families or left to fend for themselves as best they could.

The social, psychological and emotional costs of this massive social disruption in the lives of upwards of 500,000 South African children born between 1900 and 1918 have barely been noticed in South African history. One anecdote suffices to hint at this poorly documented dimension of the country's twentieth-century history. In March 1919, a Cape Town court heard that the 'coloured' pre-teenager before it on a charge of theft was,

> one of dozens of boys of his age who roam the city and sleep anywhere . . . He is a 'flu remnant'. He has no home, and does not know what has become of his parents. He does not know his age or his proper name, and has no surname, so far as he knows. He and others sleep under the Pier, in the old boxes, and in railway compartments, first-class preferred, when the opportunity offers. He looks half starved and eats garbage, or whatever he can get hold of, and says he has never been to school. (Phillips, 1990, pp. 186–7)

Having found him guilty, the presiding magistrate sent him to a reformatory for four years. *Mutatis mutandis*, this report could easily have been written yesterday about the plight of AIDS orphans in South Africa.

The loss of young mothers in 1918 – and with them all their babies as yet unborn – also left a permanent nick in the country's demographic profile, which finally worked its way through the life cycle only recently. Its impact has been felt at every social stage over the last 85 years. Evidence of this process is best documented among white South Africans, but its all-pervasive effects would have been a common national experience. In 1925 (which was the first year of school for children born in 1919), the Cape Education Department reported that enrolments in sub-A were down by 'several hundred', while by 1929 it was observed that there had been a marked 'slackening of growth' in school enrolments in the 1920s as 'children of school going age have not been increasing in number at the same rate as the total population' (Phillips, 1990, p. 175). It is likely that there will be many similar reports in South Africa in the second decade of the twenty-first century.

As for the sudden excision of a segment of the workforce by the 'Spanish' flu, it is clear that agriculture was most sharply affected, with seed left unsown in hard-hit areas like the Transkei and mature crops unharvested. Famine was a widespread consequence. Because of a loss of labour, output in the country's mines fell sharply for a few months in 1918–19, until the labour recruitment agencies could fill these gaps. 'The influenza has indeed played havoc with the profits and makes one very anxious about the future,' wrote the worried chairman of Central Mining to the president of the Chamber of Mines (Phillips, 1990, p. 3). Eighty-five years later, with the full economic impact of HIV/AIDS still developing, such evidence of how a serious epidemic can throttle key sectors of the country's economy is ominous.

Casting an eye over all these parallels between HIV/AIDS and earlier epidemics in South Africa's history, it is clear that in many of its central features – its mode of arrival, transmission and dispersion, the nature of the responses it evoked and its demographic and socio-economic impact – HIV/AIDS fits squarely into deeply rooted epidemic patterns and precedents in South Africa. That it does so suggests, in some measure at least, that such similarities arise from the very structure, composition and mode of operation of South African society. HIV/AIDS illuminates this clearly, provided one does not allow its magnitude and our historical amnesia to block out what it has in common with prior epidemics. Viewed with the benefit of such historical perspectives, HIV/AIDS appears as anything but *sui generis*.

Yet it would be misleading and one-sided to see HIV/AIDS solely in terms of its similarities with previous epidemics. As Charles Rosenberg (1992, p. 280) reminds us, to comprehend a particular epidemic, 'we must distinguish between the unique and the seemingly universal, between this epidemic at this time and place and the way in which communities have responded to other episodic outbreaks of fulminating infectious disease in the past'. If HIV/AIDS in South Africa is to be fully apprehended, its distinctive sides have to be highlighted too and incorporated into any rounded assessment.

Distinctive features of HIV/AIDS in South Africa

Broadly, these distinctive features can be put into four categories. Foremost among these is its biology. Unlike South Africa's other epidemics like bubonic plague, cholera, influenza, polio, smallpox and typhus, AIDS onset is slow and its progress relatively leisurely. On average, the period between being infected with HIV and death from AIDS or an opportunistic infection is seven to eight years in South Africa. In this respect it resembles TB and syphilis more than a fulminating epidemic disease, though, unlike TB and syphillis in the post-war period, its course is not reversible or even cheaply retarded.

From this fact have flowed several momentous social, political and economic consequences peculiar to the HIV/AIDS epidemic in South Africa. Its long, steadily draining duration has created a swelling number of AIDS invalids requiring increasing family or institutional nursing care in their dying years, and thus calling into being numerous AIDS advice, support and care groups. Parents being in this condition have produced a generation of what may be termed 'orphans in the making'. Second, its relatively gradual advance in its early phase in South Africa meant that opportunities for intervention to try and prevent its further spread by education and publicity were numerous. The result was initiatives unprecedented in South Africa's epidemic history, such as massive AIDS awareness campaigns, the introduction of intensive programmes of sex education into schools, mass distribution of condoms by the state and the official commission of safe sex videos (which the Publications Control Board banned in 1993!) and *Sarafina II*. In this respect it transformed approaches to sexual activity in South Africa out of all recognition.

Moreover, HIV's relatively slow conversion into full-blown AIDS in an individual created a generation of people living with AIDS, fit, keen and able to organize around their condition, to lobby and to draw support from sympathetic individuals and institutions. They mobilized around key issues like discrimination against HIV -positive people, the need for AIDS-delaying drugs to be made cheaper and the unacceptability of compulsory HIV testing and notification. As a result of all of these initiatives, derived ultimately from the biology of the disease, AIDS-related NGOs proliferated in South Africa. By 1993 over 700 were in existence (SAIRR, 1993/94, p. 140), not counting the specialized units and offices set up within existing institutions like insurance companies, business and law firms, trade unions, universities, churches and private and semi-private healthcare agencies like the Red Cross and the blood transfusion services. On top of these, a veritable AIDS monitoring and projection industry was born. To this surge in AIDS-related NGOs in the early 1990s neither the South African National Tuberculosis Association, nor the Poliomyelitis Research Foundation, as examples of NGOs created by public initiative during earlier epidemics, could hold a candle.

For the same basic reason – the extended window of opportunity for action provided by the slow-paced escalation of HIV into AIDS – pharmaceutical firms have found themselves in the unusual situation amidst an epidemic, of being able to have an immediate impact on the disease with their newly developed drugs. Many have been taken by surprise by the political, moral and financial implications of a position they had seldom met with before.

Pressures of a similarly unprecedented kind on government saw, even before 1994, equally novel official administrative initiatives in the history of epidemics in South Africa: the creation of a dedicated AIDS Unit within the Department of National Health; the establishment of specialized AIDS Training and Information Centres throughout the country; a request to the Law Commission to investigate all aspects of the law with regard to AIDS; and even a bid to set up a single body involving trade unions, business, the churches, the government and even the ANC government-in-waiting, the National AIDS Convention of South Africa (NACOSA), to develop a joint national policy on AIDS. What the latter points to is the second distinctive feature of the HIV/AIDS epidemic in South Africa – its political context.

Just as the epidemic was getting into its stride in the early 1990s, South Africa underwent an unprecedented political transition which put into place for the first time in the country's history a fully democratic political dispensation. This transformation produced a government with a wholly novel (for South Africa) commitment to the human rights of all South Africans, an outlook which introduced a sea change in state policy with respect to HIV/AIDS. Aware of the rapid inroads by the disease into the country's African majority in particular – a recognition which had seen it participate in NACOSA's deliberations even before the new South Africa had been born – the ANC, once in power, gave the fight against HIV/AIDS far greater priority than any of its predecessors had done when faced by an epidemic particularly prevalent among the African majority in the population.

Within months of assuming office, the ANC government identified AIDS Awareness as a special Presidential Lead Project and doubled the budget for combating AIDS, with sex education programmes in schools, public information campaigns via the mass media, free condom distribution and the expansion of the network of STD clinics being the chief beneficiaries. Alongside this enormous increase in funding for prevention and care, the ANC's promise of a compassionate approach to those with the disease, informed by a respect for human rights, began to permeate wider state interventions too. For instance, the new government overturned the policy of the police, correctional services and defence force to carry out HIV testing on all new applicants for jobs as this 'affronted the spirit' of the Bill of Rights and contravened the Labour Relations Act. Similarly, it rejected the idea of HIV/AIDS tests for all incoming hospital patients as it deemed this policy unacceptable, discriminatory and an infringement of human rights, while in the country's prisons it reversed existing policy by having condoms distributed free to all prisoners and by ending the segregation of HIV-positive inmates.

This new climate of respect for individuals' rights was not limited to government. Even before 1994, key sectors of industry and business were adopting a line on HIV/AIDS far more enlightened than they had done in the face of previous epidemics, probably as a result of overseas influence and trade union and NGO pressure. As early as 1986, the Chamber of Mines opposed the government's wish to repatriate all foreign miners who were HIV positive (SAIRR, 1986, p. 759) – in striking contrast to its stance on tubercular miners two generations earlier. The comprehensive AIDS policy developed by the Chamber of Mines, with its emphasis on the employment rights of HIV-positive miners, on counselling of those it found to be HIV positive and on instituting education programmes to prevent HIV infection, was described by a leading AIDS academic as, for its time, 'probably one of the most enlightened and responsible responses to AIDS of anybody anywhere in the world' (SAIRR, 1988/9, p. 438). The Chamber even went on to reach a rough consensus on AIDS with the National Union of Mineworkers, concluding an industrial agreement on the disease with the union in 1993. For an industry whose attitude to sick workers during earlier epidemics of silicosis, pneumonia, TB and 'Spanish' flu had been hard-line, this enlightened approach was indeed a change of heart.

The public position of business showed a similar novel degree of respect for the rights of employees. In 1988, the Association of Chambers of Commerce and Industry (ASSOCOM) came out strongly against compulsory HIV testing of workers and the dismissal of those found to be HIV positive. The former was a breach of individual's privacy, while the latter would constitute unfair dismissal, it warned. Employers should instead concentrate on AIDS education for their workforce as the best means of preventing the disease. However, the gap between this enlightened stance and the reality of testing, discrimination and dismissal in actual workplaces soon became apparent, a trend which it took decisions by the courts and the South African Law Commission to retard.

Active involvement by the latter two institutions in defence of individuals' rights again highlights that AIDS was the first epidemic in South Africa in which the rights of all infected citizens were vigorously asserted and upheld in public. It was the first epidemic to occur within a context of a burgeoning human rights culture. Whether it was prisoners insisting that their right not to be tested for HIV without their consent be respected, an HIV-positive man suing his doctor for breach of confidentiality and invasion of privacy for revealing his HIV status, an industrial court ruling that the automatic dismissal of an HIV-positive employee constituted an unfair labour practice, the Treatment Action Campaign applying to the courts to compel the government to make antiretroviral drugs available to those who were HIV positive, or the

Law Commission opposing mandatory HIV testing of prospective employees or warning insurance companies not to discriminate unfairly against prospective clients who were HIV positive, the HIV/AIDS epidemic in South Africa coincided with a transformation in state and private sector public attitudes to epidemic infection. By virtue of this consideration, too, HIV/AIDS is in a category of its own in South Africa's epidemic history.

The third dimension of the HIV/AIDS epidemic which distinguishes it from its predecessors stems, like the second, from a changed South African context. By the time the disease emerged in the 1980s, the extent to which biomedicine had penetrated into South African society was far greater than could have been the case during earlier epidemics. While it is true that biomedicine was not the only system of treatment to which a majority of the population turned in the face of HIV and its symptoms, it is likely that in a growing number of cases it was the first. No longer did biomedicine elicit the same level of popular circumspection and even hostility which vaccination or deverminization had during earlier epidemics. That AZT is an acronym probably as familiar in Mtubatuba as in Mayfair is a product of this process of the biomedicialization of South African society, which means that, in terms of the degree of acceptance of biomedicine, the HIV/AIDS epidemic takes place against a background markedly different from that of earlier epidemics in South Africa.

Fourth, the international setting in which HIV/AIDS has occurred in South Africa is so different from that of earlier epidemics as to constitute a wholly new environment. Certainly prior epidemics in the twentieth century saw South African governments trying to draw on overseas medical expertise to help them combat both epidemics and epizootics – Robert Koch during the 1896 rindepest and 1903–4 East Coast fever outbreaks (van Onselen, 1972; Gutsche, 1979; Cranefield, 1991), Professor W. J. Simpson during the bubonic plague in 1901 (van Heyningen, 1981, p. 75), the latest British thinking on treating flu during the 1918 pandemic (Phillips, 1990, p. 108), the World Health Organization (WHO) for eradicating malaria in the 1950s (Grammicia and Beales, 1988, p. 1342) and the collaboration of US laboratories in the 1950s to develop a vaccine against polio (Bettzieche, 1998, p. 58).

Yet, despite this history of a growing input from outside experts and international health authorities into South Africa's counter-measures against epidemics during the twentieth century, nothing they did can remotely compare with the scale of the huge international resources against HIV/AIDS offered to South Africa, particularly since 1994. With

WHO and UNAIDS in the lead, an extensive international anti-AIDS framework has been put into place to combat the disease around the world, with 'best practices' laid down by global health and philanthropic bodies, both official and unofficial. To a degree unparalleled in South Africa's epidemic history, this international dimension has shaped both governmental and nongovernmental policies and practices in the country. It was epitomized by the holding of the XIII International AIDS conference in Durban in July 2000, organized by UNAIDS. '[W]e count on you as a critical component part of the global forces mobilized to engage in struggle against the AIDS epidemic confronting our Continent', President Mbeki (2000) told the delegates. Even though the president's own words and deeds have not borne out this apparent readiness to welcome international advice, resources and know-how, it is clear that at most other levels of the country's fight against HIV/AIDS, international input and influence have been colossal and unprecedented.

Conclusion

HIV/AIDS is both with and without precedent in South African history. Many of its features fall firmly within the pattern of previous epidemics and the responses they evoked, the main differences being of degree not of kind – its sexually transmitted nature, the pathways along which it spread, the 'othering', blaming and stigmatization which it called forth, the demands it generated for an immediate antidote or cure and the way in which these were met, the response of the insurance industry, and the social, economic and demographic effects it produced.

Simultaneously, HIV/AIDS is novel among South Africa's epidemics too – its gradual escalation from HIV to death and all that this entails, and the fundamentally different political, medical, pharmaceutical and international environment in which it takes place. Its marrying of continuities from past epidemics with wholly new features is what is really distinctive about it. It does not stand outside of South Africa's epidemic past; it has grown out of it.

References

Ashforth, A. (2001), 'AIDS, Witchcraft, and the Problem of Public Power in Post-Apartheid South Africa', paper presented at AIDS in Context Conference, University of the Witwatersrand, 5 April.

Bettzieche, W. (1998), 'Polio, People and Apartheid: the South African Poliomyelitis Epidemics of the 1940s and 1950s with special reference to the Cape Peninsula', BA honours dissertation, University of Cape Town.

Coovadia, J. (2001), paper presented at the AIDS in Context Conference, University of the Witwaterstrand, 5 April.

Cranefield, P. (1991), *Science and Empire: East Coast Fever in Rhodesia and the Transvaal* (Cambridge: Cambridge University Press).

Crewe, M. (1992), *AIDS in South Africa – the Myth and the Reality* (London: Penguin).

Crewe, M. (2000), 'South Africa: Touched by the Vengeance of AIDS – Responses to the South African Epidemic', *South African Journal of International Affairs*, 7 (2): 23–37.

Department of Health (2000), HIV/AIDS/STI Strategic Plan for South Africa 2000–2005.

Drum (1991), 'Is AIDS a conspiracy against Blacks', 16–17 February.

Epstein, H. (2000), 'The Mystery of AIDS in South Africa', *New York Review of Books*, 20 July: 50–5.

Grammicia, G. and P. Beales (1988), 'The Recent History of Malaria Control and Eradication', in W. Wernsdorfer and I. McGregor (eds), *Malaria: Principles and Practice of Malariology*, 2 (Edinburgh: Churchill Livingstone).

Grundlingh, L. (1999), 'HIV/AIDS in South Africa: a Case of Failed Responses because of Stigmatization, Discrimination and Morality, 1983–94', *New Contree*, 46: 55–81.

Gutsche, T. (1979), *There was a Man: the Life and Times of Sir Arnold Theiler* (Cape Town: Howard Timmins).

Jochelson, K. (1999), 'Sexually Transmitted Diseases in Nineteenth- and Twentieth-Century South Africa', in P. Setel, M. Lewis and M. Lyons (eds), *Histories of Sexually Transmitted Diseases and HIV/AIDS in Sub-Saharan Africa* (Westport: Greenwood Press).

Karim, Q. A. (2000), 'Trends in HIV/AIDS Infection: Beyond Current Statistics', *South African Journal of International Affairs*, 7 (2): 1–21.

Lombaard, A. (1981), 'The Smallpox Epidemic of 1882 in Cape Town, with Some Reference to the Neighbouring Suburbs', BA honours dissertation, University of Cape Town.

Marks, S. and N. Andersson (1988), 'Typhus and Social Control: South Africa 1917–50', R. Macleod and M. Lewis (eds), *Disease, Medicine and Empire: Perspectives on Western Medicine and the Experience of European Expansion* (London and New York: Routledge).

Marwick, A. (1970), *The Nature of History* (London: Macmillan).

Mbeki, T. (2000), Speech at the XIII International AIDS Conference. Durban, South Africa, 9 July. HYPERLINK 'http://www.aid2000.org', http://www.aid2000.org.

McGrew, R. (1965), *Russia and the Cholera, 1823–32* (Madison: University of Wisconsin Press).

Phillips, H. (1990), ' "Black October": the Impact of the Spanish Influenza Epidemic of 1918 on South Africa', *Archives Year Book for South African History* (Pretoria: Government Printer).

Rosenberg, C. (1992), *Explaining Epidemics and Other Studies in the History of Medicine* (New York: Cambridge University Press).

SAIRR [South African Institute of Race Relations], various years, *Race Relations Survey*. *Sunday Times* [Johannesburg] (1998), 'Mob kills woman for telling truth', 27 December: 1.

Swanson, M. (1977), 'The Sanitation Syndrome: Bubonic Plague and Urban Native Policy in the Cape Colony, 1900–09', *Journal of African History*, 18 (3): 396–410.

Swanson, M. (1983), ' "The Asiatic Menace": Creating Segregation in Durban 1870–1900', *International Journal of African Historical Studies*, 16 (3): 401–21.

Thucydides. (1974), R. Warner, trans., *History of the Peloponnesian War*, Book Two (Harmondsworth: Penguin).

Time (2001), 'Death Stalks A Continent', 157 (6): 36–48.

Time International (2000), 'Fatal Destiny', 156 (2): 30–1.

van der Vliet, V. (2001), 'AIDS: Losing "The New Struggle"?' *Daedalus*, 130 (1): 151–84.

van Heyningen, E. (1981), 'Cape Town and the Plague of 1901', in C. Saunders, H. Phillips and E. van Heyningen (eds), *Studies in the History of Cape Town*, 4, Cape Town: Cape Town History Workshop.

van Onselen, C. (1972), 'Reactions to Rinderpest in Southern Africa 1896–7', *Journal of African History*, 13 (3): 473–88.

Viljoen, R. (1999), ' "Secrets and Smallpox": Smallpox on the Kimberley Diamond Fields in the 1880s', paper presented at the biennial conference of the South African Historical Society, University of the Western Cape.

Ziegler, P. (1982), *Black Death* (Harmondsworth: Penguin).

4

South Africa Divided against AIDS: a Crisis of Leadership

Virginia van der Vliet

Introduction

In the heady days of 1994, everything seemed possible in the so-called 'new South Africa'. Installed as president in that year, Nelson Mandela achieved the seemingly impossible – he began the process of uniting a country recently bitterly divided, and enjoyed something as close to universal respect, even reverence, as any politician is likely to experience. This theme of unity marked much of the early 1990s, with Mandela playing a central role in promoting reconciliation, particularly between black and white. It was a theme taken up by those who gathered in 1992 to plan a way forward on the AIDS front.

Although evidence of a growing epidemic had been there for a decade, the politics of the 1980s had made effective strategies impossible. Nevertheless, it became alarmingly clear that a response could not wait for a new political order to be established. In November 1991, the health secretariat of the African National Congress, unbanned the previous year, and the apartheid government's Department of National Health and Population Development, held meetings to formulate a strategy, a process that culminated in October 1992 in a national conference: 'South Africa United Against AIDS', and the formation of the National AIDS Convention of South Africa (NACOSA, 1994, p. ix). NACOSA drew together political parties, trade unions, the business sector, civic associations, religious organizations, scientists, academics, government departments, AIDS service organizations, health workers and others in an intensive programme of consultation. NACOSA convenor, Mary Crewe, writes that the working groups which were established to develop the components of the National Plan ensured that it was 'a reflection of years of experience', and that the bulk of the plan 'could have been effectively implemented in less than two years' (Crewe, 2000, p. 26).

To appreciate the significance of having united such a wide spectrum of South Africans in this unique enterprise, it is necessary to understand the political background against which it occurred.

1982 to 1994: the rocky road to a united response

Despite concerns about an impending epidemic, the response by 1992 had been both inadequate and controversial. The first two South African AIDS cases were diagnosed in 1982. The early 1980s saw the country's cases primarily confined to white male homosexuals, a pattern which peaked in 1989, then declined steeply, largely thanks to intensive self-education efforts in the gay community. The first black (African) case was diagnosed in 1987. At the time of Nelson Mandela's release in 1990, the adult HIV infection rate, measured in an antenatal survey, stood at 0.7 per cent. By 1992, this had trebled to 2.2 per cent. As it became clear that HIV/AIDS was spreading rapidly, and becoming a heterosexually transmitted epidemic concentrated in black communities, the apartheid government implemented some practical interventions. It had, for example, acted to ensure safe blood supplies, begun an annual antenatal HIV surveillance programme in public health facilities in 1990, and set up a network of AIDS Training, Information and Counseling Centers, or ATICCs. Although ATICCs were largely located in white local authorities, they had, as Crewe points out, 'amassed a wealth of experience and training. These could have been transformed and expanded and developed satellite operations' (Crewe, 2000, p. 29).

Government efforts to promote AIDS education and prevention programmes in schools and elsewhere were at best ignored, at worst counter-productive. Sex education in South African schools, black and white, had always been a contentious issue, but in the dying years of apartheid, such programmes would have been impossible. The schools in the black townships had become 'sites of struggle' caught up in the political turmoil which marked much of the 1980s. Even had they been functioning normally, any government programme would have been met with suspicion and resistance. As it was, 'targeted' advertising campaigns with different message for white and black, were decried as 'typical of government racist propaganda'. Critics argued that if government had consulted black political organizations and trade unions, more appropriate messages could have been devised.

In the political climate of the times, and the policy of non-collaboration with government, any such overtures on the government's part would almost certainly have been rebuffed. Still in the 'silent' HIV phase, AIDS was dismissed by many as a government fabrication; the acronym was said to stand for 'Afrikaner Invention to Deprive us of Sex'. Conspiracy theories abounded. Advocating condom use or the restrictions implied in safer sex, raised suspicions that the real aim was to reinforce what many saw as government's 'genocidal' family-planning programme. On the other hand, if government was seen to be failing to promote safer sex it was attributed to the apartheid regime seeing AIDS as a way of controlling population growth! In November 1988 *Sechaba*, the official publication of the ANC in exile, questioned the African origin of the virus, suggesting, instead, that it may have been developed 'in the secrecy of the laboratories of many imperialist countries' (p. 28). Others believed that it was sprayed in police tear gas, or deliberately spread to black prostitutes by infected ex-ANC guerrillas who were working for the police.[1]

The situation was not improved by the efforts of the right wing to link AIDS to a call to reverse the process of political change. In February 1991, for instance, *Die Afrikaner* (6 February 1991), a newspaper of the ultra-conservative Herstigte Nasionale Party, accused the government of suppressing the information that HIV could be transmitted in casual contact, because it threatened the process of desegregating public amenities. An anonymous pamphlet, 'AIDS – the Facts', believed to come from the Conservative Party, accused the government of 'shockingly' increasing the danger of infection to 'low risk groups' (a euphemism for whites) by desegregating facilities such as hospitals, schools, swimming pools and blood banks.[2]

Other pamphlets carried similar messages; they differed only in the unrestrained viciousness of some of their attacks. One, entitled 'Welcome to the New South Africa', purporting to come from the 'White Consciousness Movement,' after describing gruesome episodes of violence, and pointing to the state's inability to protect its citizens, went on to warn that AIDS would ensure 'up to 25 million people will be dead or dying by the end of the century. And up to 7 million will be raving mad before dying.' After painting a lurid picture of AIDS being transmitted in desegregated schools, in non-racial sports and by domestic workers (and of global economic collapse), it concluded: 'There will be a *New South Africa* after the *Apocalypse* at the other side of the Valley of the Shadow of Death. Will you be there with us or will you have joined your "new brothers" to their doom?' Like all such apocalyptic political visions, it offered salvation. 'If you have any survival instinct left, support those who fight for you even if you do not always agree with them.'[3] Such responses bring to mind Susan Sontag's remarks in her essay *AIDS and its Metaphors*:

> The taste for worst case scenarios reflects the need to master fear of what is felt to be uncontrollable. It also expresses an imaginative complicity with disaster. The sense of cultural distress or failure gives rise to the desire for a clean sweep, a *tabula rasa*. No one wants a plague, of course. But yes, it would be a chance to begin again. (Sontag, 1989, p. 87)

Other pamphlets circulating at the time linked AIDS to Africa, to neighbouring states or to returning ANC exiles, presumably hoping to create divisions in the black community, fear among whites, and embarrassment for the government. One, purporting to come from the ANC, advised black men to have sex with Indian women, because they had 'antibodies to the virus'. The pamphlet also alleged that South Africa had paid Israeli scientists R1 billion for the virus, and urged blacks to destroy white racists. Nelson Mandela, then deputy president of the ANC, publicly denied any ANC connection with the pamphlet. It was seen by the ANC as 'no more than an amateurish effort to create uncertainty and panic, especially in the white community' (*Sunday Times Extra*, 22 April 1990).

The AIDS issue also surfaced in parliament. In May 1990, Conservative Party (CP) member, Dr F. H. Pauw, accused ruling National Party vote canvassers of reassuring its white members that black majority rule posed no threat because AIDS would ensure that blacks became a minority within five years (*Debates of Parliament*, 18 May 1990, col. 9761) – an unlikely outcome where 75 per cent of the country's population are black. In her reply, Health Minister, Dr Rina Venter, retorted that such beliefs were more representative of the CP, and quoted CP member Clive Derby-Lewis as saying: 'If AIDS stops black population growth, it would be like Father Christmas.' Venter rejected 'this fooling around with such a serious matter', and appealed to parliament not to make AIDS a political issue (*Debates of Parliament*, 18 May 1990, col. 9797).

It was a vain plea. As Refiloe Serote, of the Township AIDS Programme, observed, 'the political and racial divisions, created and inflamed by apartheid, make everything to do with AIDS "political" ' (*WorldAIDS*, 1990, p. 5). The turbulent climate of the 1980s and early 1990s made devising an apolitical, pragmatic response to the epidemic improbable, and the chance of the apartheid government implementing it, virtually nil. As anti-apartheid activist, Dr Ivan Toms, argued at the time, there was 'no possibility that the present government could, even if it [had] the inclination, run an effective campaign to limit the spread of HIV infection. It has no credibility or legitimacy whatsoever among blacks' (Toms, 1990, p. 14).

It clearly was an issue the new government would have to address. The African National Congress (ANC) had become increasingly concerned that the South Africa they inherited could fall prey to an epidemic of the proportions they had seen ravage many countries in sub-Saharan Africa in the 1980s, including Tanzania and Zambia, in which many of them had spent years of political exile. In April 1990, soon after the apartheid government's president, F. W. de Klerk, un-banned the ANC, representatives of the movement, and of a number of other anti-apartheid organizations, met in Maputo, Mozambique, at a conference on health and welfare. AIDS was on the agenda. The 250 delegates passed a resolution calling for immediate action by 'progressive' organizations in the face of an impending AIDS 'crisis'. Delegates were urged to play a leading role in AIDS campaigns 'situated within the broader struggle for political change', with senior leadership urged to become involved, in order to overcome the suspicion around AIDS that the apartheid government's attempts at information campaigns had aroused (*History in the Making*, 1991, p. 9). It was at this meeting that Chris Hani, head of Umkhonto we Sizwe, the armed wing of the ANC, and general secretary of the South African Communist Party, was to say: 'We cannot afford to allow the AIDS epidemic to ruin the realization of our dreams.' Having seen the epidemic close-up while in exile, he warned that, 'unattended [AIDS would] result in untold damage and suffering by the end of the century' (Marais, 2000, p. 4). Despite these strong words, senior ANC representatives failed to raise the issue at political rallies or public meetings at home (Crewe, 1992, p. 73).

The Congress of South African Trade Unions (COSATU), which would become part of the ruling government alliance in 1994, had sounded the alarm on AIDS in 1989, passing a resolution to provide education and protect workers' rights, and to fight the social conditions that fuelled the epidemic. In June 1991, COSATU held a conference devoted to developing an AIDS programme. David Morake, the conference organizer, criticized efforts by the apartheid government and employers as 'racist' and 'counter-productive', and said COSATU recognized that 'worker education is now the responsibility of the unions' (*Weekly Mail*,

28 June–4 July 1991). A few unions did attempt to put AIDS programmes in place, but in the turbulent political and labour climate of
the 1990s, AIDS was often low down on the list of union priorities. Mark
Heywood of the AIDS Law Project notes that in 1996 the Department of
Health's HIV/AIDS and STD Directorate sent out a questionnaire on the
issue to 150 trade unions: only twelve responded. Given that HIV/AIDS
was undoubtedly something which would be critical to workers,
Heywood expressed surprise that there had been 'hardly a squeal from
the official guardians of working class people', who seemed, he said, 'to
have little time, capacity and – dare we say it – will to deal with these
issues' (Heywood, 1997, pp. 28–9).

Despite repeated statements and assertions about plans to get
involved in the AIDS issue, little was actually done, and the ANC journal *Mayibuye* was forced to admit that South Africa's democratic movement had not seen its 'deep sense of urgency . . . translated into
practice' (*Mayibuye*, 1991, p. 37). By 1992, although South Africa was in
the throes of a massive, complex political transition, it was clear that
comprehensive planning to deal with the looming AIDS crisis could not
wait, and the NACOSA initiative was born.

It was very much a product of the times – what the 1997 South
African STD/HIV/AIDS Review would later call: 'an effective and democratic way of developing a representative and united response to the
HIV/AIDS epidemic' (Marais, 2000, p. 12). It covered the six key elements fundamental to most such plans – education and prevention,
counselling, health care, human rights and law reform, welfare and
research[4] – and was praised by those in the AIDS field in South Africa
and abroad as an enlightened and comprehensive strategy. Two of the
eight-member drafting committee – Dr Nkosazana Dlamini-Zuma and
Dr Manto Tshabalala-Msimang – would go on to become consecutive
health ministers in the new South African government (NACOSA, 1994,
p. 11). NACOSA believed its strategy would be 'the one with the most
credibility and legitimacy upon which the government can act', and
saw itself continuing to function 'as a collaborator and watchdog on the
government's National AIDS policy and commitment' (NACOSA, 1994,
p. 4).

After the April 1994 elections, with Dlamini-Zuma then Minister of
Health, the NACOSA strategy was endorsed as the National AIDS Plan,
and its rapid implementation eagerly anticipated. What followed was a
disillusioning experience for those who had hoped South Africa's successful handling of AIDS would 'astonish the world' as much as its transition to democracy had done (Crewe, 2000, p. 28).

1994 to 1999: a troubled transition

NACOSA had envisaged that the National AIDS Plan programme would be located in the office of the president, a formula that had worked well in Uganda (Rwomushana, 2000). Such a location would prioritize AIDS and ensure that it would be recognized as far more than simply a health matter. In South Africa, although it was endorsed by the Cabinet – important for multisectoral support – and designated a 'Presidential Lead Project' in the Reconstruction and Development Programme, it was situated firmly in the Department of Health, where, a decade later Mary Crewe writes: it 'remains un-consulted, unimplemented and largely ignored' (Crewe, 2000, p. 28).

Looking back, one could say that AIDS had arrived at the best of times, and at the worst of times – the best because with the transition to democracy under Nelson Mandela, a charismatic leader with immense moral authority, to lend credibility and legitimacy to government interventions, and with hordes of dedicated people willing to help as evidenced by the NACOSA network, South Africa was finally in a position to confront the epidemic, and to shed the political baggage that HIV/AIDS had acquired; the worst, because the disease had been politicized in the run-up to the transition, and the fragmented health system inherited from apartheid needed major restructuring, requiring the integration of sometimes reluctant, even obstructive, old and new bureaucrats. Tensions between local, provincial and national governments over policy, programmes and budgetary allocations often paralysed implementation. Hein Marais talks of 'feuding' between levels, with mutual blame for lack of delivery. 'At play, it seemed, were fascinating, but debilitating struggles for legitimacy, influence and power' (Marais, 2000, p. 17).

It also was a time when the new government would prioritize positive programmes, such as housing, jobs, education and wider healthcare issues. AIDS warnings and the message of safer sex were not subjects congenial to those savouring the euphoria of freedom.

By 1996 it was clear that the plan was floundering. Two years after its implementation, HIV levels had almost doubled – from 7.6 per cent in 1994 to 14.2 per cent in 1996. The vision of a 'South Africa United Against AIDS' was fading fast, as discord and confusion took over.

A major review of the strategy in 1997 noted, among other problems, the lack of political leadership around the issue (*South African STD/HIV/ AIDS Review*, 1997). Many had hoped that Mandela, like President Yoweri Museveni of Uganda, would personally lead South Africa's AIDS crusade. Justin Parkhurst ascribes Museveni's success to his unique position in coming to power after years of civil strife, suggesting that a transition to peace is a time particularly suited to radical policy reform (Parkhurst, 2001, p. 75). Although Mandela made a major speech on HIV/AIDS at the World Economic Forum in Davos, Switzerland, in February 1997, he seldom highlighted the issue in South Africa. He was aware of its significance, as his Davos speech makes clear. 'When the history of our time is written, it will record the collective efforts of societies responding to a threat that has put in the balance the future of whole nations. Future generations will judge us on the adequacy of our response' (*Cape Argus*, 6 February 1997). Although the South Africa campaign called for 'a New Struggle' – a reference to the 'old' struggle against apartheid – such fighting talk was seldom heard from South African platforms. Mandela, by virtue of his age, and the conservatism surrounding open public discussion of sexual matters among South Africans, black and white, found the topic uncomfortable. This failure surely will be seen as one of the few major weaknesses of his presidency.[5]

Implementation difficulties were compounded by a series of scandals and blunders. In 1995, the Department of Health had commissioned a musical, *Sarafina II*, intended to take AIDS education to the masses. An inappropriate, all-star, big budget production, it devoured R14.2 million of a slender AIDS budget. Using unauthorized expenditure, based on a flawed tendering process, its message was far from clear. It drew heavy criticism not only from political opponents, but also from AIDS organizations. Apart from the criticism that the money could have been better used in local projects, with a better understanding of AIDS issues, they were alarmed at the increasingly high-handed, non-consultative way that Health Minister Dlamini-Zuma was making decisions around HIV/AIDS. Despite her stated policy of accountability and transparency, AIDS organizations felt that they were being marginalized. Some even felt that cuts to their funding – from R19 million to R2 million in 1998 – were in part motivated by spite because they had tried to hold the Department to account (Marais, 2000, pp. 33–4).

Sarafina II marks a watershed in relations between the Health Department and civil society. A NACOSA briefing to the Parliamentary Portfolio Committee on Health (3 September 1996) states: '*Sarafina II* has done immense damage to the individuals and organizations active in the AIDS field. The process was not transparent and this has resulted in a rift between the Department of Health, NACOSA and the NGOs, as well as public derision about and hostility to HIV/AIDS work and programs.'[6] This breakdown of the solidarity, which had characterized early relations between the Health Department, and what Mary Crewe has called 'the AIDS world',[7] and public criticism, confusion, even cynicism, about HIV/AIDS programmes, is a process which undermines the AIDS efforts down to the present day.

In 1997, while the *Sarafina II* matter was still under investigation, the government found itself embroiled in yet another controversy, involving their support for a substance, Virodene PO58, an industrial solvent (dimethylformamide) once tested as a cancer therapy, but abandoned as being ineffective and toxic. This time not only the health minister, but the entire cabinet, including Deputy President Thabo Mbeki, became entangled in the affair, as they sought endorsement for its use as a treatment for AIDS. It was a scientific issue on which cabinet was ill-equipped to pass judgement. The researchers touting it had ignored the established ethical and procedural protocols for drug research, and Virodene had been branded as dangerous by the Medicines Control Council (MCC), the country's drug regulatory body. Peter Folb, director of the MCC and a (white) ANC member, faced pressure from both Dlamini-Zuma and Mbeki to approve the drug. Frustrated by his repeated refusal, Dlamini-Zuma finally rounded on him: 'You're ANC. Why won't you back me on this?' (*Washington Post*, 6 July 2000). 'The following year, government shut down the MCC replacing it with a new control body' (Marais, 2000, p. 13).

In a long dispute over the affair, the opposition Democratic Party (DP), which had accused the ANC of having a financial link with the developers of Virodene, exchanged bitter words with the ANC. At one stage Dlamini-Zuma exploded that 'the DP hates ANC supporters. If they had their way we would all die of AIDS' (Marais, 2000, p. 13). Thabo Mbeki himself, in a newspaper article, pointed to the fate of millions infected with HIV/AIDS in sub-Saharan Africa, and wondered if 'those who kicked up all these duststorms' around Virodene 'did not have precisely these results in mind' (*Rapport*, 8 March 1998 – author's translation from Afrikaans).

In October 1998, the heat around HIV/AIDS went up a few degrees when Minister Dlamini-Zuma announced that she and her nine provincial health ministers had decided not to make AZT (zidovudine), a drug which could cut vertical transmission of HIV from infected mothers to their babies by 50 per cent, available. The government would concentrate rather on prevention (*Sunday Times*, 11 October 1998). When critics noted that AZT was *aimed* at prevention, she countered that, despite Glaxo Wellcome, AZT's manufacturer, drastically cutting the price of the drug, preventing mother-to-child-transmission (MTCT) remained too expensive because it required testing, counselling, formula feeding and technical support.

These arguments and suggestions that AZT, and its successor for MTCT prevention, nevirapine, were toxic or created drug resistance, are still part of a fiery debate in South Africa. Some have accused those advocating drug use of operating with a hidden agenda – deliberately foisting toxic substances on the black population, or serving the interests of the pharmaceutical industry. It was in the wake of Dlamini-Zuma's AZT decision, that the activist organization, the Treatment Action Campaign (TAC), was formed, its object to ensure enhanced prevention, and care for those infected with HIV/AIDS. With broad links into civil society, it aimed to pressure both government and the pharmaceutical companies into making treatment more accessible and affordable (Marais, 2000, p. 39).

Dlamini-Zuma's stance also drew criticism from health professionals on ethical and medical grounds. Economists disputed her case on the basis of cost-benefit analysis of MTCT prevention. There also were the beginnings of international scrutiny, as *Nature* carried a report that researchers were considering boycotting the prestigious thirteenth International AIDS Conference – AIDS 2000 – due to be held in Durban, South Africa in July 2000, if the government did not relent (Cherry, 1998).

In January 1999, the first signs of political rebellion against national policy saw the Western Cape, a province not under ANC control, decide to go ahead with providing AZT and free formula feed at two Cape Town clinics in communities with substantial HIV prevalence. The province was accused of playing games with the lives and hopes of vulnerable people, of making AIDS a political football (Crewe, 1999, p. 30), but the Western Cape branch of NACOSA disagreed. The initiative finally had given some meaning to the much-vaunted notion of a partnership against AIDS, in so far as it drew together people of different political persuasions and organizations in a concerted effort to deal with HIV/AIDS (NACOSA, 1999, pp. 5–6).

By 1999, Dlamini-Zuma's position had become untenable. She had stonewalled on AZT, been embroiled in bitter disputes with the pharmaceutical industry, alienated those working in the AIDS field, and presided over a series of minor and major public relations disasters. Given that the media, the opposition parties and the leadership of many in AIDS organizations were white, it was perhaps inevitable that she translated criticism against herself into a counter-charge of racism – a charge which in turn drew anger and derision from blacks in the field (Marais, 2000, p. 33).

1999 to 2002: the Mbeki years

After South Africa's second democratic election in June 1999, Mandela stepped down and Thabo Mbeki was elected President. Dlamini-Zuma changed cabinet portfolios to become Minister of Foreign Affairs, and Dr Manto Tshabalala-Msimang became Minister of Health. Tshabalala-Msimang's arrival was a breath of fresh air. Within weeks, she met with NACOSA, the pharmaceutical industry, doctors involved in MTCT prevention, and, on a visit to Uganda, consulted with those involved in HIV/AIDS prevention and their nevirapine MTCT project. She came back from that trip 'absolutely inspired' that AIDS was a battle South Africa could win (*Pulsetrack*, 6 August 1999). The enthusiasm was not to last.

In October 1999, President Mbeki informed the National Council of Provinces that his Internet research had revealed that AZT was toxic (*Pulsetrack*, 29 October 1999). Shortly thereafter, Tshabalala-Msimang suggested that AZT weakened the immune system and could lead to disabling 'mutations' in babies (*News24.com*, 29 November 1999).

There was dismay in the AIDS world. Professor Hoosen Coovadia of the University of Natal, who was to chair the AIDS 2000 conference, said of the government's 'quixotic' response, that they stood 'on their own, in conflict with every informed opinion, including my own, in South Africa'. He suggested that such 'amazing statements with no basis in fact' might be the result of 'bad advisors or a preoccupation with the pharmaceutical industry's impact on South Africa' (*Reuters Health*, 2 December 1999).

The launch of the government's South African National AIDS Council (SANAC) in January 2000 was greeted with anger and despair. There had been repeated calls for a multi-sectoral national AIDS commission, along the lines of that in Uganda; instead, the nation got an anaemic body with fifteen cabinet ministers (who had shown little enthusiasm for AIDS issues in the Inter-ministerial Committee established in 1997), and a hodge-podge of 'sector' representatives. The 600-plus organizations involved in HIV/AIDS had one representative; high profile organizations like the AIDS Law Project and TAC had none. There were three members representing 'sport', the hospitality industry and 'celebrities', and two traditional healers – but no scientists, medical practitioners or representatives of bodies such as the Medicines Control Council or the Medical Research Council. For those who had hoped for a strategic think tank, a muscular body that could take control of the rudderless AIDS programme and steer it away from the looming AIDS disaster, SANAC was a bitter disappointment.[8]

Worse was to follow. Mbeki's personal scepticism about AZT proved to extend to a wider mistrust of what he called 'the science of AIDS', and his questioning led him into the camp of the so-called 'dissidents', who questioned whether HIV existed, whether it was simply a harmless 'passenger' virus, whether AIDS was a 'lifestyle' disease precipitated by using recreational drugs (or even AZT), and whether, if there was indeed increased morbidity and mortality in Africa, that they were simply the result of poverty aggravating old disease patterns. Attracted by these alternative theories, in early 2000, Mbeki set up the 'Presidential International Panel of Scientists on HIV/AIDS in Africa' to establish 'the facts'.[9] Predictably, the inclusion of well-known dissidents such as Peter Duesberg and David Rasnick on the panel caused uproar in the scientific and medical fraternity (van der Vliet, 2001, p. 171). Mbeki appeared to hope that the diverse panel could come up with some kind of compromise position. One panellist commented, 'The absurdity of this panel is without question . . . The President wants to know that we came to an agreement' (*Independent online*, 7 July 2000).

Then, in April 2000, Mbeki baffled world leaders, including UN Secretary General Kofi Annan, US President Bill Clinton and Britain's Prime Minister Tony Blair, in a letter hand-addressed to each, in which he made an impassioned plea to revisit the issue of AIDS in Africa. In the media, this extraordinary letter has often been distorted to suggest that it said outright that HIV did not cause AIDS. Had this been the case, the government AIDS prevention and vaccine programme Mbeki outlined would not make sense, since they depend on AIDS being a sexually transmitted disease with a viral etiology. He did, however, say that the search for a response to the 'specifically African' epidemic required that all opinions needed to be considered. In an alarmingly intemperate defence of the dissident position, he portrayed them as being terrorized and intimidated in their fight to have their voices heard, much as the 'racist apartheid tyranny' once did in South Africa.[10]

His letter provoked strong negative reactions, locally and internationally. Professor William Malegapuru Makgoba, president of the Medical Research Council, wrote of the 'lengthening list of politically driven decisions regarding the South African AIDS crisis', and warned that the country was 'rapidly becoming a fertile breeding ground for the types of pseudo-science embraced by politicians' (*Sunday Times*, 21 May 2000). With the AIDS 2000 conference just weeks away, conference chairperson, Professor Coovadia made a similar plea for Mbeki to keep clear of scientific debates (*Sunday Independent*, 25 June 2000). In response, Coovadia and his co-authors met with a swingeing personal attack in a press article by Tshabalala-Msimang and two other cabinet ministers, questioning their academic credentials, and suggesting that they were operating as 'frontline troops of the pharmaceutical industry' (*Sunday Independent*, 2 July 2000).

Clearly, the old pharmaceutical industry bogey, apparent since Dlamini-Zuma's time, was still strong. Mbeki seemed to share this view. Responding to the demand for AZT to prevent MTCT, he professed to be taken aback by the determination of many South Africans 'to sacrifice all intellectual integrity to act as salespersons of the product of one pharmaceutical company' (*Agence France Presse*, 2 April 2000) – a view possibly reinforced by the dissidents' notion that mainstream scientists are, perhaps 'largely unwittingly', part of a pharmaceutical industry conspiracy to sell anti-AIDS drugs (Epstein, 2000, p. 50).

With the AIDS 2000 conference due to open on 10 July, the journal *Nature* (6 July 2000) published what came to be called the Durban Declaration,[11] in the hope of clarifying, once and for all, the scientific position on HIV and AIDS. Signed by 5000 scientists, including local members of the president's panel, Nobel Prize winners, and directors of leading research institutions and medical societies, the document was dismissed by Tshabalala-Msimang as an 'elitist document' signed only by health scientists. 'You can't have a certain exclusive group of people saying this is what we believe about HIV and AIDS' (*Independent online*, 3 July 2000). Coovadia dryly commented, 'science is elitist' (*Business Day*, 14 July 2000). Parks Mankahlana, head of communications in the president's office, warned that if the drafters gave the Declaration to the president or the government, it would find 'its comfortable place among the dustbins of the office' (*Woza News*, 1 July 2000).

The controversy ensured that the eyes of the world would be focused on Mbeki when he opened the AIDS 2000 conference. Many saw it as an opportunity for him to pull back into the mainstream. Instead, he sidestepped the issues completely, offering for much of his speech the findings of a 1995 World Health Organization report which argued that the world's biggest killer was extreme poverty – a theme in line with dissidents like Charles Geshekter, a US historian, and one to which Mbeki frequently returns.[12]

The deep disappointment Mbeki's speech evoked, perhaps helps to explain the rousing reception given to South African High Court judge, Edwin Cameron, when he addressed a plenary session of the conference (Cameron, 2000). A long-time AIDS activist, gay and HIV-positive, Cameron criticized the government's 'grievous ineptitude' in its handling of AIDS, and Mbeki's 'flirtation' with the dissidents which had 'shaken almost everyone responsible for engaging the epidemic. It has created an air of disbelief among scientists, confusion among those at risk of HIV, and consternation amongst AIDS workers.' He quoted Dr Mamphela Ramphele, ex vice-chancellor of the University of Cape Town, and currently Managing Director of the World Bank, saying that giving official sanction to scepticism about the cause of AIDS was 'irresponsibility that bordered on criminality'. Coovadia saw, in the huge ovation that Cameron received, a red light flashing: the uniformity of criticism coming from the conference and the expressions of solidarity with Cameron showed strong disapproval of government. Coovadia warned that the gap between the government and its critics had not been bridged – it was in fact widening (*Business Day*, 14 July 2000).

Closing the conference, former president Nelson Mandela urged people to make every effort 'to rise above our differences and combine our efforts to save our people. History will judge us harshly if we fail to do so, and right now.' In a plainspoken, no-frills delivery, he called for large-scale interventions to prevent MTCT, and spoke of how the safer sex message was working in Uganda, Senegal and Thailand. The time had come, he said, to move from rhetoric to action, to mobilize 'all of our resources and alliances, and to sustain this effort until this war is won'.[13] As the audience responded with a tumultuous standing ovation, there were those who hoped that Mandela might have helped set South Africa back on track – that we would finally see a 'South Africa United Against AIDS'.

It was a false dawn. No unequivocal acceptance of the 'HIV-causes-AIDS' position by Mbeki followed, and, instead, he retreated further into semantics, conspiracy theories and bad science.[14] Finally his own constituency stepped in. Alliance partners, COSATU and the South African Communist Party (SACP), and even some elements of the ANC, stated publicly that the link between HIV and AIDS was irrefutable; any questioning of this fact was unscientific and likely to confuse people.[15] In October 2000, it became clear that Mbeki's position was not only causing a rift in the alliance, but doing his image at home and abroad immense damage; Mbeki informed the ANC that he was withdrawing from 'the public debate' on the science of HIV and AIDS (*Sunday Times*, 15 October 2000).

Again, some hoped this would move South Africa past the whole damaging controversy, and into a coherent government response. However, Mbeki's move was a tactical withdrawal rather than a recantation. In his New Year speech in 2001, Mbeki did not mention HIV/AIDS directly. Some of the heat went out of the issue, but it continued to simmer. In early April, the presidential AIDS Advisory Panel released its interim report.[16] At 134 pages, with thirteen pages of recommendations, and costing an estimated R2.5 million, the report looked substantial, but one suspects it was something of an embarrassment to the government. While Tshabalala-Msimang said that the objective of the panel had been to 'pursue debate on scientific and public policy issues in a dispassionate manner' (*Pulsetrack*, 5 April 2000), bringing together thirty-three 'experts' with diametrically opposed views had generated little apart from acrimony and confusion. The exercise had raised Mbeki's profile, largely to his detriment, although he became something of a hero among the dissident movement. Their web pages featured his photograph, and thousands signed their support for what they termed his 'call for an open scientific debate'.[17] Although Tshabalala-Msimang's statement noted that the debates of the panel had not 'provided grounds for government to depart from its current approach to the HIV/AIDS problem which is rooted in the premise that HIV causes AIDS' (*Pulsetrack*, 5 April 2000), the report itself presents two opposing sets of recommendations from the orthodox and dissident scientists. AIDS activists were incensed. They believed the whole farcical 'debate' had set back the HIV/AIDS programme by years, with people now questioning the necessity for safer sex and the validity of HIV testing.

The panel report soon was overshadowed by the long-awaited settlement of a dispute between the government and the pharmaceutical industry. In 1997, South Africa had drawn up legislation, which would have allowed it to use parallel imports and compulsory licensing to access cheap drugs. Concerned about intellectual property rights, the plan was challenged by thirty-nine manufacturers and the Pharmaceutical Manufacturers Association of South Africa (*Financial Mail*, 9 March 2001, p. 30). While the case originally dealt with dry legal issues around patent rights on drugs in general, AIDS activists led by the Treatment Action Campaign (TAC) succeeded in diverting attention on to the issue of access to drugs for HIV/AIDS sufferers. Their demonstrations and protests, designed to draw worldwide media attention, presented a parallel case phrased in moral and ethical terms, rather than the legal minutiae of the court case.

Under the glare of the international spotlight, the case proved a public relations disaster for the pharmaceutical industry. The *Wall Street Journal* (6 March 2001) talked of industry executives concerned that the 'vilification of the industry' would become so widespread that governments, in both poor and rich countries, might become emboldened to take away drug company patents. Already generic manufacturers were offering tempting packages to government and NGOs, such as Médecins Sans Frontières (*New York Times*, 7 February 2001). On 19 April, the pharmaceutical industry withdrew its case. Predictably, there was dancing in the streets. For a brief moment, the AIDS world and the government danced together. Tshabalala-Msimang was jubilant. 'This is a victory not just for South Africa but for Africa and the whole developing world. I would like to say thank you to the whole world for supporting us' (*Daily News*, 19 April 2001). However, the elation soon received a cold shower. At a press conference, the minister announced that as far as government was concerned, the drugs remained unaffordable, infrastructure to distribute them effectively was lacking, and there were still concerns about their safety (*Agence France-Presse*, 20 April 2001; *Associated Press*, 20 April 2001). To date, little has come of this victory, a failure which, as a *Business Day* editorial at the time suggested, would leave 'the impression that government is more interested in scoring points off the multinationals than providing care for millions of poor HIV/AIDS sufferers' (*Business Day*, 20 April 2001).

In the week in which the case was withdrawn, the ANC website published a detailed report, drawing selectively on US guidelines, pointing to the immense difficulties and dangers involved in antiretroviral (ARV) treatment, a situation which it said 'does not admit of inhuman games and clever intellectual point-scoring. It does not allow for the propagation of unscientific slogans that "the time for scientific enquiry is over".' It appeared to pin its hopes for a solution on the presidential advisory panel (*Pulsetrack*, 25 April 2001).

That the dissidents on the panel still influenced Mbeki became clear, when he again spoke publicly of HIV/AIDS on e-TV on 24 April 2001. He said he would not be prepared to take a public HIV test because it would send a message that he supported a particular scientific viewpoint. 'I go and do a test – I am confirming a particular paradigm.' Mbeki also rejected growing calls for ARV drugs for AIDS patients, saying they were not yet proven safe. 'I think it would be criminal if our government did not deal with the toxicity of these drugs,' he said. 'Let's stop politicizing this question, let's deal with the science of it' (*Associated Press*, 24 April 2001).

For many, such issues amounted to delaying tactics, and activists found the lack of a sense of urgency exasperating. TAC's Zackie Achmat said after the case that they hoped government would have a treatment plan in place by 1 December 2001, World AIDS Day, and would roll out antiretrovirals in the public sector by New Year (*Agence France-Presse*, 20 April 2001). From a government which had not even begun to address the issue of ARV treatments, that was obviously a wildly optimistic expectation, but the activists clearly hoped there would be some pay-off for their monumental efforts. They had managed to turn a mundane legal wrangle into an international *cause célebre*, thanks to their exertions, including an international 260 000 signature 'Drop the Case' petition.[18] As government walked away from the ARV issue, activists could reasonably feel that they had been used as a moral battering ram to destroy the pharmaceutical case by those who had a very different agenda.

South Africa, in fact, was still wrestling with the most basic drug provision issue – the use of AZT or nevirapine (viramune) to prevent HIV-infected pregnant women passing on the virus to their babies. The HIVNET trials in Uganda in 1999 (Guay et al., 1999) had shown that one dose of nevirapine each to mother and baby could cut transmission of the virus by 50 per cent, and the SAINT trials (Moodley et al., 2000) in South Africa confirmed this. By October 2000, UNAIDS advocated that drug regimens to prevent MTCT 'should be included in the minimum standard package of care' for HIV-positive women, and that there was 'no justification to restrict use to research settings'.

With an estimated 5000 babies born HIV-positive each month, the possibility of preventing 30 000 HIV infections a year would represent at least one small ray of light on the gloomy South African HIV/AIDS landscape. The drug's manufacturer, Boehringer Ingelheim, had offered the drug free to developing countries for five years. But there were interminable delays in getting nevirapine registered for MTCT prevention. After over a year of foot dragging, the MCC finally registered it for this purpose in April 2001. The Department of Health was supposed to be testing it at two pilot sites in each province from the beginning of April 2001 (*Health-e News*, 19 April 2001) but even this limited programme was again stalled, ostensibly because it had to be approved by cabinet. Mark Heywood, of the AIDS Law Project, fumed: 'There is no justifiable reason to refer a matter of public health policy, in line with the government's strategic AIDS plan, back to the Cabinet . . . Everybody, apart from a few headcases, accepts nevirapine as a useful tool to fight HIV infections' (*Mail and Guardian*, 10 May 2001). There have been repeated rumours that the stalling on nevirapine is deliberate, (*Sunday Independent*, 8 April 2001; *Business Day*, 9 April 2001), due to what some have called 'top level political interference' (*The Star*, 11 April 2001).

In the face of the delays, the Western Cape province, an area under the control of the New National Party, had, in January 1999 (*Die Burger*, 9 April 2001), begun to use AZT at some antenatal clinics in black townships with high levels of HIV infection, despite ANC accusations that it was using dangerous and toxic drugs, with blacks as guinea pigs, in a manner reminiscent of the biological warfare of the apartheid era. In January 2001, the Western Cape, now under the control of the Democratic Alliance party, extended MTCT prevention to further clinics, using nevirapine on an 'off-label' basis.[19] The Cape Town township of Khayelitsha was also the site of the first provincial pilot project to provide triple therapy to treat AIDS patients in collaboration with a Médecins Sans Frontières team (*Cape Argus*, 25 May 2001), and the authorities began establishing rape crisis centres where rape survivors could be given counselling, care, and free AZT prophylaxis against HIV transmission.

Such rape interventions had proved highly controversial elsewhere in the country. In the province of Mpumalanga, for instance, the Greater Nelspruit Rape Intervention Project (GRIP), launched in 2000, and staffed largely by black women volunteers (a project welcomed by the hospitals where they operated), was repeatedly harassed by the provincial authorities, and the Mpumalanga health minister, Sibongile Manana, who accused the project of attempting to poison black people, and 'trying to overthrow the government' (*The Guardian*, 12 June 2001). The dispute over distributing ARVs not only to rape survivors, but also to pregnant women, resulted in lawsuits, the resignation of a number of doctors (in an area where hospitals are already under staffing pressure), and the axing of Rob Ferreira Hospital superintendent, Dr Thys von Mollendorff, in February 2002 (Samayende and Arenstein, 2002, pp. 11–13).[20]

It was clear that despite Mbeki's call to depoliticize AIDS, it was still an issue saturated with politics, and Mbeki's influence on the topic was far from over. In a tough interview with BBC's Tim Sebastian on his *Hard Talk* show on 6 August 2001, Mbeki repeated his now-familiar argument that the diseases killing South Africans were caused by immune deficiencies, but that the virus was only one of many factors precipitating this condition, and the government needed a 'comprehensive' response to all the causes. When Sebastian suggested that Mbeki's critics, including the labour unions, and AIDS workers in Soweto, felt Mbeki's stance had 'muddied the waters' and damaged AIDS campaigns, Mbeki replied that was 'absolute nonsense'. Sebastian questioned Mbeki's priorities in the face of a projected seven million AIDS deaths in the next ten years; Mbeki responded by saying the largest single cause of death among men aged 16 to 45 years was violence, which accounted for 54 per cent of such deaths.[21]

Mbeki's claims were based on a study using 1999 statistics (*Agence France-Presse*, 8 August 2001). While they certainly confirmed Mbeki's view of how terrible violence was in South Africa, they reflected the deaths of people infected five to ten years earlier – a time when HIV infections were low. As the HIV/AIDS epidemic matures, such retrospective data are of little value in policy formation.

The same can be said of Mbeki's next venture into statistics where, in a letter to Health Minister Tshabalala-Msimang, he quoted 1995 World Health Organization (WHO) 'causes of death' tables for South Africa which appear on the Internet, and suggested that HIV/AIDS only accounted for 2.2 per cent of the recorded deaths (*Business Day*, 10 September 2001). If such figures were accurate, Mbeki suggested, perhaps health and social policy priorities needed reevaluation, as did the country's HIV/AIDS statistics, and the programmes at state medical research institutes. Mbeki wrote that these figures would undoubtedly 'provoke a howl of displeasure and a concerted propaganda campaign' from those who had convinced themselves that HIV/AIDS was the biggest single cause of death, but 'we cannot allow that government policy and programs should be informed by misperceptions'.[22]

Quite apart from the age of the WHO figures, such data are often skewed by the 'invisibility' of AIDS as a cause of death. Because AIDS deaths may carry social and financial consequences, and doctors are not obliged to give HIV/AIDS as an underlying cause of death from tuberculosis or pneumonia, death certificates are not necessarily a useful guide to actual AIDS deaths, and will always underestimate actual incidence.

The sudden need to challenge those who believed the country faced a runaway epidemic, was probably influenced by the imminent release of a study by the Medical Research Council (MRC) – a state body – which concluded that, in the period 1999 to mid-2001, AIDS had indeed become the leading cause of death in South Africa. In the year 2000, 40 per cent of deaths among those aged 15 to 49, and 25 per cent of total deaths, including children, were from AIDS-related illnesses.[23] The findings clearly caused consternation in government. In a letter to the *Sunday Times* (14 October 2001), Tshabalala-Msimang and two cabinet colleagues wrote that Statistics SA was the official body dealing with statistical matters in the country, and that 'official statistics' would be released towards the end of the year.[24] The MRC study was part of a project conducted by an interdepartmental task team; current data, including the MRC report, could not be relied upon, and were at most 'just a work-in-progress'. That the report – and the public demand for its release which had preceded it – had shaken government was clear from the tone of their article, which talked of 'lynch mobs', 'the delirium of witchhunts', 'the tearing of hairs', 'beating of drums' and 'a sense of hysteria all round'.[25]

Professor Malegapuru Makgoba, the president of the MRC, had first made public the alarming change in mortality profiles at a meeting of the Presidential AIDS Advisory Panel early in 2000, and in November warned that if the epidemic went unchecked it would claim between five and seven million South Africans by 2010, 'which compares with the Holocaust figure of six million' (*Independent online*, 21 November 2000). Clearly, these were figures the government would prefer not to hear, hence the delayed release, despite pressure from AIDS activists, trade unions, religious leaders and others. When cabinet reluctantly agreed to release the findings, *The Star* (2 October 2001) reported Tshabalala-Msimang as saying that she found it 'highly regrettable that employees of the MRC, who themselves are government employees, should have chosen to act in ways which place themselves in a hostile position vis-à-vis the government, and it will be necessary for this serious situation to be attended to'.[26] Wisely, Makgoba did not comment. Knowing the figures would cause uproar, he had ensured that they had been checked and rechecked, and, he said, 'commented upon and reviewed by a panel of leading world authorities on demography, epidemiology and medical statistics' (*Business Day*, 4 October 2001).

Statistics SA was also called on by government to challenge the MRC findings, but its comment was snarled up in issues unrelated to the fundamentals of a changing mortality profile.[27] Many of the limitations in the report's data, and the models to which it refers, were acknowledged by the five authors of the MRC report themselves. As one of them, Professor Rob Dorrington, of the University of Cape Town's Centre for Actuarial Research, told a subsequent press briefing, the Statistics SA comment was 'riddled with half-truths and misunderstandings', suggesting they had 'little knowledge or experience in this area' (*Independent online*, 16 October 2001).

The government response in impugning the MRC study, was attacking, in Makgoba, a man who had been a staunch supporter of Mbeki's vision of an African renaissance. It had also once again come into conflict with its trade union alliance partner, COSATU. In a joint campaign with TAC and religious leaders, COSATU demanded that government reprioritize its spending to reflect the findings of the MRC report. Accusing government of being in denial, when the reality of the epidemic was obvious, even in the numbers of their members they were burying, they called for the epidemic to be declared a national emergency (*The Sunday Independent*, 22 September 2001).

Coercing science into the service of politics has always been a dangerous game; when your constituency confronts the fallacies in your position on a daily basis, it comes with considerable political risk.

Popular sentiment was also inflamed by growing reports of child-rape, in some cases of infants less than a year old. Horrible enough in their own right, their relation to a widespread myth that sex with a virgin was a cure for AIDS added a fatal dimension to the crime. In a youth survey by the *loveLife* organization, *Hot Prospects, Cold Facts* (March 2001), 7 per cent of those interviewed believed sex with a virgin could cure AIDS, and 18 per cent did not know.[28] Dr Ivan Toms, director of Cape Town's health services, pointed out that the danger to young girls was twofold – on one hand the myth itself, on the other the probability that very young girls became targets because they were less likely to be infected. The virgin myth he said, had 'created a huge crisis' (*Sunday Times – Metro Supplement – Western Cape*, 28 October 2001). While political leaders have come out with appropriate expressions of shock and horror, one sees little of the strong public information campaign needed to counteract the myth, from not only political figures, but also the whole range of influential community leaders, from traditional leaders and healers, to pop stars and sports heroes. While it may be a sensitive issue to address, unfortunately almost everything that needs saying on the HIV/AIDS issue is bound to offend someone.

It is one of the ironies of South Africa that a country with one of the most gender-sensitive constitutions, including a Commission on Gender Equality, should also experience very high levels of violence against women (Jewkes, 2001). The inability to negotiate safer sex because of gender inequality is a major driving force in the HIV/AIDS epidemic. While the leaders have tended to sidestep the issue, ANC women's groups have been more forthright. They have issued statements not only on the virgin myth, but on rape and violence against women generally, from the ANC Women's League and the ANC Women's Caucus. Caucus chairwoman, Lulu Xingwana, said of the virgin myth that it was an 'ignorant, unfounded and perverse belief', and both groups have called for life sentences for men who knew they were HIV-positive, yet raped babies and children (*Sunday Tribune*, 3 November 2001).

Symptomatic of increasing tensions within the ANC on HIV/AIDS issues was the report by the Parliamentary Joint Standing Committee on the Improvement of the Quality of Life and Status of Women which was released on 14 November 2001. In the report – 'How best can South Africa address the horrific impact of HIV/AIDS on women and girls?' – the Committee, dominated by ANC women members, and chaired by

ANC MP Pregs Govender, recommended not only that antiretrovirals for rape survivors and to prevent MTCT be made available in the public health system, but, citing the successful provision of such drugs in Brazil, that national guidelines for providing ARVs on a wider scale be urgently addressed (*The Sunday Independent*, 17 November 2001; *Sunday Times*, 25 November 2001).[29]

As 2001 ended, the attack on government policy was once again led by TAC. After four years of trying to persuade government to institute an MTCT prevention programme, TAC finally made good on its threat to take the government to court on the issue. The application, launched by TAC, Dr Haroon Saloojee, principal paediatric specialist at Soweto's Chris Hani Baragwanath Hospital, and the Children's Rights Centre, was filed in the Pretoria High Court on 22 August 2001. The court application ran to over 600 pages and was supported by more than 250 doctors.[30] It demanded that the government institute a comprehensive MTCT reduction programme, using nevirapine, within a clearly defined time frame. The minister of health and all nine provincial health MECs were named as respondents. The case finally came to court on 26 November (although excluding the Western Cape health MEC, since the province was already complying with the demands). By this stage, it had drawn huge support from healthcare specialists, AIDS activists, scientists, union leaders, religious leaders and international organizations like Oxfam and Médecins Sans Frontières. Mark Heywood, TAC national chairman and head of the AIDS Law Project, told a news conference in Johannesburg that he found it regrettable that a government for which the people had struggled, had to be taken to court in pursuit of people's constitutional right to life, and to compel government to fulfil its constitutional obligations (*Pulsetrack*, 22 November 2001). For its part, the government was to argue that it was not the court's role to make policy decisions, that government had to consider the operational and budgetary implications of such a programme, and that research on nevirapine was inconclusive (*Health-e News*, 22 November 2001).

Although the government was ostensibly fighting the case on the limited issue of drugs for MTCT prevention, it was clear that it saw this as the thin end of the wedge. Not only were demands for wider use of ARVs coming from TAC and AIDS activists, but increasingly from within the government's own constituency, as the Govender report and calls from COSATU made clear. TAC also had outlined, in its Bredell Consensus, plans to widen its demands.[31]

When Judge Chris Botha delivered his landmark judgement on 14 December it was predictable that the government would take the case on appeal to the Constitutional Court. In this seventy-two-page judgement, Botha ordered the state to provide nevirapine to prevent MTCT in all public health facilities, and to report back to the court by 31 March 2002 on how a nationwide comprehensive plan to prevent MTCT would be implemented. He warned: 'About one thing there must be no misunderstanding: a countrywide MTCT prevention program is an ineluctable obligation of the state.'[32]

In opting to take the matter to the Constitutional Court, Tshabalala-Msimang insisted that the judgement had to be challenged because it suggested that the courts had the right to make health policy. It could, she said, 'throw executive policy-making into disarray and create confusion about the principle of the separation of powers, which is the cornerstone of our democracy' (*South Africa Government Online*, 19 December 2001).

Judge Botha had been aware of this concern. In his judgement, 'When the court, being part of the judicial arm of government, sits in judgement on the reasonableness of steps taken by the executive arm in the fulfillment of its constitutional obligations it is exactly a perfect example of how the separation of powers should work.'[33]

The Bill of Rights in South Africa's Constitution is justifiable; the courts have the power to hold government to its promises, but government argued that while, under section 28:1c, every child has the right to basic healthcare services, the right to nevirapine – or any specific treatment – was not guaranteed. The government case also hinged on a constitutional proviso of 'available resources'. This argument looked thin in terms of the enormous evidence of the cost-benefits of nevirapine treatment, produced to support TAC's case.[34] It also came at a bad time for the government, when a massive budget allocation for arms procurement was getting a public airing. When Judge Botha denied the government side leave to appeal an execution order, granted to TAC, that made the provision of nevirapine compulsory in all state facilities with the capacity to provide the service, until the full appeal was heard on 2 and 3 May, the Minister of Health and her MECs requested the Constitutional Court for leave to appeal. The Court rejected the request on 4 April 2002.

The government's image was further dented by the scandal surrounding a hospital in Kimberley providing ARVs to a nine-month-old baby which had been raped and sodomized; the Northern Cape health MEC hauled the hospital over the coals for flouting government health policy, which specifically states that ARVs 'should not be issued to the victims of rape or sexual assault' (*Mail and Guardian*, 11 January 2002). It is difficult to imagine an incident which could have cast this policy in a more callous light, and at a time when the whole nevirapine issue was under the international spotlight.

In response to this and other incidents, and the growing despair among doctors, faced daily with patients they cannot help, though they know the treatment exists, the South African Medical Association (SAMA), which represents 17,000 South African doctors, two-thirds of whom are employed in the public sector, came out in support of its members who, in contravention of government policy, prescribe ARVs to those who have been raped. SAMA also expressed support for the use of ARVs aimed at MTCT prevention. Government policy, they maintained, cannot determine medical ethics (*South African PA*, 15 January 2002). There were reports, too, of medical personnel flouting policy on the provision of nevirapine to pregnant mothers, often paying for it out of their own pockets.

Anita Kleinsmidt, of the AIDS Law Project, has said that doctors under the current government increasingly feel that they are facing the same conflicts as doctors in the apartheid era. 'They are becoming prisoners of politics . . . What the government is doing is irrational, and the more people say so the better' (*Saturday Star*, 11 January 2002).[35]

Criticism of government HIV/AIDS policy grew increasingly sharp in 2002, coming from AIDS activists, the judiciary, academics, medical personnel, religious and business leaders. World media, too, carried highly critical attacks. Critiques in Britain's *Prospect* (21 February) and *The Economist* (23 February) and the US *Newsweek* (4 March) suggested that government attempts to 'improve communications' faced an uphill battle.

But surely of more concern to Mbeki were attacks from government's own political allies. In Parliament in February, cabinet colleague, Mangosuthu Buthelezi, the Minister of Home Affairs and leader of the KwaZulu-Natal based Inkatha Freedom Party, attacked the government stance on restricting nevirapine, and reiterated that province's decision to defy government policy (*The Star*, 12 February 2002). Days later, Gauteng premier, Mbhazima Shilowa, outlined plans for the ANC-controlled province to roll out nevirapine to all infected pregnant women, and other provinces hinted at similar intentions (*The Sunday Independent*, 23 February 2002). Shilowa may have been influenced by his COSATU roots; COSATU had come out strongly against the policy, as had the third member of the ruling tripartite alliance, the South African Communist Party (*The Sunday Independent*, 23 February 2002). Political icons Mandela and former Archbishop Desmond Tutu had also pleaded in vain for more rational drug policies. When former US president, Jimmy Carter, on a visit to AIDS projects in South Africa in March 2002, accompanied by Mandela, suggested that African countries poorer than South Africa had achieved more in AIDs prevention, and called on Mbeki's 'full and unequivocal support' for anti-AIDS campaigns, ANC spokesperson Smuts Ngonyama, issued a statement saying: 'We do not need the interference and contemptuous attitude of president Carter or anybody else.' He added: 'We find it alarming that president Carter is willing to treat our people as guinea-pigs, in the interest of the pharmaceutical companies' (*SABC News*, 10 March 2002).[36]

In the face of all this opposition, many had hoped that the meeting of the ANC National Executive Committee (NEC) in March 2002, particularly following a strong plea from Mandela for greater ARV access, would move the debate into less contentious, more constructive territory. The statement issued by the NEC (22 March 2002), 'Lend a caring hand of hope',[37] dashed these expectations. While talking of the need for 'unity of purpose and action among all of us', it demonstrated again how far the ANC was from being able to disentangle politics and science – a critical step in getting back any semblance of the unity which once characterized the efforts of South Africans to address the epidemic.

The NEC statement appeared to short-circuit any chance of support for provincial plans to extend nevirapine provision; such decisions would be 'taken collectively by the Ministers and MECs, based on national guidelines, norms and standards', once research was evaluated, a process due to start in December 2002.[38] In the general dismay at the NEC response, its suggestion that the efficacy of the use of ARVs following sexual assault or needle-stick injury (in healthcare workers) was unproven, and that 'these should not be provided in public health institutions for this purpose', virtually passed unnoticed. It is a suggestion which would have caused public outcry elsewhere, given that ARVs are internationally routinely given to health workers following needle-stick injuries. It has been suggested that the NEC response was motivated by spite against doctors, who had grown increasingly defiant in the face of government policy.

Ominously, the statement noted the meeting's resolution that the government was 'duty-bound to pose scientific questions', and welcomed the continuing work of the presidential Advisory Panel. It vowed that the ANC and the government would 'not be stampeded into precipitate action by pseudo-science, an uncaring drive for profits or an opportunistic clamor for cheap popularity'. Scientists like Makgoba, however, believed the re-emergence of dissident views spelled disaster for AIDS efforts, and would lead to yet further confusion and denial. Government, he said, had simply refused or denied the information coming from the world's leading AIDS experts (*The Sunday Independent*, 23 March 2002).[39] Such concerns were heightened by reports that an extraordinary discussion document had been circulated at the NEC. Entitled 'Castro Hlongwane, Caravans, Cats, Geese, Foot & Mouth, and Statistics: HIV/ AIDS and the Struggle for the Humanization of the African', it was apparently being sent to ANC offices for distribution to party members countrywide. Espousing fundamentalist dissident views, it claimed that nobody had 'seen' the HI virus, that the Elisa HIV test was faulty, that ARVs were poison, and that poverty and underdevelopment were the main causes of 'AIDS' deaths. But it also put a peculiarly South African spin on the issue, claiming that orthodox AIDS theory was a conspiracy pushed by an 'omnipotent apparatus' posing as 'friends of Africa' with the aim of dehumanizing Africans. The document implied that it was referring to forces which did not share Mbeki's stance. Quoting Herbert Marcuse's *Eros and Civilisation*, which speaks of our epoch as 'a period when the omnipotent apparatus punishes real non-conformity with ridicule and defeat' (2002, p. 14), the document saw a conspiracy between, among others, the media and scientists to sell the idea of an African AIDS epidemic, largely to force the consumption of ARVs. It attacked 'Eurocentric' science and 'mental colonization' (p. 128) and insisted that Africa must reject the idea that it is 'a victim of a self-inflected "disease" called HIV/AIDS' (p. 132). It suggested, too, that the MRC had ascribed to 'the faith about HIV/AIDS' in order to help pharmaceutical companies sell drugs.[40]

Peter Mokaba, ANC MP and NEC member, and a major protagonist of the dissident position, defended the document: 'We cannot be stampeded into any one position by people whose interest is merely to sell antiretrovirals', and who did not have the welfare of South Africans at heart. Dr Saadiq Kariem, the ANC's national health secretary, saw it differently. 'There's a small minority of very senior people in the party who support the dissident view.' Kariem was angry that the document had not been cleared by the health committee; Mokaba's campaign to spread the word was irresponsible. 'The implications of this are enormous and disastrous', completely undermining the safer sex message, he said (*The New York Times*, 31 March 2002).

Mokaba's response to Kariem's criticism was an interesting comment on the debate on HIV/AIDS within the ANC. Kariem, he said, should not have publicly criticized a document endorsed by the ANC's NEC. 'If he was an ANC person, as he claims, he knows the protocols in the ANC.' Accusing him of being a 'very ill-disciplined member,' Mokaba vowed to check on Kariem's membership in the system, adding: 'The [AIDS] strategy of our government is the best in the world' (*Cape Times*, 3 April 2002).[41]

April 2002 to April 2003: postscript

In April 2002, as the Wellesley College Conference (for which this chapter was prepared) got underway, news broke of a 'turnaround' in government policy. *The Boston Globe* (19 April 2002) carried the front-page headline 'South Africa lifts its Barrier to AIDS Drugs', and called it 'a dramatic policy reversal'. A closer reading of the changes outlined in the cabinet statement, however, suggested only cautious advances.[42]

Research at pilot sites would continue, as would the temporary provisions of nevirapine required by the court judgement. Some additional research sites would be created where appropriate capacity existed, but, although the government was working on a plan for a universal rollout of a nevirapine programme, this would not happen before current research was evaluated at the end of 2002.

The only new intervention mentioned was the plan to 'endeavour' to provide a comprehensive package of care, including ARV HIV prophylaxis for rape survivors, although there were warnings that devising a national protocol to achieve this was unlikely to be finalised in less than six months (*Daily News*, 18 April 2002).

There was also a hint of softening on ARV treatment, acknowledging that such drugs could 'improve the quality of life' of infected people, but it was clear that government was very aware of the financial and health infrastructural obstacles the provision of such treatment would face, and there was no suggestion of any plan to provide such treatment in the state system.

While it was not a 'dramatic' turnaround, the statement did suggest there was some government appreciation of the need for a different approach – and for a consensus on what that approach would be. In interviews at the time, Mbeki, too, seemed to have realized this, saying that he was prepared to do more than he had in the past to provide leadership on the HIV/AIDS issue. 'It is critically important that I communicate correct messages' (*The Star*, 23 April 2002).

It was also becoming clear that if Mbeki was to achieve his wider goals, particularly on the international stage, he needed to put the HIV/AIDS controversies behind him. He could not afford to have press conferences on other initiatives dominated by hostile questions about his stance on AIDS. At a press conference, for instance, to discuss a G8 meeting on the ambitious recovery plan for Africa, the New Partnership for Africa's Development (NEPAD), Canadian journalists ignored his attempts to speak about the meeting and 'flayed him with questions on his HIV policies' (*The Guardian*, 26 June 2002).

Following the April cabinet statement, government alliance partner COSATU, which supported TAC in the pending court case, called on the government to drop its Constitutional Court appeal against the high court ruling to provide nevirapine. COSATU secretary-general, Zwelinzima Vavi, said there was 'no logic' in continuing with such action after the 17 April statement (*Pulsetrack*, 26 April 2002). The call went unheeded. For its part, TAC was sceptical about the government's intention to roll out nevirapine. Citing the government's past 'irrationality and unreasonableness' the TAC's Zackie Achmat said: 'We will accept an undertaking only if it is on order of the court' (*SABCnews.com*, 3 May 2002).

The case was heard in May and the judgement, delivered on 5 July 2002, denied the government leave to appeal against the high court ruling. Geoff Budlender, lawyer for TAC, noted that not only did this mean that government was now legally obliged to implement a nationwide nevirapine programme 'without delay', but that the judgement had demonstrated that constitutional rights were justiceable, and that government was accountable to the courts.

Budlender saw it, too, as 'a turning point in relations between government and civil society'. In the euphoria of the transition, civil society had, he said, become quiescent, and 'as the government became more confident, it had become less open and less responsive to the views of those outside it'. In the dispute over nevirapine, civil society had regrouped. The judgement, he believed, represented 'a new depth and maturity in our new democracy' (*Mail and Guardian online*, 12 July 2002).

Budlender clearly believed that the government would immediately comply with the judgement. Provision of nevirapine was patchy, to the extent that in December TAC launched an urgent contempt of court application against the worst offender, Mpumalanga's recalcitrant health MEC, Dr Sibongile Manana, for failing to implement the court order. Tshabalala-Msimang was cited as a second respondent for failing to ensure Manana's compliance (*TAC.org*, 17 December 2002). Tshabalala-Msimang responded: 'If she (Manana) goes to prison, I'm going with her' (*SABCnews.com*, 11 February 2003).

It was typical of the provocative style that has come to characterize the minister. She has repeatedly been quoted making imprudent, even outrageous, statements which she subsequently denies having said. For instance, when *Newsday's* award-winning health and science writer, Laurie Garrett, interviewed her about the Constitutional Court ruling at the International AIDS Conference in Barcelona in July 2002, Garrett records that the Minister responded 'with obvious rage': 'We will implement because we are forced to implement . . . I must give my people a drug that isn't approved by the FDA. I must poison my people' (*Newsday*, 8 July 2002).[43] She subsequently flatly denied saying it.

The minister also has effectively stalled a grant of $72 million from the Global Fund for HIV/AIDS, Tuberculosis and Malaria to KwaZulu-Natal's Enhancing Care Initiative, ostensibly because 'proper application procedures were not followed' (*Daily News*, 12 June 2002), but many believe that a major reason for the government's response was the inclusion of antiretroviral treatment in the initiative. Addressing a National AIDS Council youth summit, she accused the Global Fund of 'trying to bypass the democratically elected government and put it (the money) in the hands of civil authorities' (*SAPA*, 20 July 2002). Days before, in a tense stand-off with Peter Piot, head of UNAIDS, at the Barcelona conference, she reportedly told him that South Africa was capable of managing and funding its own AIDS programmes 'without outside interference' (*Mail and Guardian*, 12–18 July 2002). In an interview for the conference news service, Piot noted: 'Effective responses are possible only when they are politically backed and full-scale.' He believed NEPAD's inadequate approach to AIDS had led to the G8 countries' lukewarm response to the plan the previous month. Perhaps pointedly, he commented that 'it is better to bypass a government that is not doing what it should, and give funding direct to non-governmental organizations' (Medical Research Council of South Africa, September 2002).

For many activists, the last straw was the reappearance of a dissident centre-stage. Dr Roberto Giraldo, an eminent US nutritionist, according to Tshabalala-Msimang, was first invited to address the Department of Health in November 2002, and then a meeting of Southern African Development Community (SADC) health ministers in January 2003.

While nobody would deny the crucial role good nutrition plays in building the immune systems of both HIV-infected and uninfected people, Giraldo's position is more radical. He believes AIDS researchers have focused too much on sex, which he says has 'little or nothing to do with AIDS', and that AIDS can be effectively prevented, treated and overcome by a healthy diet (*The Star*, 8 January 2003).

Reporting back to the parliamentary health portfolio committee in March, the minister claimed that the nutritional intervention launched by the Department of Health had produced 'astounding results' (*Parliamentary Monitoring Group*, 18 March 2003), and advocated such food items as garlic and olive oil for boosting the immune system. TAC walked out. They warned that the health minister had squandered her 'last chance' to avert a planned civil disobedience campaign protesting government's failure to agree to a national treatment plan (*The Natal Witness*, 19 March 2003).

How does a minister with such a string of gaffes and blunders behind her – and the strong suspicion that she herself is an AIDS 'denialist' – retain her portfolio? Political commentator, Anthony Johnson, writes: 'If she is not censured, disciplined or fired for her sayings and doings, there is a simple explanation. It's because Thabo Mbeki wants it that way' (*Cape Times*, 18 March 2003).[44] However low a profile Mbeki keeps on the AIDS issue these days, nothing he has done refutes Johnson's hypothesis.

A year after the so-called 'turnaround', then, the message coming out of government remains confusing. On 9 October 2002, the cabinet issued a second statement acknowledging that ARVs could 'improve the condition of people living with AIDS', and that government was 'actively engaged' in addressing such treatment. A task team comprising Department of Health and National Treasury officials was investigating 'the conditions that would make it feasible and effective to use ARVs in the public health sector' (*South Africa Government Online*, 9 October 2002).

Yet at the ANC party congress, in Stellenbosch in December 2002, Mbeki barely mentioned AIDS. By contrast, the ANC statement on its development strategy, issued at the congress, said: 'Given the progression of the AIDS epidemic . . . our program of transformation should not only acknowledge this danger, but it must also put the campaign against it at the top of our agenda' (*News24.com*, 19 December 2002). With five million South Africans infected, many of them ANC members, it is hard to see how such a campaign could avoid the issue of ARV treatment for very long.

Mbeki's state of the nation address at the opening of Parliament on 14 February 2003, again devoted just two sentences, in a twenty-one-page speech, to AIDS (*South Africa Government Online*, 14 February 2003). The Budget speech on 26 February announced major additional HIV/AIDS funding, but again said nothing directly about ARVs. However, tucked away on page 329 of the *Estimates of National Expenditure* was the clue that some of this funding might be destined for ARVs: 'Investigations on the introduction of a national antiretroviral program are far advanced, and recommendations are close to finalization.'

It is hard to square that conclusion with the vitriolic battle between government and AIDS activists raging at the time of writing this postscript. The battle has its roots in a National Treatment Congress in June 2002, co-hosted by TAC and COSATU. The call for a national treatment plan, including antiretrovirals, that emerged from that gathering was subsequently taken to the National Economic Development and Labour Council (NEDLAC), where NEDLAC's component sectors – government, business, labour and community – established a senior HIV/AIDS task team in September 2002 to begin negotiating a plan. The team met in October and November, with TAC and COSATU favouring World AIDS Day (1 December), as a date for the agreement to be signed. However, business and government both said further consultation was necessary before their principals could sign the agreement. Just what *was* agreed in the framework agreement is far from clear, as government and TAC have issued conflicting statements. TAC insists that all members had agreed on the text finalized on 29 November 2002, apart from 'less than five paragraphs' bracketed for further discussion; the government insists that, while consultation continues, there is no such agreement.

The government response reiterates that a task team consisting of officials from the National Treasury and the Department of Health is evaluating the cost implications of a treatment plan, and looking at infrastructural and sustainability issues. No plans for antiretroviral treatment will be considered until that report, expected some time in April 2003,[45] is complete.

While the team evaluating the implications appear to be made up of competent civil servants with orthodox views on AIDS, intent on doing a thorough job, there is scepticism about the outcome: 'statements by ministers over the past year suggest that its political masters have already made up their minds about the efficacy of the drugs' (*Mail and Guardian*, 4 April 2003).

The team's deliberations are happening against a backdrop of an ongoing protest and civil disobedience campaign by TAC, directed at the government's failure to sign the NEDLAC plan. TAC and its supporters have kept the issue in the public eye, locally and internationally. Since February 2003, they have marched on Parliament, shouted the minister down at a health conference, marched on police stations to lay charges of culpable homicide (manslaughter) against the Health Minister and the Minister of Trade and Industry for having 'unlawfully and negligently caused the death of men, women and children', and handed memoranda to the Human Rights Commission and the Commission on Gender Equality, demanding that these constitutional bodies address the government's failure to provide treatment.

In TAC's e-newsletter of 12 April 2003, Zackie Achmat outlines the events that led to the civil disobedience campaign. He ends: 'These wounds between ourselves and the government will not be healed easily.' That became apparent at a gathering to welcome Richard Feachem, the executive director of the Global Fund for HIV/AIDS, TB and Malaria, on 8 April 2003. A small group of TAC protesters had gathered outside, waving posters. Instead of the welcoming address the audience had expected, Tshabalala-Msimang 'launched into a blistering, sarcastic attack that left senior government officials, Feachem and the rest of the high-profile audience cringing', according to the *Mail and Guardian* report (11 April 2003). In a blatantly racist attack, she accused 'a white man' of masterminding the civil disobedience campaign, using Africans, who wait for 'the white man' to deploy them. The attack was obviously directed at TAC's Mark Heywood, who was in the audience. Her repeated reference to 'a white man' eventually led to an angry interchange in which Heywood called the minister a liar.

Feachem had come expecting to sign agreements handing the government and KwaZulu-Natal millions of dollars in Global Fund money. Instead, he was not only given a first-hand insight into the acrimony and belligerence which currently characterize the whole debate on AIDS treatment, but was also sent away empty-handed, after the minister had told the gathering that the reason government had 'not moved with speed is because the Global Fund had to set their house in order and not that SANAC was not ready. Geneva was not ready' (*Mail and Guardian*, 11 April 2003). Almost a year after the grants were first made, a government statement cited 'relatively complex legal processes which made it impossible to finalise agreements'. It promised that the agreements would be signed in May 2003, and that programme implementation would begin by the end of May (*South Africa Government Online*, 11 April 2003).

There were, of course, the predictable responses to the whole fiasco – disappointment, dismay, cynicism, outrage, stubborn defiance – but no sign that all sides were any closer to getting around a table to thrash out a rational response that would take into account both the very real need for, and the constraints around, treatment. The players seemed further apart than ever.

However heroic, efforts by health professionals (including many in the Department of Health), NGOs, civil society, the private sector, and the international community are difficult to sustain if doubts and contradictions continually subvert them – and more particularly if the source of these lies at the very centre of policy-making.[46] In the end, Mbeki's personal doubts – and of those around him who support them – are not as Mbeki has claimed, simply 'asking questions'. They undermine the very foundations of the HIV/AIDS strategy and any hope of recapturing that vision of a country united against the epidemic.

As Dr Ashraf Grimwood, at the time chairman of NACOSA, once summed it up, 'South Africa's history of addressing AIDS is the most appalling debacle. We have shot our allies, knifed our neighbors, and instead of attacking the enemy, attacked each other' (*Financial Mail*, 19 November 1999).

Why did South Africa go wrong?

There is no simple answer to this question. Rather, the explanation requires a jigsaw of pieces, some still not at hand. Part of the answer lies in the nature and timing of the South African epidemic – that it coincided with the transition to democracy; that it came in the wake of apartheid and a long history of discrimination; that it is a sexually transmitted infection; and that it is a racially differentiated epidemic. These factors go some way to accounting for South Africa's singular failure to deal with the disease.

While the transition made a credible strategy possible, it also presented stumbling blocks. In trying to weld together new and old systems, it was inevitable that no programme would work as smoothly as it would have done in a stable democracy, with a non-partisan, well-trained, experienced bureaucracy (Marais, 2000, pp. 14–29). Lack of implementation through poor management in the health system, massive under-spending of AIDS budgets, and under-funding of NGO's, have characterized the process. Under the circumstances, the unaffordability of drugs, thanks to exorbitant pharmaceutical industry prices, and the toxicity of ARVs were convenient excuses for poor delivery. The 1994 vision of government and civil society mutually involved in implementing the strategy fizzled out, as donor funding shifted directly into government hands, and the participatory decision-making style of the anti-apartheid struggle was superceded by the top-down style of Dlamini-Zuma. As Helen Schneider of the Centre for Health Policy at the University of the Witwatersrand, writes: 'Ultimately, policy contestation around AIDS in South Africa can be understood as a series of attempts by the state to legitimately define who has the right to speak about AIDS, to determine the response to AIDS, and even to define the problem itself' (Schneider, 2001, p. 21).

Ironically, given the resources and enthusiasm that were available in 1994, had government provided the leadership and funding, the AIDS programme might have been one of its success stories. It was understandable, too, that a country emerging from years of civil strife, under a new government, would want to concentrate on the positive goals of that new society, such as housing, jobs, education and healthcare, rather than the threat of an as-yet-invisible epidemic.

As apartheid's barriers to internal migration dissolved, and the rural poor flooded into the squatter camps around the major cities, the rapid urbanization process, too, drove the epidemic. Dense populations of people in the most sexually active cohort, away from the normative constraints of village life, have always encouraged high levels of sexual activity. Where there is a continuous rural–urban shuttle, as there is in South Africa, HIV can be carried into even the most remote areas (van der Vliet, 1996, pp. 77–81).

The transition also brought with it a wave of returning exiles, many of whom had belonged to the military wing of the ANC, and had been stationed in African countries with very high infection rates. Whereas apartheid had, ironically, isolated South Africa from direct contact with the epidemic to the north, freedom opened the borders. It was an extremely politically sensitive issue, one most easily addressed by silence.[47]

Although one of the wealthiest countries in Africa – the World Bank estimated annual GNI per capita in 2000 at $3020 (World Bank, 2002)[48] – apartheid has ensured that South Africa was also one of the most unequal in the distribution of that income. That inequality, and the poverty of black citizens, was later to be seized upon as an explanation of the rampant spread of HIV/AIDS. While poverty undoubtedly plays a part in the epidemic (and will undoubtedly deepen as a consequence of AIDS), it is a dangerous refuge for the 'denialists'. It implies that the poor are uniquely at risk, encouraging a fatalism which undermines people's will to protect themselves, and it leaves the affluent with a false sense of security. Already reports from the teaching and healthcare sectors in South Africa and elsewhere in Africa, suggest that the relatively privileged are no less at risk. Suggesting that HIV/AIDS is, like TB, directly linked to poverty, as some dissidents like Charles Geshekter claim, means one escapes all the difficult issues around sexual behaviour change – shifting blame on history (Schlemmer, 2000). Campaigns today address risk *behaviour*; linking HIV/AIDS with poverty reverts to a risk *group* emphasis, once again stereotyping those at risk.

While apartheid has systematically undermined social and family life, with, for instance, the migrant labour system, forced relocations, and pass laws, the mid-1980s saw community upheaval on an unprecedented scale; a time of political turmoil and violence in the townships, with blacks bent on overthrowing the government by making the country 'ungovernable'. Schools were turned into 'sites of struggle', with the battle cry 'Liberation before Education'. Young activists – the 'comrades' or 'Young Lions' – became central to the politics of 1984–6.

Many of the youth took to the streets and engaged in often violent, sometimes deadly, confrontations with the police. Adults felt they had lost control of their young, and psychologist Saths Cooper remarked that there was 'very little normality in the lives of politicized children. No good familial relationships, no normal schooling, no integrated existence. Norm restraints were nonexistent' (Johnson, 1988, p. 120).[49] It is the children of these turbulent years, inured to risk, and now in their twenties and thirties, who today bear the brunt of the HIV/AIDS epidemic. In 2000, 31 per cent of those aged 25–29, and 23 per cent of those aged 30–34 were infected (Department of Health, 2001).

South Africa's HIV statistics are based largely on the annual antenatal HIV surveys conducted since 1990 in public health facilities nationwide. Eighty per cent of pregnant women use these facilities and 85 per cent of the women tested in 2000 were black (Department of Health, 2001, p. 4). Although Tshabalala-Msimang has said that future surveys would attempt to include private sector clinics – hence more affluent women, including whites – such figures are not as yet available. However, rates among whites are generally believed to be low.[50] Had the disease affected all racial categories equally, the politics of the epidemic in South Africa may well have looked quite different.[51] Instead, South African blacks are disproportionately affected and, indeed, AIDS is at present pre-eminently a disease of sub-Saharan Africa, which has meant that all the baggage of 'race' and 'culture' have been packed in with the issue.

From the beginning, the African connection has met with vehement opposition from Africans and their sympathizers. Even the seemingly innocuous scientific search for the origins of HIV in primate populations has been interpreted as an attempt to 'blame' AIDS on Africa. Richard and Rosalind Chirimuuta see such associations as just another example of the world's profoundly racist views of the continent. Such notions, they wrote, 'cohabit easily with racist notions that Africans are evolutionarily closer to sub-human primates' (1987, p. 1). Years later, in a sharp exchange of correspondence with Tony Leon, leader of the

opposition Democratic Party, Mbeki accused Leon of failing to under-
stand the significance of theories that 'alleged transmission of HIV from
(African) animals to humans' and 'the message it communicates to
Africans' (*Mail and Guardian*, 6 October 2000).

The Chirimuutas believed, too, that, given 'the association of black
people with dirt, disease, ignorance and an animal-like sexual promiscuity', it was 'almost inevitable that black people would be associated
with [AIDS'] origin and transmission' (Chirimuuta and Chirimuuta,
1987, p. 1). It was a theme reiterated fourteen years later by President
Mbeki in a speech given at the University of Fort Hare in October 2001.
He talked of those who are 'convinced that we are but natural-born,
promiscuous carriers of germs, unique in the world, they proclaim that
our continent is doomed to an inevitable mortal end because of our
unconquerable devotion to the sin of lust'.[52]

That HIV/AIDS is sexually transmitted sets off fears that the epidemic
will reinforce the kind of racial/sexual stereotypes outlined above. The
document circulated in the ANC NEC in March 2002 again confirms
that this fear in part underpins the 'denialist' position. One caustically
sardonic passage reads: 'Yes, we are sex crazy! Yes, we are diseased! Yes,
we spread the deadly HI virus through our uncontrolled heterosexual
sex! In this regard, yes, we are different from the US and Western
Europe! Yes, we, the men, abuse women and the girl-child with gay
abandon! Yes, among us rape is endemic because of our culture! Yes, we
do believe that sleeping with young virgins will cure us of AIDS! Yes, as
a result of all this, we are threatened with destruction by the HIV/AIDS
pandemic! Yes, what we need, and cannot afford because we are poor,
are condoms and anti-retroviral drugs! Help!' (*Mail and Guardian*, 22–29
March 2002).[53]

Like the note of hysteria in the right-wing 'Apocalypse' pamphlet,
quoted at the beginning of this chapter, the tone of the NEC document
speaks of the extreme distress of people faced with uncontrollable situations. The writing of dissidents must be very reassuring. Charles
Geshekter writes, for instance, of the way orthodox AIDS believers 'try
to change African sexual practices . . . a crusade reminiscent of Victorian
voyeurs whose racist constructs equated black people with sexual
promiscuity'. He finds it 'a scandal' that the diseases of poverty are
being blamed on a sexually transmitted virus (*The Globe and Mail*, 15
March 2000).

The passage in the NEC document quoted above, is not only intended
to crush suggestions that any of the behavioural 'aberrations' listed
might be driving the epidemic, but would also serve to discredit claims

that gender inequality and resistance to behaviour change are major factors in South Africa's failure to control the disease. However, a growing body of South African research paints a gloomy picture of women's vulnerability to infection – of their inability to negotiate safer sexual relationships, of high levels of domestic violence and rape, of macho sexual attitudes, and dangerous myths around HIV/AIDS.[54]

These are uncomfortable, politically unpopular areas to deal with in South Africa. Addressing the National Institute of Allergy and Infectious Diseases in Bethesda, Maryland in May 2001, Makgoba said: 'Sex is regarded as a taboo in Africa – you don't speak openly about it. We all know that this is a sexually transmitted disease and that's the bottom line, and we're doing everything except focusing on the real major factor that determines whether or not you get the disease' (*Reuters Health*, 16 May 2001).

Sexually transmitted diseases are in many societies seen as indicators of social transgression, of the violation of 'ideal' norms of conduct, thus shameful or stigmatized. This is true also in much of South Africa, from rural traditionalists to urban Christians (Green, 1994, ch. 7).[55] Where sexual behaviour has also been part of the kind of racial stereotyping suggested above, it is dangerous territory to enter. For this reason, the problem of denial in South Africa is twofold – the denial of the epidemic itself, and the denial of the behaviour that underlies it.

With little sign that behaviour change is turning the epidemic around, increasing numbers of South Africans may be looking to drugs for salvation. That, however, is certainly not on the government's agenda, as the long-standing nevirapine controversy demonstrates. While cost and the lack of infrastructure may be the real (and rational) reasons underlying government resistance, the issue is clouded by the dissident view that the drugs are toxic, especially if HIV/AIDS is actually not a disease at all.

The resistance must also be seen against an almost paranoid view of the pharmaceutical industry. For some this links to residual socialist leanings and a suspicion about multinationals in general, but for others the distrust is more specific. Conspiracy theories abound: that drug companies are experimenting on Africans, using them as guinea pigs in unethical drug experiments (in the manner suggested in John Le Carré's 2001 novel, *The Constant Gardener*); the belief that the AIDS story is being fabricated by the industry in collusion with the CIA or other Western bodies to push expensive drugs; that activists and scientists who believe in the use of ARVs are in the pay of the industry; or even that drug companies already have the cure, but are waiting until they have made enough money from their drugs (or enough Africans have died) before they will release it. Mokaba argued, for instance, that the AIDS drugs are deadly, and that the epidemic is a fiction created by the drug companies to boost profits by forcing poor countries to buy drugs, and by financing researchers to terrorize the public with lies about AIDS (*New York Times*, 31 March 2002).[56]

Against a background of apartheid, in which many believed the government was investigating drugs to sterilize blacks, and using poisons to kill those who opposed them, paranoia is understandable, but it allows very dubious information to be circulated at the highest policy-making levels. In September 2000, Tshabalala-Msimang circulated a chapter from William Cooper's 1991 book, *Behold a Dark Horse*, which suggested that the HI virus had been specially engineered by the world's ruling elite 'to reverse the explosive population growth' of the mid-twentieth century (*Mail and Guardian*, 5 September 2000).

In October 2000, it was reported that Mbeki himself, in an ANC caucus meeting, suggested that he and his government were the target of a hostile campaign by powerful international forces, including the CIA and big international drug companies. This was because the questioned link between HIV and AIDS, and South Africa was challenging the world economic order (*Mail and Guardian*, 6–12 October 2000). Although the account came from a number of ANC MPs at the meeting, there were denials from others, accusing the press of a massive propaganda campaign. One of the most vociferous dissidents on Mbeki's Advisory Panel, David Rasnick, wrote in *Business Day* (9 May 2001), that Mbeki's solitary crusade to ask questions about orthodox AIDS views, made 'Mbeki and South Africa threats to the business interests, prestige, and US global hegemony'. Fingering the CIA, FBI and the National Security Agency, Rasnick asserted that 'millions of US dollars are being spent to monitor and neutralize Mbeki and other African leaders. Much of this money is used to "orchestrate" the public media and press of targeted countries.' The ANC's refusal to repudiate publicly the dissident position – indeed as the recent NEC meeting shows, to give it recognition – makes the ANC denial of the caucus story rather less convincing.

Plagues throughout history have spawned conspiracy theories, and HIV/AIDS has produced a bumper crop. In the general population, such themes may prove dangerous because they undermine educational and medical information. In the hands of policy-makers, who circulate rather than denounce them, they are potentially disastrous. Given the paranoia surrounding HIV/AIDS, what is perhaps surprising is the ready acceptance of the dissident line. In its massive undermining of any prevention message, it could be seen as the most diabolically genocidal conspiracy of all, yet, baited with a morsel of hope, it is eagerly swallowed by the desperate.

The Mbeki factor

Much of what has happened on the political front in South Africa's AIDS epidemic has bewildered analysts, both locally and internationally, but the most perplexing piece in the puzzle is the role of President Mbeki himself. Why should an intelligent, sophisticated man who believes passionately in an 'African Renaissance', an 'African Century', refuse to deal with the epidemic in the rational way that, say, Uganda's Yoweri Museveni, Botswana's Festus Mogae or Senegal's Abdoulaye Wade have done? One answer might lie precisely in this passionate belief itself. It is surely impossible to hold this vision for the continent, and at the same time concede that tens of millions of young adults are infected and dying. AIDS is doing to Mbeki's 'African Century' what the slave trade did to the continent in centuries past. It is snatching away the young and able-bodied, and it will take generations to recoup the losses. Faced with such a painful reality, denial, or grasping at the prospect of some alternative explanation, is understandable. Both can lead to 'genocide by omission'.

In his letter to world leaders, Mbeki talked of the epidemic the continent confronted as a 'uniquely African catastrophe', and felt 'a simple superimposition of Western experience on African reality would be absurd and illogical'. South Africa's task, he argued, was 'to search for specific and targeted responses to the specifically African incidence of HIV/AIDS' (*Washington Post*, 19 April 2000). That Mbeki should have become personally obsessed by this pursuit is perhaps not surprising. Clearly, he was hoping his research on the Internet and elsewhere, and his Advisory Panel's contribution, would come up with an 'African solution to an African problem'. Quarraisha Abdool Karim, the first director of South Africa's national AIDS programme post-1994, has in fact suggested that the enthusiastic reception for Virodene by the cabinet, including Mbeki in 1997, was partly driven by this need to show the world that 'Africans can do this. Virodene became our redemption' (*Washington Post*, 6 July 2000).

Mbeki was groomed for intellectual leadership from an early age; some suggest that this has made him intellectually arrogant. In 2000, Mondli Makhanya, then political editor of the *Sunday Times*, commented: 'A hallmark of the Mbeki presidency has been what can only be described as an intellectual superiority complex.' Makhanya believed it was associated with a decline in debate within the ANC, combined with dissent 'merely whispered in hidden corners'. If the trend was to be reversed, he believed, HIV/AIDS was the area where it would be possible to remind Mbeki that he could be wrong, and others right. Mbeki's response to an ANC challenge on this issue, and his response to popular opinion, would reveal 'whether his vision of a new Africa led by people who do not see themselves as demigods is real, or whether it is just a sexy catch phrase he dreamt up one boring Sunday afternoon at Sussex University' (*Sunday Times*, 24 September 2000).

Elements in the ANC have, in the time since Makhanya wrote, registered their deep concern, but there is still no unequivocal evidence that Mbeki has changed his mind, much less admitted he made a mistake. Moreover, to question the party line from within is to provoke accusations of disloyalty. AIDS researcher, Professor Salim Karim, who himself has faced such charges, says the health ministry itself is divided. 'There are very committed people working in the government. They don't want people to die of AIDS, but there is an inability to act because they don't want to be seen criticizing the President' (*The Guardian*, 12 June 2001). A recurrent theme in the AIDS issue since the beginning has been that 'if you're not for us, you're against us', a line that makes open debate difficult, and encourages intellectual bullies. Steven Friedman, of the Centre for Policy Studies, writes that with a two-thirds majority in Parliament, and the ANC leadership's pressure for uniformity among its elected officials on all issues, the chances for vigorous debate within the party are currently very limited. In bodies such as SANAC, 'professionals and other key actors who are not considered sufficiently loyal to the ANC leadership on this issue have been excluded. Government has insisted on relegating them to the margins because it wants to show that it is in charge of AIDS policy and will not be ordered around by its critics' (*Business Day*, 25 March 2003).

It could all have been very different. Where Mandela's presidency brought reconciliation, Mbeki's promised delivery. A *New York Times* article (7 May 2000) describes him as 'an intensely driven, hands-on leader who is reluctant to leave critical decision making to others'. The report quotes Tom Lodge, professor of political science at the University of the Witwatersrand, commenting on Mbeki's AIDS panel: 'In one way, of course, it's an admirable indication of an extremely conscientious and intelligent chief executive. But I think he's also a compulsive interferer.' Lodge believes Mbeki should have left to the experts those things which require expertise. Later, following Mbeki's opening address to the controversial panel, Lodge said that Mbeki's actions suggested 'a lack of clear vision, advisers who are either too weak or timid to give him advice he does not like, and an inability to admit mistakes'. Once optimistic about Mbeki's coming to office, he said: 'What we're seeing are all the symptoms of a weak presidency. I think that the projection of Mbeki as a strong, decisive president who would provide leadership on key issues was a misrepresentation' (*Newsday*, New York, 22 May 2000).

Mbeki's hypersensitivity to criticism, especially where he believes there is a racist dimension to comment,[57] and his suspicions, some say paranoia, concerning the pharmaceutical industry, the media, and conspiracies aimed at him and his government, make it particularly difficult for him to deal effectively with AIDS. In April 2002, for instance, he again responded to the controversy around ARVs, by writing in the ANC online journal, *ANC Today* (5–11 April 2002), that much of the country's disease burden could be traced to poverty. He rejected the view that 'the only health matters that should concern especially the black people are HIV/AIDS, HIV, and complex anti-retroviral drugs, including nevirapine'. Maintaining that 'in pursuit of particular agendas' there was 'a studied and sustained attempt to hide the truth about diseases of poverty'. To be influenced by these agendas would lead to further deterioration in the nation's health: 'We are both the victims and fully understand the legacy of centuries-old and current racism on our society and ourselves.'

His position on HIV/AIDS has undoubtedly done Mbeki's image great damage, both locally and internationally. The positive advances during his term, particularly in the field of economic policy, are being overshadowed by the furore around AIDS. As time passes, Mbeki comes more and more to bear the hallmarks of the classic tragic hero – a man so driven by a vision that, combined with a fatal dose of hubris, he is unable to heed the warnings all around him, and destroys himself.

In March 2003, faced with a rising tide of protest, the government placed an advertisement – 'Let's build a people's contract to fight HIV/AIDS' – in newspapers countrywide. The message ended: 'Our energies should be spent fighting AIDS, not one another' (*Cape Times*, 20 March 2003). Given the government's own track record, that is a plea that continues to ring hollow.

Notes

1   See van der Vliet (1994) for a fuller account of these issues.
2   Pamphlet in author's archive.

3   Pamphlet in author's archive.

4   Marais (2000), pp. 11–14; Crewe (2000).

5   Mandela has become increasingly outspoken on HIV/AIDS issues, including the need to provide antiretroviral drugs, in the past two years. David Dimbleby, who interviewed him for a two-part BBC documentary, broadcast in March 2003, 'Nelson Mandela: the Living Legend', writes that Mandela said that in the early 1990s he had faced resistance from audiences when he mentioned AIDS. He was warned that to talk about it might lose him election. 'I wanted to win and I didn't talk about AIDS' (http://news.bbc.co.uk/1/hi/world/africa/2808313.stm).

6   The briefing notes appeared as an insert in *AIDS Bulletin* (1996), 5 (2), September.

7   For a brief outline of the 'AIDS world' structure, see Schneider (2001), pp. 18–21.

8   See *South African Health Review 2001*, by the Health Systems Trust for comment, www.hst.org.za.

9   The Ministry of Health, Pretoria, circulated an explanatory pamphlet in national newspapers in April/May 2000 – 'What did you hear about AIDS today?'

10 The full text of this letter is available online at www.washingtonpost.com, 19 April 2000.

11 Text at www.nature.com.

12 Mbeki also gave a very brief outline of the government's AIDS strategy: awareness, prevention, targeting poverty and opportunistic diseases, a 'humane' approach to those affected, including orphans, and further research on antiretrovirals. Oddly, he did not mention the state's support of vaccine initiatives. The full text of the speech is available at www.aids2000.com.

13 The full text of the speech is available at www.aids2000.com.

14 'Mbeki fingers the CIA in AIDS conspiracy', *Mail and Guardian*, 6–12 October 2000; 'Mbeki – Africa's challenges', *Time (Europe)*, 11 September 2000.

15 COSATU Seventh National Congress, 18 September 2000, www.cosatu.org.za/congress/cong2000/.

16 For full text see www.gov.za.

17 www.virusmyth.com.

18 www.tac.org.za.

19 Drugs may be used for purposes not specifically indicated where research indicates their value. In the case of nevirapine, the drug had been used to prevent MTCT elsewhere, but there had been long and inexplicable delays in MCC registration for this purpose in South Africa (*Cape Argus*, 20 April 2001).

20 In a hearing in the Public Service Bargaining Council in March 2003, Manana's legal representatives finally withdrew charges of misconduct and insubordination against von Mollendorff. Manana has also dropped her legal attempts to evict GRIP volunteers, at the insistence of the public protector (*News24.com*, 10 March 2003).

21 A transcript of this interview, and a statement from the office of the presidency, refuting certain media 'interpretations' of the interview, are available on *South Africa Government Online*. The transcript is dated 6 August 2001, the statement 7 August 2001.

22   The letter and tables appear in full in *Business Day*, 10 September 2001.

23   The full report is available at www.mrc.ac.za/bod.

24   When Statistics SA released its estimates in November 2001, it broadly confirmed MRC findings (*Afrol.News*, 10 November 2001). In November 2002, a Statistics SA report, commissioned by cabinet, broadly confirmed the MRC findings. A study based on 'cause of death' in South Africa from 1997 to 2001, as reflected in a sample of death certificates, found 'a steep rise in mortality due to HIV, TB, influenza and pneumonia' (www.gov.za/2002/causesdeath.pdf), accounting for over 21 per cent of deaths over the period. With up to 50 per cent of HIV patients developing TB, and influenza, pneumonia and 'ill-defined causes' (8.2 per cent) often masking actual AIDS deaths, plus the fact that the period surveyed reflected years when HIV levels were lower than in the MRC study, the trend in mortality was indisputable.

25   This letter is available at www.gov.za, under statement on MRC's report on HIV/AIDS.

26   In March, it was reported that the health minister was on the warpath to find out who had leaked the MRC report to the press. The investigation raised concerns about government interference in academic freedom (*The Star*, 21 March 2002). It was a concern reiterated by Makgoba in September, when he said the MRC was being put under great political pressure to toe the party line and become 'the trusted scientific voice that justifies unscientific findings or pseudo-science' (*Health-e news*, 4 September 2002).

27   www.gov.za/reports/2001.hivdeaths.pdf.

28   The LoveLife project was initiated by the Henry J. Kaiser Family Foundation. The youth survey is available at www.kff.org/content/2002/20020305b/. See also Leclerc-Madlala (2002).

29   For full report see www.gov.za. Govender resigned her parliamentary seat in mid-2002 (*Mail and Guardian*, 31 May 2002). In February 2003, at a TAC march on Parliament demanding drugs for HIV/AIDS sufferers, she addressed the urgent plea for antiretroviral treatment to President Mbeki, reminding him that the young women demanding drugs 'are your African Renaissance' (www.web.uct.ac.za/org/agi/new/preg.htm).

30   For court papers see www.tac.org.za.

31   At a meeting of activists, health and policy experts in October 2001, it was agreed, as part of this consensus, that '[e]nsuring expanded, equitable and sustainable access to life-saving and prolonging medicines is a moral and legal responsibility for government, business, international agencies and private health-care funders'. See www.tac.org.za.

32   The full judgement is available at www.tac.org.za.

33   Ibid.

34   Research on the cost and feasibility of not only preventing MTCT, but of antiretroviral treatment for those infected, has gathered momentum since the court case. See Boulle, et al. (2002), Nattrass (2003), and TAC Fact Sheet (2002).

35   This warning is particularly significant in light of the finding of the Truth and Reconciliation Commission's Report, which noted that, while there was little evidence of direct involvement of the medical profession in gross violations of human rights, 'the health sector, through apathy, acceptance of the *status quo* and acts of omission, allowed the creation of an environment

in which the health of millions of South Africans was neglected, even at times actively compromised and in which the violations of moral and ethical codes were frequent' (TRC Report, 1998, p. 250). Correspondence in the *South African Medical Journal* (April 2002) also warns of doctors becoming accomplices in 'atrocities' by not providing ARVs (*Business Day*, 17 April 2002).

36 This suspicion of the drug industry has been fuelled by the delay experienced by nevirapine manufacturer, Boehringer Ingelheim, in getting the drug registered with the US Food and Drug Administration. The delay has been the result of technical irregularities in records from the Uganda trials, where its safety and efficacy for MTCT prevention was first established. Although UNAIDS, the WHO and the US National Institute of Allergy and Infectious Diseases have said there was no reason to stop prescribing nevirapine for MTCT prevention, the MCC may review its registration of the drug for MTCT prevention.

37 www.anc.org.za/ancdocs/pr/2002/pr0320a.html.

38 Provincial rollout is still uneven. While the Western Cape has achieved 100 per cent coverage (*Independent online*, 21 March 2003), Mpumalanga's health MEC, Sibongile Manana, has been threatened with court action as she continues to flout a Constitutional Court judgement ordering the provision of nevirapine (*SABC News.com*, 11 February 2003). A government update on 19 March 2003 was vague as to the precise level of coverage. 'Most provinces are now extending this comprehensive package to more facilities and at last count about 658 hospitals and clinics were providing the service' (www.gov.za). At a Health Standing Committee on 16 April 2003, the Western Cape legislature also agreed to provide 'triple cocktail' antiretroviral therapy to all HIV-positive babies and toddlers in provincial hospitals, where they could benefit from the treatment (*Pulsetrack*, 16 April 2003).

39 An article in the British medical journal, *The Lancet* (23 March 2002, Vol. 359, No. 9311) by some of South Africa's top AIDS researchers, unequivocally advocating universal access to nevirapine for HIV-infected pregnant women, will doubtless face a similar reception.

40 Full document at http://132.230.108.107/people/sitas/seminar-Freiburg-2002/Castro-Hlongwane.pdf.

41 It is perhaps significant, too, that Mokaba is heavily critical of the continued alliance between the ANC, COSATU and the SACP. In September 2001, Mokaba declared the alliance 'dead' (*Mail and Guardian*, 18 January 2002). Both COSATU and SACP have in turn been highly critical of the ANC and government stance on nevirapine and on the dissident position on HIV/AIDS. Some believe that Mokaba represents the most right-wing element of the ANC broad church, motivated by an exclusivist form of Africanism (*Business Day*, 20 Sept 2001).

42 www.gov.za, speeches 17 April 2002.

43 Nevirapine manufacturer, Boehringer Ingelheim, has suspended its application to have the drug registered to prevent MTCT with the US Food and Drug Administration (FDA) after some aspects of the Uganda trials, on which the application had been based, were found not to have met FDA record-keeping requirements. There was no question of the validity of the study (*NIAID News*, 22 March 2002).

44   At the height of the KwaZulu-Natal débâcle, when activists, political opposi-
     tion and the Anglican Archbishop of Cape Town, Njongonkulu Ndungane,
     were all calling for the minister's resignation, the ANC issued a statement
     saying that 'the President remains convinced of her capacity to lead the
     Ministry and no amount of pressure will force the President to review his
     opinions of his cabinet' (*The Star*, 18 July 2002).
45   TAC's version of events is available at www.tac.org.za. For the government
     perspective, see the report of the Parliamentary Health Portfolio Committee,
     19 March 2003, at www.pmg.org.za/docs/2003/viewminute.php?id=2581.
46   See Health Systems Trust (2002) for a review of the wider current HIV/AIDS
     issues. The review also outlines the problems of a comprehensive pro-
     gramme, inadequately implemented. Full report available at www.hst.
     org.za.2002 saw the introduction of increasing numbers of private sector ini-
     tiatives in the workplace which included antiretroviral treatment. See Health
     Systems Trust (2003), Ch.12, 'AIDS and the Private Sector' (www.hst.org.
     za/sahr.2002).
47   In 2003, a comparable problem arises from the huge number of illegal immi-
     grants into South Africa from neighbouring countries, particularly
     Zimbabwe, who have come as economic or political refugees. Not only are
     they often from high-incidence countries, but also in the age cohorts most
     likely to be sexually active. If South Africa's HIV/AIDS treatment improves,
     they might also come seeking expensive medical care.
48   Ironically, the only wealthier listing is Botswana at $3300 – with 38 per cent
     of its women testing HIV positive at antenatal clinics, it has the highest
     infection rate in the world.
49   For brief accounts of this period see Seekings (1993) and Everatt and Sisulu
     (1992).
50   Among voluntary blood donors (recruited from low-risk groups) the HIV
     prevalence per 100 000 in 1996 was estimated to be 209 for whites, 509 for
     Indians, 1048 for coloured/mixed race and 20 515 for blacks (Karim, 2000).
51   That the first serious epidemic in South Africa was in the white gay commu-
     nity did not help matters, given that there was a substantial degree of homo-
     phobia among black South Africans, and thus a refusal to be associated with
     what they perceived to be a gay disease (Gevisser and Cameron, 1994).
52   The ZK Matthews Memorial Lecture: 'He Wakened to His Responsibilities'
     (Fort Hare, 12 October 2001). For full speech, see www.gov.za.
53   The *Mail and Guardian* article provides a useful outline. For selected excerpts,
     see the document produced by the ANC in March 2002, www.7mac.com/
     7MAC/investigations/ANC_summary.htm.
54   See Wood and Jewkes (1997), Jewkes (2001), Wood and Jewkes (2001) and
     Human Rights Watch (2001).
55   Green also provides a useful analysis of the prevalence of sexually transmit-
     ted diseases in Africa, and their complex relationship to the prevalence of
     HIV/AIDS (Green, 1994).
56   Mokaba died in June 2002 at the age of 43. His death was widely believed to
     be due to AIDS, although his doctor.gave the cause as pneumonia.
57   See his correspondence with Tony Leon, leader of the opposition Democratic
     Party, in 2000. Excerpts at www.aegic.com/news/dmg/2000/mg001001.
     html.

News sources consulted

Newspapers and news magazines

The Boston Globe – Boston
Business Day – Johannesburg
Cape Argus – Cape Town
Cape Times – Cape Town
Daily News – Durban
Die Afrikaner – Pretoria
Die Burger – Cape Town
The Economist – London
Financial Mail – Johannesburg
The Globe and Mail – Toronto
The Guardian – London
Mail and Guardian – Johannesburg
The Natal Witness – Pietermaritzburg
The New York Times – New York
Newsday – New York
Newsweek – US
Prospect – London
Rapport – Johannesburg
Saturday Star – Johannesburg
The Star – Johannesburg
The Sunday Independent – Johannesburg
Sunday Times – Johannesburg
Sunday Tribune – Durban
TIME Europe
Wall Street Journal – New York
Washington Post – Washington, D.C.
Weekly Mail – Johannesburg

Electronic sources

www.aegis.com – *Aegis AIDS Education Global Information System*
www.afp.com – *Agence France-Presse*
www.afrol.com – *Afrol News*
www.anc.org.za/ancdocs/anctoday – *ANC Today*
www.ap.org – *Associated Press*
www.gov.za – *South Africa Government Online*
www.health-e.org.za – *Health-e News*
www.iol.co.za – *Independent online*
www.mrc.ac.za – *Medical Research Council of South Africa*
www.news24.com.za – *News24.com*
www.pmg.org.za – *Parliamentary Monitoring Group*
www.pulsetrack.co.za – *Pulsetrack*
www.tac.org.za – *Treatment Action Campaign*
www.reutershealth.com – *Reuters Health*
www.sabcnews.com – *SABC News online*
www.sapa.org.za – *South African Press Association*
www.woza.co.za – *Woza News*

References

AIDS Bulletin, Vol. 5 (2), September 1996.

ANC National Executive Committee (2002), 'Castro Hlongwane, Caravans, Cats, Geese, Foot & Mouth, and Statistics: HIV/AIDS and the struggle for the Humanisation of the African' (March).

Boulle, A., Kenyon, C., Skordis, J. and Wood, R. (2002), 'Exploring the Costs of a Limited Antiretroviral Treatment Program in South Africa', *South African Medical Journal*, 92: 811–17.

Cameron, Edwin (2000), 'The Deafening Silence of AIDS', The First Jonathan Marin Memorial Lecture, 10 July (the full text is available at www.aids2000.com).

Cherry, Michael (1998), 'US Scientists may Boycott AIDS Congress', *Nature*, 396: 504.

Chirimuuta, Richard C. and Rosalind J. (1987), *AIDS, Africa and Racism* (Derbyshire: Bretby House).

Crewe, Mary (1992), *AIDS in South Africa: the Myth and the Reality* (London: Penguin Forum Series).

Crewe, Mary (1999), 'Face of the Future', *Siyaya*, 6: 28–31.

Crewe, Mary (2000), 'South Africa: Touched by the Vengeance of AIDS', *South African Journal of International Affairs*, 7 (2): 23–37.

Debates of Parliament (1990), Second Session, Ninth Parliament, 16–18 May, Col. 9797.

Department of Health (2001), *National HIV and Syphilis Sero-prevalence Survey of Women Attending Public Antenatal Clinics in South Africa: 2000* (Pretoria: Department of Health).

Epstein, Helen (2000), 'The Mystery of AIDS in South Africa', *The New York Review of Books*, 20 July.

Everatt, David and Sisulu, Elinor (eds) (1992), *Black Youth in Crisis: Facing the Future* (Johannesburg: Ravan Press).

Gevisser, Mark and Cameron, Edwin (eds) (1994), *Defiant Desire: Gay and Lesbian Lives in South Africa* (Johannesburg: Ravan Press).

Green, Edward C. (1994), *AIDS and STDs in Africa: Bridging the Gap Between Traditional Healing and Modern Medicine* (Pietermaritzburg: University of Natal Press).

Guay L. A., Musoke, P. and Fleming, T. (1999), 'Intrapartum and Neonatal Single-dose Nevirapine Compared with Zidovudine for Prevention of Mother-to-child Transmission of HIV-1 in Kamapala, Uganda: HIVNET 012 Randomized Trial', *Lancet*, 354: 795–802.

Health Systems Trust (2002), *South African Health Review 2001*.

Health Systems Trust (2003), *South African Health Review 2002*.

Heywood, Mark (1997), 'So What About the Working Class?', *AIDS Bulletin*, 6 (3): 28–9.

History in the Making (1990), 'HIV and AIDS in Southern Africa: Draft Maputo Statement, 15/4/1990', Vol. 1 (5): 8–12 (Johannesburg: South African History Archive).

Human Rights Watch (2001), *Scared at School: Sexual Violence against Girls in South African Schools* (New York: Human Rights Watch).

Jewkes, Rachel (2001), 'Violence against Women: an Emerging Health Problem', *MRC News*, 32 (3) Medical Research Council.

Johnson, Shaun (1988), ' "The Soldiers of Luthuli": Youth in the Politics of Resistance in South Africa', in Shaun Johnson, (ed.), *South Africa: No Turning Back* (London: Macmillan Press).

Karim, Quarraisha Abdool (2000), 'Trends in HIV/AIDS infection: Beyond Current Statistics', *South African Journal of International Affairs*, 7 (2): 1–21.

Leclerc-Madlala, S. (2002), 'On the Virgin Cleansing Myth: Gendered Bodies, AIDS and Ethnomedicine', *African Journal of AIDS Research*, 1 (2): 87–95.

LoveLife (2001), *Hot Prospects, Cold Facts: Portrait of Young South Africa*, LoveLife/Henry J. Kaiser Foundation.

Marais, Hein (2000), *To the Edge: AIDS Review 2000* (Pretoria: Centre for the Study of AIDS, University of Pretoria).

Mayibuye (1991), 'Campaigning against AIDS', April, Johannesburg.

Moodley, D. et al. (2000), 'The SAINT trial: Nevirapine (NVP) versus Zidovudine (2DV) + Lamivudine (3TC) in Prevention of Peripartum Transmission', AIDS 2000 – The 13th International AIDS conference, Durban, South Africa.

NACOSA (1994), *A National AIDS Plan for South Africa: 1994–1995* (Pretoria: NACOSA National Secretariat, July).

NACOSA (1999), *NACOSA Western Cape Annual Report 1998–1999* (Cape Town: NACOSA Western Cape).

Nattrass, Nicoli (2003), 'The Costs of HIV Prevention and Treatment Intervention in South Africa', Centre for Social Science Research – Working Paper No. 28.

NIAID (National Institute of Allergy and Infectious Disease) (2002), 'Review of HIVNET 012', 22 March, Washington, DC.

Parkhurst, Justin (2001), 'The Crisis of AIDS and the Politics of Reponse: the Case of Uganda', *International Relations* 15 (6).

Rwomushana, John (2000), 'Breaking the Silence Surrounding AIDS: Uganda's Success Story', *South African Journal of International Affairs*, 7 (2): 67–72.

Samayende, Sizwe and Arenstein, Justin (2002), 'Sacked for Putting his Patients' Interests First', *Focus*, 25: 11–13.

Schlemmer, L. (2000), 'The President's Search for Scapegoats is Part of a Shrewd Strategy for Political Survival', *Focus*, 20, December.

Schneider, Helen (2001), 'A Struggle for Symbolic Power', *Siyaya*, 8: 18–21.

Sechaba (1988), 'AIDS and the Imperialist Connection', 22 (11): 23–8.

Seekings, Jeremy (1993), *Heroes or Villains? Youth Politics in the 1980s* (Johannesburg: Ravan Press).

Sontag, Susan (1989), *AIDS and its Metaphors* (New York: Farrar, Strauss, Giroux).

South African STD/HIV/AIDS Review: Final Report (1997), Medical Research Council.

Toms, Ivan (1990), 'AIDS in South Africa: Potential Decimation on the Eve of Liberation', *Progress*, Fall/Winter: 13–16.

TAC (Treatment Action Campaign) (2002), 'The Costs and Benefits of Preventing and Treating HIV/AIDS'.

TRC (1998), 'Findings and Conclusions', *Truth and Reconciliation Commission of South Africa Report*, 5 (6): 250–1.

van der Vliet, Virginia (1994), 'Apartheid and the Politics of AIDS', in Douglas A. Feldman (ed.), *Global AIDS Policy* (Westport: Bergin and Harvey).

van der Vliet, Virginia (1996), *The Politics of AIDS* (London: Bowerdean).

van der Vliet, Virginia (2001), 'AIDS: Losing the "New Struggle"?', *Daedalus*, 130 (1): 151–84.

Wood, Katharine and Jewkes, Rachel (1997), 'Violence, Rape and Sexual Coercion: Everyday Love in a South African Township', *Gender and Development*, 5 (2): 41–6.

Wood, Katharine and Jewkes, Rachel (2001), 'Dangerous Love: Reflections on Violence among Xhosa Township Youth', in Robert, Morrell (ed.), *Changing Men in Southern Africa* (New York: Zed Books; Pietermaritzburg: University of Natal Press).

WorldAIDS (1990), 12, November (London: Panos Institute).

World Bank (2002), *2002 World Development Indicators* (Washington, DC: World Bank).

5
Assessing the Demographic and Economic Impact of HIV/AIDS

Jeffrey D. Lewis

The demographic impact

Examining the demographic impact of HIV/AIDS provides a bird's-eye view of the human dimension of the pandemic. It necessarily deals in aggregate numbers – shares of the population that are infected, average number of years from infection until death, mortality rates – and may seem somewhat clinical and dispassionate. But as other chapters in this volume illustrate so clearly, underlying these aggregate statistics are the personal passions and struggles of millions of individuals who have been forced to confront a disease that threatens life and family in ways that those of us unaffected are hard-pressed to understand.

One cannot overestimate the adverse impact of HIV/AIDS on African development. AIDS has virtually wiped out the social and economic gains achieved with such difficulty over the last three decades. Life expectancy has been reduced by 25–30 years in the worst-affected countries. AIDS now ranks as the number one cause of death in Africa, twice as high as acute respiratory infection, the next biggest cause. In South Africa, most estimates suggest that during the current decade, twice as many people will die from AIDS as from all other non-AIDS causes combined (Dorrington et al., 2001, pp. 23–5). Unlike earlier global epidemics, AIDS strikes hardest at the productive adult population, rather than the young and the old. The resulting loss of incomes produces disastrous consequences for households, including the emergence of a generation of AIDS 'orphans' whose upbringing strains informal networks and formal safety nets.

Figure 5.1 illustrates how fast HIV has spread in sub-Saharan Africa, as measured by estimates of prevalence rates among adults. The four maps provide a visual affirmation that the countries in southern Africa have

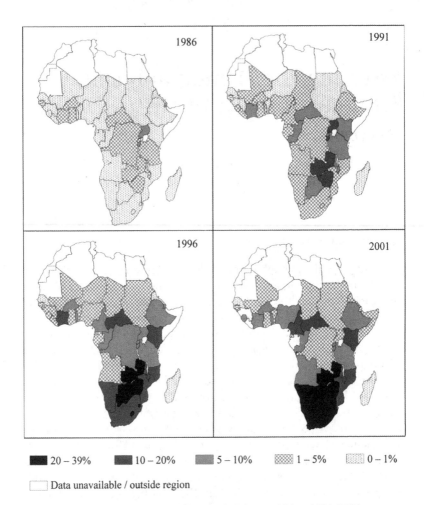

20 – 39%   ■ 10 – 20%   ■ 5 – 10%   ▨ 1 – 5%   ▦ 0 – 1%

Data unavailable / outside region

Figure 5.1   HIV prevalence in adults in sub-Saharan Africa, 1986–2001
Source: UNAIDS/WHO (July 2002b).

been affected the worst. In 1986, HIV prevalence rates were low
throughout sub-Saharan Africa. Only Burundi and Uganda exhibited
rates approaching double digits. But HIV spread quickly and within a
decade and a half all of southern Africa faced prevalence rates in excess
of 20 per cent.

By the end of 2002, it was estimated that 70 per cent of all persons
living with HIV/AIDS were located in sub-Saharan Africa. This amounts

to nearly 30 million African men, women and children. By way of comparison, in North America there were around 980,000 people living with HIV/AIDS. If North America had the same prevalence rate as South Africa, the number of persons with HIV/AIDS would rise from just below 1 million to over 36 million.[1] One can only imagine the attention the epidemic would receive in the United States if this were the case.

To some extent, South Africa's relative isolation during the final years of apartheid insulated it from the early spread of the epidemic. Economic embargoes imposed on South Africa by the rest of the world and security-based restrictions on the movement of people resulted in South Africa, in 1991, having adult prevalence below 1 per cent even as the epidemic raced forward in neighbouring countries. South Africa's political opening that began in the early 1990s created conditions that encouraged the spread of the disease. HIV prevalence rates among South Africans are now among the highest in the world. Since the onset of the AIDS epidemic, estimates are that more than 1 million South Africans have died of AIDS-related causes. By 2010, this number is projected to grow to more than 6 million deaths. By 2008, overall life expectancy in South Africa is forecast to fall from its pre-epidemic high of sixty-five years to only forty years. In 2001, there were an estimated 660,000 AIDS orphans in South Africa; by 2010, this is expected to rise to almost 2 million, or about 5 per cent of the total population.[2]

Modification of high-risk behaviours could reduce AIDS-related death rates, which in turn would slow the expected decline in life expectancy and reduce the number of AIDS orphans. But long delays between infection and death mean that behaviour change today would only begin to reduce the number of AIDS deaths in five years' time with the full effect lagging by a decade or more. The grim statistics of projected increases in mortality outcomes over the next ten years will be hard to change regardless of the success of current programmes to slow the spread of HIV.

It is easy to toss around figures on national prevalence rates and the numbers of current and future infected persons. But as these are only estimates, calculated from a narrow empirical base, Figure 5.2 displays the most important 'building block' in such calculations – survey results obtained from pregnant women seeking antenatal care from public health clinics in South Africa. In South Africa and elsewhere, data obtained from such locations (called Sentinel Surveillance Sites) constitute the only systematic source of clinical information over time concerning the severity of the disease.

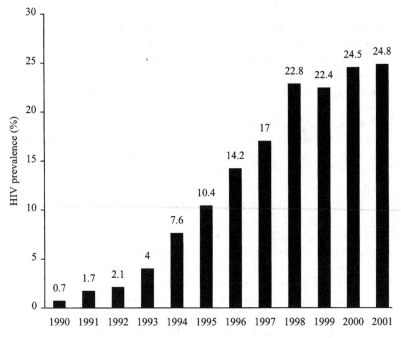

Figure 5.2 HIV prevalence among pregnant women in South Africa 1990–2001
Source: Department of Health, South Africa (2003), Section 4.2.1.

The picture that emerges is consistent with the observation about the relatively late arrival of HIV in South Africa. In 1990, the prevalence among pregnant women was below 1 per cent. Since then, it has risen almost exponentially. By 2001, virtually one-quarter of all South African women receiving support from public antenatal clinics were HIV positive.[3] The apparent dip in the rate in 1999 following the sharp surge in 1998 gave rise to hopes that efforts to curtail further diffusion were starting to yield results. But the return to an underlying rising trend in 2000 and 2001 suggests that 1998 was an outlier, not a turning point.

Moving from these survey results to prevalence estimates for the total adult population occurs through use of epidemiological and demographic models that combine the limited available data (including prevalence rates among pregnant women) and estimates of other key parameters that will influence the spread of the disease (for example, prevalence rates among high-risk groups, such as commercial sex workers, and the frequency of condom usage). These models are used to generate a more comprehensive picture of the past, present and future course of the epidemic, including prevalence rates for different age groups, the numbers of infected persons, the expected number of AIDS-related deaths, and so forth.

The three panels portrayed in Figure 5.3 illustrate the view of the South Africa epidemic that emerges, drawing on one of the available models.[4] The first panel highlights how AIDS is concentrated in the productive cohorts. Prevalence rates among the 30–44 age group is expected to reach a staggering 35 per cent before 2010. Overall prevalence, including everyone 15 years of age and older, is expected to peak this decade at slightly more than 15 per cent. Note that these models, however, do not predict a continuous increase in prevalence rates – in keeping with other epidemics, HIV/AIDS tends to trace out an 'S' - pattern over time. After an initial slow start, the spread of the disease accelerates as transmittal occurs throughout the population. As the pool of uninfected persons shrinks, its composition also shifts towards those less likely to be infected (because of location, behaviour, or other factors affecting risk) so that the growth in the number of new cases slows.

The second panel in Figure 5.3 illustrates the prolonged impact of the disease, driven in part by the extended period between infection and appearance of full-blown AIDS symptoms. The limited available evidence, from industrial as well as emerging economies, suggests that the median time from infection to death is eight to ten years for patients without access to ART regimens. Many who are infected now could live for a decade or more before exhibiting symptoms. While the number of South Africans infected with HIV already exceeds 5 million, the increase in the number of AIDS deaths lags well behind, and will begin to rise sharply only towards the end of the decade. But even with rapid increases in the number of AIDS-related deaths, South Africa's total population will continue to rise. This is because fertility rates likely will remain high enough to offset the population reducing impact of premature deaths due to AIDS. These same trends also suggest significant changes in the age distribution of the population with increasing percentages of the young and old dependent on a relatively smaller cohort of prime aged adults.

The third panel in Figure 5.3 shows the impact on mortality rates, showing three standard mortality measures. *IMR*, the infant mortality rate or the probability of an infant dying before its first birthday, is not much affected. The probability of a child dying before the age of five, *5q0*, rises somewhat over time, the result primarily of mother-to-child

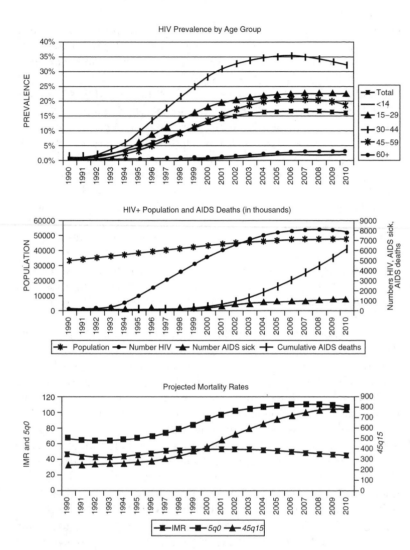

Figure 5.3   Demographic profile of HIV/AIDS in South Africa
Source: Dorrington et al. (2001).

transmission of HIV. Most striking is the impact on survival rates through adulthood. The third line, *45q15*, shows the probability that a 15-year-old will die before reaching 60 years of age. For South Africans, this probability rose from around 25 per cent prior to the AIDS epidemic to almost 80 per cent at present. In other words, four out of five 15-year-olds living in South Africa today are not expected to live until they are 60, with many of them dying as a result of AIDS.

The increased probability of death due to AIDS during adulthood is the major factor behind the drastic reduction in life expectancy in South Africa and other African economies. Figure 5.4 summarizes estimates of life expectancy since 1950 for five African economies that are among the worst hit by AIDS, including forecasts until 2025. The better health indicators that characterized higher income Botswana and South Africa are apparent in the higher life expectancies in these countries achieved up until 1990–5. The later arrival of HIV into South Africa is also evident in the delayed life expectancy downturn. But the precipitous decline in life expectancy apparent in the four other nations – Botswana, Uganda, Zambia and Zimbabwe – is also well under way in South Africa. Current estimates suggest that by the end of this decade, South African life expectancy will drop to only 42 years. Put another way, as a result of HIV/AIDS, a South African child born in 2000 has a life expectancy around ten years lower than one born five years earlier, while a child born in 2005 will likely have its life expectancy shortened by an additional six years. From another vantage point, the sharp recovery of life expectancy in Uganda over the next two decades

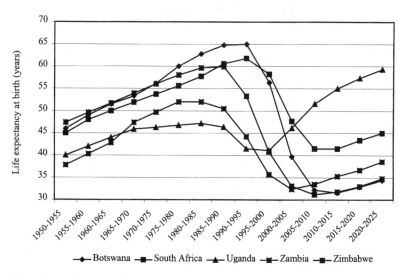

Figure 5.4 Changes in life expectancy, 1950–2025
Source: Data obtained from United Nations (2003).

provides a tangible affirmation of the benefits of 'success' that can emerge from concerted efforts to limit the further spread of the disease.

The economic dimension

Dramatic demographic consequences can be expected to have equally dramatic economic consequences. But understanding the economic consequences of HIV/AIDS lags well behind the predictions of demographic impacts. During the early phase of the epidemic, HIV/AIDS was viewed primarily as a 'health' problem, to be addressed by the medical profession and health departments. In the industrial nations, where prevalence rates hovered around 1 per cent or less, efforts quite sensibly focused on interventions designed to educate and change behaviour among at-risk populations, and on improvements in health and safety standards (such as blood handling and blood bank protocols) to minimize these risk factors. The economic impact, at a macro level, was likely too small to detect, and there was little reason for a broader multidisciplinary perspective.

But in developing countries, especially in Africa, as prevalence rates rose steadily higher, the neat compartmentalization of AIDS as 'only' a health problem became harder and harder to justify. Anecdotal evidence began to emerge of how AIDS was adversely affecting particular groups – specific firms, groups of farmers, different professions, etc. In South Africa it quickly became apparent that the mining sector was particularly hard hit, in part due to its extensive reliance on migrant labour spending extended periods away from families. As more and more sectors were affected, it became increasingly apparent that there were measurable macroeconomic impacts.

Moving past such piecemeal information to more consistent assessments of sectoral burden has proved difficult in South Africa and elsewhere. This stems from the culture of secrecy that has emerged around firm or industry impacts, and their response. There continues to be a strong individual stigma associated with being HIV positive, and this appears to have carried over into the public positions of firms or institutions, which have been extremely reluctant to acknowledge the extent of the problem and identify measures that are being undertaken to address it.

Another reason why it is so difficult to evaluate the macroeconomic impact of the epidemic is that it affects so many different aspects of social, political and economic life at the same time. Economics tends to frame questions in a manner designed to isolate the impact of one factor at a time. Such analysis requires assumptions of *ceteris paribus*, 'holding all else constant', or employs regression techniques that try to measure the statistical significance of some effect while 'controlling for other factors'. But AIDS does not allow us to assume that other things are not changing – in a society battered by the pandemic, there is no such thing as 'holding all else constant'.

To organize the discussion of the economic impact of HIV/AIDS on the South African economy, Table 5.1 identifies three groups – firms, households and government – and briefly presents the main impact channels for each. After considering some recent evidence on the impact on each group, separately, an attempt is made to assess the magnitude of the aggregate economic consequences of the pandemic.

Firms

AIDS affects firms through its impact on costs, on productivity, and on the demand for products. Competitiveness can be directly and adversely affected as firms are obliged to increase worker-related expenses for health benefits or insurance that are utilized more as result of the epidemic. Even without monetary outlays, the economic costs can be substantial. Absenteeism rises both directly, as workers begin to show AIDS symptoms and require more sick leave, and indirectly, as AIDS deaths

Table 5.1 Major channels of HIV/AIDS impact on the economy

For firms:	
• insurance/benefits up	⇒ affects costs, profits, savings
• disruption/absenteeism	⇒ affects overall productivity
• worker experience down/morbidity	⇒ affects labour productivity
• critical sectors hit harder	⇒ affects overall growth potential
For households:	
• loss of income/orphans	⇒ vulnerable households require transfers
• caring for HIV/AIDS	⇒ changed expenditure patterns, reduced savings, asset sales, lower investment in human capital
For government:	
• AIDS spending up	⇒ affects other spending, deficit
• production structure shifts	⇒ affects revenue from VAT, trade taxes
• household incomes, spending shift	⇒ affects income tax receipts, transfers
• education sector affected	⇒ human capital investment down
• health sector squeezed	⇒ demand surges, supply capacity down

Source: Arndt and Lewis (2000), Table 1.

increase and co-workers take leave to attend increasingly frequent funerals. In the medium term, firm productivity will be hit, as the death of so many workers means that firms must constantly hire replacements, which raises training costs and lowers the average work experience – and hence productivity – of the labour force. Firms faced with continuous pressures to hire and train new workers to replace those departing from disease or death are also more likely to adopt production techniques that use relatively fewer workers and more machines, an outcome not necessarily desirable in South Africa where the unemployment rate is around 40 per cent.[5]

Systematic analyses of the impact of AIDS on firms in different sectors have been relatively few, either in South Africa or elsewhere. One exception is a study carried out by a group of researchers based at Boston University (Rosen et al., 2003). Their approach is to construct a framework that identifies the direct and indirect costs that will be incurred in the future by the firm as a result of one of its employees becoming infected today. The different categories of costs encompass those discussed already – morbidity-related costs (higher medical costs, absenteeism, productivity), termination-related costs (death and disability benefits, lower experience), and turnover costs (recruiting, training). The time dimension is especially important, since many of the costs of an additional worker becoming infected today will not be borne by the firm for many years. Many infected workers will remain symptom-free and fully productive for as long as ten years. To capture this feature, this research calculates the net present value of all current and future costs associated with the additional infection; in other words, the amount of money the firm would have to pay out *today* to compensate fully for all future expenses.

The Boston University team applied this methodology to six different firms, five in South Africa and one in Botswana. The firms were selected because they operated in different sectors, were located in different parts of the region, and had different labour force profiles. The firms also allowed HIV testing of their labour force, so that a fairly accurate picture of current prevalence rates could be obtained. Table 5.2 presents indicators on the six firms. Because of continuing sensitivity of firms to possible negative publicity from this analysis, they have been identified only by letters (Company A, Company B . . .).

There are striking differences in HIV prevalence rates across the firms. Regional differences account for some of the variance. Company C, which has the highest prevalence rate (29 per cent), is located in Botswana where infection rates are among the highest in the world.

Table 5.2 HIV prevalence and the AIDS 'tax' in six Southern African firms

Company Studied	A	B	C	D	E	F
Year of study	1999	1999	2000	2001	2001	2001
Industry	Utility	Agribusiness	Mining	Metals	Retail	Media
Location	South Africa	KwaZulu Natal	Botswana	KwaZulu Natal	KwaZulu Natal	South Africa
Size of workforce	>25,000	5,000-10,000	500-1,000	500-1,000	<500	1,000-5,000
HIV prevalence (percent of labour force)	7.9%	23.7%	29.0%	23.6%	10.5%	10.2%
AIDS 'tax'[a]	3.7%	1.8%	5.9%	1.9%	0.4%	2.4%

[a]The AIDS 'tax' is defined as the total annual cost of AIDS as a percentage of salaries and wages.

Source: Adapted & reprinted by permission of *Harvard Business Review*: "The AIDS "Tax"" from 'AIDS is Your Business', by Sydney Rosen et al., February, 2003. Copyright © 2003 by the Harvard Business School Publishing Corporation; all rights reserved.

Company A, with the lowest prevalence rate (7.9 per cent), has operations located throughout South Africa, including high and low prevalence areas. Labour force characteristics are also associated with prevalence rates. Companies B, C and D all have high prevalence rates and are intensive in the use of unskilled labour as compared to Companies A and F with low prevalence rates and relatively more skilled workers.

It is not possible to do justice to the rich results from these case studies, but two additional findings are worth highlighting. First, the relative importance of different costs varies enormously among firms in the study, underscoring the point that AIDS has highly differentiated effects across various sectors of the economy, rather than a uniform 'macro' impact. Figure 5.5 shows the composition of the additional costs for Company A (a large utility operating throughout South Africa) and Company B (an agribusiness in KwaZulu-Natal). For Company A, 46 per cent of the total cost, measured in net present value terms, of an additional AIDS infection among its workforce comes from the sizeable retirement/disability payment it is obliged to make when workers leave the firm. For Company B, retirement payments are negligible and the biggest costs are morbidity-related resulting from absenteeism (36 per cent) and lower productivity (57 per cent). What explains the difference? Company B does not provide retirement/disability payments to most of its workers. Company A does. Even though the HIV prevalence

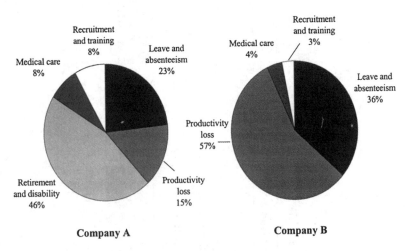

Figure 5.5 Distribution of the costs of a new infection
Source: Rosen et al. (2002).

rate in Company A is a relatively low 7.9 per cent, compared to 23.7 per cent for Company B, Company A will be liable for substantial cost increases as the disease progresses through its labour force. Second, not only are the composition of costs different among firms, but so are the absolute magnitudes. Table 5.2 presents the overall impact of HIV/AIDS by expressing the aggregate (present value) cost of AIDS to each firm as a share of total salaries. In other words, the imputed AIDS 'tax' indicates what each firm implicitly pays relative to its wage bill in order to cover the current and future costs of infected workers. The size of the tax varies: from 5.9 per cent in firm C, the Botswana mining company operating in a high prevalence environment where substantial medical and retirement payments are provided, to 0.4 per cent for the KwaZulu-Natal retail company, a firm that offers most of its employees' minimal benefits. Paradoxically, it is those firms that offer the most extensive benefits to workers that are the most adversely affected, an outcome which will have implications as firms struggle to remain competitive domestically and globally.

In a world of increasing competitive pressures, the imposition of unforeseen AIDS-related costs on firms, not surprisingly, leads to efforts to manage or reduce those costs. There is some evidence that this is already occurring. Some South African firms have been reducing benefits, raising eligibility requirements, or relying on different types of screening mechanisms to avoid incurring HIV/AIDS related costs (Rosen and Simon, 2003). Not all firms are taking this route. Some have taken the opposite tack of offering full medical coverage, including expensive ART, to infected workers. But some of those that have done so have also found it necessary to scale back, confronted with the challenge and cost of meeting the enormous clinical and financial demands. Efforts by firms to try to 'shift' the financial burden of HIV/AIDS from the private sector to households or government, each of which faces its own constraints, pose an important challenge for the future.

Households

There is no shortage of impact channels through which AIDS affects the economic status and well-being of households. The direct and catastrophic effects of having one or more adult members who have AIDS include income loss due to illness, home care and extraordinary medical expenses over several years, and, after the individual dies, additional funeral expenses. But there are indirect effects as well. With income loss and increased medical spending, expenditure patterns will change, possibly reducing spending on education, health and food, with adverse consequences especially for children. Existing extended family networks will be strained as the death of parents means that children will need to be cared for by others, often grandparents. The need to mobilize resources to compensate for lost income and costs of care will reduce or eliminate household assets, with adverse effects in areas such as small business development or food and income security.

Despite the obvious importance of household effects, this has proven the hardest arena in which to get any clear evidence on what is happening. As with the firm perspective, there are a number of recent studies that are starting to fill in the gaps in our understanding of how households are coping with the epidemic. It is important to stress that this is not just an academic enquiry. Understanding what the impacts are and how households respond is crucial to designing future interventions that might alleviate some of the adverse consequences.

One valuable study is a longitudinal survey that is being carried out in Free State Province, South Africa (Booysen, 2002). The household sample comprises of 400 households, segmented along two dimensions. First, half of the households are rural, and half are urban. Second, and more unusually, half of the households are drawn from a group in which at least one member was known to have HIV/AIDS, while the other half was drawn from the general population. (This 'other' half also includes a number of households with HIV positive members.) Identifying and surveying a sub-sample known to be affected by HIV avoids some of the usual difficulties associated with inferring impact on households when it is not certain whether there is any household member who has HIV/AIDS or not.

The results available now are from the first round of the survey, and shed light on different household behaviour at the point the survey was taken, rather than over time as will be possible once the second round is completed. But even these initial results are striking. They reveal in stark terms the enormous disease burden that is imposed on households affected by AIDS. Table 5.3 summarizes information obtained from the survey on the frequency and causes of illness among the sample households. People living in an affected household were three and a half times more likely to have been ill in the last month. Among ill people, nearly three-quarters of those in AIDS-affected households were ill for more than half of the previous 30 days, a quarter were hospitalized, and half were unable to perform daily tasks during the period. AIDS, tuberculosis and pneumonia accounted for over 40 per cent of diagnoses for those in affected households (around 85 people), while the same diagnoses represented only 6 per cent for unaffected households (4 people).

Table 5.3 Illness in AIDS affected and unaffected households

	Affected	Unaffected
Among all households	(n=202)	(n=204)
At least one ill member in last 30 days	73%	20%
At least one member died in last 6 months	20%	1%
Among ill people	(n=203)	(n=53)
Ill for more than 14 of the past 30 days	72%	54%
Hospitalized	27%	9%
Not recovered	73%	55%
Unable to perform daily tasks	50%	19%
Diagnosis	(n=204)	(n=54)
HIV/AIDS	17%	2%
Tuberculosis	21%	4%
Pneumonia	4%	0%
Flu/cold	15%	30%
Other	43%	64%

Source: Booysen et al. (2002), Tables 2 and 11.

Twenty per cent of affected households had experienced a death in the last six months, compared to only 1 per cent of unaffected households.

It is not surprising that this differential disease incidence in affected and unaffected households translates into economic outcomes as well – including differential expenditure patterns, savings, and so on. One illustration of this, based on the survey results, concerns the pattern of savings for households, and in particular the purposes for which households 'drew down' their savings during the six months prior to the survey. The level of 'dis-saving' differed substantially among household groups. For affected households, the average household that utilized savings spent the equivalent of twenty-one months of savings, whereas unaffected households using savings spent only five months' worth. How affected households used their savings differed as well (Figure 5.6). For affected households, the largest uses were funeral expenses (40 per cent) and medical expenses (24 per cent). In other words, nearly two-thirds of savings went for AIDS (or at least illness) related costs. For unaffected households, the pattern is more 'normal'. There was some spending for funerals (8 per cent), but the largest shares went to asset maintenance (31 per cent) and education (30 per cent), which did not appear at all in the affected households' spending.

These results highlight the long-lasting economic impact of HIV/AIDS on households. Families with members who have AIDS may be less able to engage in human capital formation and asset accumulation.

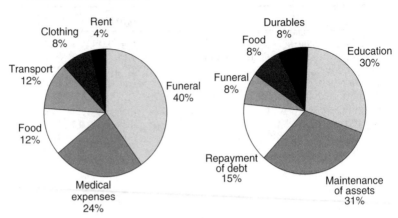

Figure 5.6   Utilization of savings
Source: Booysen (2002), Figure 6.

HIV/AIDS prevents families from pursuing investment strategies needed to ensure future economic well-being both by reducing the household's earnings potential and increasing income instability.

Government

The effect of the AIDS epidemic on government programmes and spending occurs through a number of different channels. Most directly, government bears much of the cost of additional AIDS-related spending aimed at slowing the spread of the disease – public awareness and education campaigns, condom distribution initiatives – as well as the cost of care for those population groups dependent on the public healthcare system. Next, the government plays a dominant role in service delivery in key human development sectors, health and education, for which the epidemic poses major challenges. The prevalence rate among teachers is above average, leading some southern African economies to an outcome where the number of teachers dying of AIDS each year exceeds the annual output of all teacher training institutions. The epidemic also may encourage long-term shifts in economic structure that will lead to future budgetary pressures. In South Africa, reductions in revenues may result if the profitability and tax potential of the mining sector are significantly affected. Increased service demands can be anticipated as a result of expanded care for orphans and overall service delivery will be impaired due to the rapid loss of skilled professionals in the public service.

The direct costs of providing healthcare for those affected by HIV/ AIDS are the most immediate spending needs. Sensible estimates of how those costs might evolve are difficult to produce, dependent as they are on assumptions about who will provide care (public versus private sector providers), what costs will be at different stages of the disease, and what types of treatment will be covered (especially whether ART costs are included or not). But regardless of the particular assumptions, it is clear that the public sector burden will be enormous. One study estimates that the annual average cost of care for an infected person with full AIDS symptoms could be around R17,000 in the public sector (around US$2000), approximately two-thirds of South Africa's current per capita income (Steinberg et al., 2000). When these high patient expenditures are combined with the expected growth in those with full symptoms, the strain on the public budget is evident.

Figure 5.7 shows an estimate of how public sector spending on healthcare will evolve over the next decade in real terms. Total health care spending will double, with the growth entirely due to spending on HIV-related illness. And these figures do not include any public spending on ART treatment! The costs are driven by providing expensive in-patient care to patients in the latter stages of the disease.

The economy-wide impact of HIV/AIDS

The previous discussion focused on the impact of HIV/AIDS on specific groups within the economy: on individual firms, households and

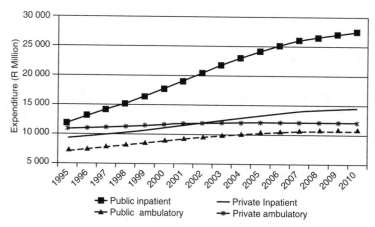

Figure 5.7 Projected healthcare spending for public and private sector
Source: Steinberg et al. (2000), Figure 9.

government. At a more aggregate level, what is the sum of these impacts? What are the macroeconomic consequences of the HIV/AIDS pandemic? One approach to providing answers is to try to quantify and add up all the effects on each of the specific groups. Such an approach would encounter numerous difficulties. First, the number of distinct effects that would have to be considered is huge. Second, estimating the overall impact involves more than just adding up individual effects. In some instances, different factors may affect growth or income in opposite directions, with the potential that the effects may partially offset one another, rather than add up. For example, it might be the case that slower population and labour force growth will reduce the need to construct new schools, thereby lowering government capital spending requirements.

The empirical challenges plus the conceptual ambiguity of the 'adding-up' approach has led analysts to determine aggregate effects in different ways. One method, which builds on the empirical literature on growth determinants, employs cross-country regression techniques. This type of analysis explains growth performance using a wide range of determinants – investment rates, openness to trade, resource endowments, literacy rates, and so on. The possible impact of AIDS can be examined by including an AIDS-related indicator, typically the national HIV prevalence rate, among the variables determining growth, and identifying both the magnitude and significance of the AIDS variable on growth.

While the growth regression approach does take advantage of available cross-country data, it is not without its drawbacks. Because it measures statistical *correlations* among variables, it is not able to shed light on the *causal* mechanisms that lead to growth. Stated differently, it has nothing to say about *how* AIDS reduces growth, or for that matter how trade, or any other growth determinant, either increases or decreases growth in national income. Growth regressions also yield estimates of the importance of different factors for the 'average' country, which means that important heterogeneity among countries may be lost. But despite these limitations, cross-country growth regressions can still be useful in identifying the importance of a particular factor, such as AIDS, in comparison with other determinants of growth.

Figure 5.8 shows the findings of one cross-country growth regression that includes adult HIV prevalence in its analysis (Bonnel, 2000). With a prevalence rate of 10 per cent, per capita GDP growth, on average, is reduced by 0.8 per cent annually; for a prevalence rate of 20 per cent, per capita growth drops by 1.1 per cent annually. These results confirm

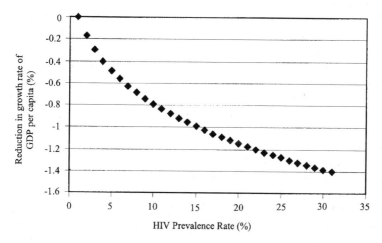

Figure 5.8 Growth impact of HIV (1990–97) (80 developing countries)
Source: Bonnel (2000), Figure 4.

the anticipated negative correlation between HIV/AIDS prevalence and macroeconomic growth. The results also suggest that the magnitude of these effects is large. For the last several years, South Africa has had GDP per capita growth of between 1 and 2 percent. With a national HIV prevalence rate of over 10 per cent, the growth regression findings suggest that if South Africa did not have an HIV/AIDS pandemic, growth rates would have been closer to 2–3 percent.[6]

Another method for assessing the macroeconomic consequences of HIV/AIDS is to construct a model of the economy that includes many of the effects AIDS has on specific economic groups. One type of model that can be constructed is a computable general equilibrium (or CGE) model. Such models have been applied to issues of trade strategy, income distribution, and growth and structural change in developing countries. Because they specifically model the behaviour of firms, households and government, CGE models allow incorporation of the range of AIDS-related effects described earlier – changing household spending, higher firm costs, increased government spending on health – within a consistent economy-wide framework.

The CGE model can be used as a simulation laboratory to examine how the different impact channels affect growth and other key macroeconomic variables. First, a hypothetical 'no-AIDS' scenario is constructed, under the assumption that the pre-epidemic status quo was maintained. Next, the different AIDS-related impacts are added in: lower labour force growth due to premature deaths; lower labour productivity as a result of worker illness; reduced total productivity as result of absenteeism; lower average skills and training costs; increased spending by households on medical and related expenditures; and higher government spending on health and social services. By introducing these effects one at a time, the AIDS scenario can be constructed to see how much each factor contributes to the reduction in growth compared to the 'no-AIDS' case.

Two aspects of the CGE analysis of AIDS in South Africa are worth presenting (Arndt and Lewis, 2000). First, the exercise suggests that the impact on South African GDP growth should be significant over the medium term. As Figure 5.9 shows, GDP growth could be substantially reduced over the rest of the decade as a result of the epidemic. The shortfall in GDP growth rates, due to AIDS, rises from about 0.5 percentage points in 2000 to 2.5 percentage points by 2010. The cumulative impact means that GDP would be 19 per cent lower in 2010 than in the absence of AIDS, or 8 per cent in per capita terms. Once again these are large effects.

Second, decomposing the total decline in GDP into the contribution of different components yields the following results. The bulk of the impact on growth does not come from the *direct* effect of the decline in labour supply. Reduced labour supply accounts for only one-eighth of the total drop in GDP. Decreases in the productivity of factors of production are substantial, accounting for a combined 42 per cent of the estimated decline. The largest impact, some 45 per cent of the decline in GDP, somewhat surprisingly, is attributed to lost government savings.

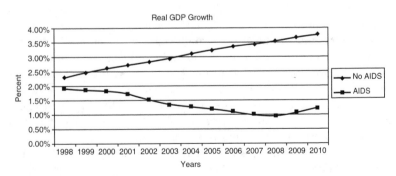

Figure 5.9   Impact of AIDS on GDP growth, 1998–2010
Source: Arndt & Lewis (2000), Figure 1.

The damage is done by the fiscal 'crowding out' that occurs as higher health expenditures lead to larger deficits which displace private investment and reduce growth. It should be emphasized that these findings are not definitive predictions, since they involve comparisons with a hypothetical no-AIDS status quo and are driven by somewhat arbitrary assumptions about the magnitude of the different impact channels. But the results do highlight the pervasive influence of the pandemic on the economy. It is not just households with members who have HIV/AIDS who must bear the burden of the diseases. All South African households bear the burden as HIV/AIDS weakens the entire economy.

Conclusion

Nearly a quarter of a century after its emergence, Africa is still coming to grips with the impact of HIV/AIDS. Understanding the sweeping demographic impact of the pandemic is increasingly apparent in the statistics. AIDS deaths in South Africa already exceed one million, with millions more to follow by the end of the decade. An entire generation is being forced to cope with the death of one or both parents, with the number of AIDS orphans projected to reach 2 million by 2010. A wave of sickness and death is already sweeping through South Africa, and its impact will be felt throughout this decade and beyond by the millions of households that will be directly affected. Beyond the widespread personal and human losses created by the pandemic lies a second level of effects. South Africa's economy, which has been struggling for two decades, is another indirect victim of the pandemic. HIV/AIDS adds one more 'tax' on South African firms trying to compete in a global market and burdens a government already facing pent-up demand for services that lie beyond its means. Just as the society needs more resources to confront HIV/AIDS, the adverse impact of the epidemic on human capital, on productivity, and on government finances could impose a macroeconomic cost which would run as high as 1 per cent or more of the growth in GDP per capita, which is already too low to create enough jobs and alleviate widespread poverty.

Whether one views HIV/AIDS from the vantage point of a medical professional or public health specialist, or as a demographer or an economist, it is clear that confronting the pandemic will require the active involvement and commitment of all groups within society – individuals, households, firms and government – in a concerted campaign to limit and reverse the spread of the disease, and to deal with the enormous challenge of dealing with the millions of lives damaged or destroyed.

Notes

*Jeffrey Lewis is Economic Adviser in the International Trade Department and the Prospects Group at the World Bank. The views expressed are those of the author and should not be attributed to the World Bank, its Executive Directors or the countries they represent.

1 Estimates of people living with HIV/AIDS by region are from UNAIDS (2002a). According to the Nelson Mandela/HSRC Study of HIV/AIDS (2002), South Africa's HIV prevalence rate (population two and older) is estimated at 11.4 per cent. North America's population in 2002 is 319 million yielding an estimated 36.4 million HIV positive persons if North America had the same HIV prevalence rate as South Africa.

2 Estimates of South Africa's cumulative AIDS deaths are from Dorrington et al. (2001). Life expectancy forecasts are taken from United Nations (2003). The number of living AIDS orphans, 0–14 years of age, is from UNAIDS (2002b) and projections for future numbers of orphans is from Steinberg et al. (2000).

3 Testing in antenatal clinics provides the only time series evidence on HIV prevalence rates. However, the recently completed cross-section study, the Nelson Mandela/HSRC Study of HIV/AIDS (2002), provides an alternative estimate of HIV prevalence based on a random sample of almost 9000 individuals who were tested for HIV. This study yielded a 17.7 per cent HIV positive rate in 2002 for females, 15–49 years of age. This rate is lower by about one-quarter than the rate for pregnant women obtained from the Sentinel Surveillance Sites, in part because the latter study, by construction, samples a sexually more active population.

4 The figures are taken from Dorrington et al. (2001) who use a model developed by the Actuarial Society of South Africa called the ASSA 600 model. Versions of this model are available publicly through the Internet and other sources, so that researchers can vary assumptions and parameters in order to investigate alternative scenarios about how the epidemic will progress. (See http://www.assa.org.za/aidsmodel.asp).

5 Forty per cent refers to the 'broad unemployment' rate which includes those currently not working but actively seeking employment as well as those discouraged workers who have given up even looking for a job.

6 Closer inspection of the growth regression results yields a somewhat surprising result. The growth 'costs' of AIDS increase with higher prevalence rates, but at a decreasing rate. In evaluating whether this makes sense, it is worth returning to a point made at the beginning of the chapter. There may exist a 'threshold' effect, so that relatively low HIV prevalence has little if any macro impact, whereas rates above some threshold would tend to have an increasing impact. The relationship depicted in Figure 5.8 suggests the opposite. At low prevalence levels, the first 5 per cent of HIV prevalence 'costs' 0.5 percent in growth terms; the next 5 per cent only about 0.3 per cent, and so forth. This finding warrants further investigation.

References

Arndt, C. and Lewis J. D. (2000), 'The Macro Implications of the HIV/AIDS Epidemic: a Preliminary Assessment', *South African Journal of Economics*, 58 (5) (December).

Bonnel, R. (2000), 'HIV/AIDS and Economic Growth: a Global Perspective', *South African Journal of Economics*, 58 (5) 5 (December).

Booysen, F. le R. (2002), 'Financial Responses of Households in the Free State Province to HIV/AIDS-related Morbidity and Mortality', *The South African Journal of Economics*, 70 (7), pp. 1193–1215.

Booysen, F. le R., Van Rensburg, H. C. J., Bachmann, M., Engelbrecht, M., Steyn, F. and Meyer, K. (2002), 'The Socio-economic Impact of HIV/AIDS on Households in South Africa: Pilot Study in Welkom and Qwaqwa, Free State Province', report for USAID on Economic Impact of HIV/AIDS in South Africa. Bloemfontein, Centre for Health Systems Research and Development, University of the Free State. Available as: http://www.uovs.ac.za/faculties/humanities/chsrd/research.asp.

Department of Health, South Africa (2003), 'Summary Report: National HIV and Syphilis Sero-Prevalence Survey in South Africa', Directorate: Health Systems Research, Research Coordination and Epidemiology.

Dorrington, R., Bourne, D., Bradshaw, D., Laubscher, R. and Timaeus, I. M. (2001), 'The Impact of HIV/AIDS on Adult Mortality in South Africa', *Technical Report, Burden of Disease Research Unit, Medical Research Council* (September).

Mandela, Nelson/HSRC (2002), *Full Report: Nelson Mandela/HSRC Study of HIV/AIDS*.

Rosen, S. and Simon, J. (2003), 'Shifting the Burden: the Private Sector's Response to the AIDS epidemic in Africa', *Bulletin of the World Health Organization*, 81, pp. 131–7.

Rosen, S., Simon, J., Fox, M., MacLeod, W., Vincent, J. and Thea, D. (2002), 'Investing in the Epidemic: the Cost of Aids to Businesses in Africa', Center for International Health, Boston University School of Public Health, http://www.international-health.org/aids_economics/Publications.htm.

Rosen, S., Simon, J., Vincent, J., MacLeod, W., Fox, M. and Thea, D. (2003), 'AIDS is Your Business', *Harvard Business Review*, February.

Steinberg, M., Kinghorn, A., Söderlund, N., Schierhout, G. and Conway, S. (2000), 'HIV/AIDS – Facts, Figures, and the Future', chapter 15 in Health Systems Trust, *South African Health Review 2000*, United Nations (2003). *World Population Prospects: the 2002 Revision and World Urbanization Prospects: the 2001 Revision*, Population Division of the Department of Economic and Social Affairs of the United Nations Secretariat, http://esa.un.org/unpp, 5 May 2003.

UNAIDS/WHO (2002a), 'AIDS Epidemic Update'.

UNAIDS/WHO (2002b), 'HIV/AIDS in sub-Saharan Africa', www.unaids.org/barcelona/presskit/epigraphics/SSAfrica0702_en.ppt.

UNAIDS/WHO (2002c), 'South Africa: Epidemiological Fact Sheets', 2002 Update.

6
HIV/AIDS in South Africa: Can the Visual Arts Make a Difference?

Marilyn Martin

It is probably art historically and theoretically – and politically – incorrect to start a paper by quoting Clement Greenberg, arguably the preeminent art critic of the twentieth century, but one who has been out of favour for some time. I have indeed questioned my decision to do so and I hope that at the end of this chapter, you and I will understand why. I suspect that it has to do with my strong sense that art is undergoing profound changes, that we are experiencing the swing of the pendulum that characterizes the history and theory of aesthetic production – from romanticism to classicism, from the linear to the painterly, from figuration to abstraction. Being somewhat disconcerted by signs of a return to abstract painting must have made me receptive to Greenberg's words that I read recently.

> I say that if you have to choose between life and happiness or art, always choose life and happiness. Art solves nothing, either for the artist himself or for those who receive his art. Art shouldn't be overrated. It started to be in the late eighteenth century, and definitely was in the nineteenth. The Germans started the business of assessing the worth of a society by the quality of art it produced. But the quality of art produced in a society does not necessarily – or maybe seldom – reflects the degree of well being enjoyed by most of its members. And well being comes first. I deplore the tendency to over-value art. (Accone, 2002)[1]

As a firm and committed believer in the potential of art as a transformative power in society, I was taken aback by the bluntness of Greenberg's statement. Why does one have to choose between art and life? Are they not one and the same thing? In South Africa we have not assessed the worth of our society by the quality of art produced (art is simply not that important), but rather the quality of the art in relation to society and in particular the extent to which art is a reflection of, and a catalyst within, society. We know that art played a role both inside and outside South Africa in the struggle for political liberation, beginning with Dumile Feni (1939–91) in the 1960s. The 1980s saw the production of an extraordinary body of work stimulated by opposition to apartheid and made in the face of adversity. Artists found technical, formal and expressive ways to engage political and social questions, affirming that art and culture can interrogate centralized processes and develop ideas and metaphors that can influence and change society. It made the world sit up and take notice. The cultural and academic boycott was highly successful in isolating South Africa from the rest of the world. I can release Greenberg's modernist, formalist statement that 'art solves nothing' and let it go, for I know that art does offer solutions.

What concerned me deeply about Greenberg's ideas was his comment on the relationship between the quality of art produced in a society and the extent to which it reflects the degree of well-being enjoyed by the majority. South African art started coming into its own during the darkest years of oppression. Since April 1994, when the first democratic elections were held, South African artists have participated in exhibitions, art biennials and festivals throughout the world, and individuals like David Goldblatt and William Kentridge have been honoured with retrospective exhibitions in major institutions in the United States and elsewhere. Never has the reputation of our visual art been greater and the aesthetic production as sought after as it is right now.

Yet we are a society deeply flawed and in serious trouble. Everybody has twice had the chance to vote, human rights are enshrined in the constitution and education is available to all. But the cultural topography of segregation and division, privilege and deprivation has in many cases endured without change, and the shift in political power has not brought economic empowerment. More than a million jobs have been lost since 1994. The white minority, together with a black elite, control the economy, while the majority of South Africans are sinking into the quicksand of poverty and are unable to realize their constitutional rights. A dominant culture of greed and profligacy has emerged, fuelled by a macroeconomic policy that seeks to make the South African economy competitive in the international arena, but that cannot meaningfully address the inherited inequities of the apartheid system, let alone transform them. The health and education sectors are in crisis and violent crime, financial fraud, corruption, drug dealing, homelessness, child prostitution, rape, xenophobia and racism plague the country.

The devastation brought upon South Africa by HIV/AIDS and the crisis around policy and action are subjects of this volume, so I need not go into any detail or offer statistics in this regard. I do wish to mention, however, that censorship is reappearing in general and in particular with regard to HIV/AIDS. Recently radio host Tim Modise and SABS-Safm were cleared of charges of 'sedition' by the Broadcasting Complaints Commission after allegations were made by Anita Allen, one of South Africa's leading AIDS dissidents (Beresford, 2002). She had the support of Professor Sam Mhlongo, head of Family Medicine at Medunsa (Medical University of South Africa). Modise and other investigative broadcasters, such as Sally Burdett, Nadia Levin and John Perlman are branded anti-science and anti-government as a result of their efforts to bring newsworthy information about HIV/AIDS to the South African public.

The institutional framework for the arts, culture and heritage has changed significantly and for the better since 1994. The list of new policies, structures and legislation generated by the Department of Arts, Culture, Science and Technology is impressive, but adequate funding and efficient implementation are lacking in all areas and some are in crisis. The government is spending R68 billion (about $6.8 billion) on arms and R408 million (about $4.8 million) on a presidential jet, while the budget for the country's major museums, heritage and funding bodies for film, performing arts, visual arts, crafts and literature amounts to R495 million (about $4.95 million) in the 2002–3 financial year. A recent survey on the radio found that only 2 per cent of the South African population want Lottery money allocated to arts, culture and heritage.

All the above tempts me to agree with Greenberg, at least for the moment, that the quality of art produced in South Africa right now does not reflect the degree of well-being of the majority of its citizens. And it raises the question: what role can the arts play in contemporary South Africa, if any? For the politically engaged artist under apartheid there was no doubt about the identity of the target. After 1994, both the challenges and the possibilities have become more complex, ambivalent and unpredictable. The course of South African art changed from confrontation to reconciliation and during the honeymoon years of the new democracy there were calls for artists to put aside political considerations and find new themes and images. To stop and smell the flowers, some suggested, but this was short-lived.

Today the artist's social responsibility is once again debated. History, memory and identity are central to the enquiry and artists often address their roles as individuals within a historical process, and engage with the past, while remaining aware of contemporary challenges. The Truth and Reconciliation Commission (TRC), which was created to record and cleanse the pain of the past through a series of public hearings, has given rise to art works that chillingly invoke scenes recounted in testimony. Under apartheid, incidentally, few artists who made works critical of the regime experienced repercussions, unless they were also political activists. And while political journalism, theatre productions, festivals, pornography and music suffered bans, few exhibitions of works of visual art were banned. This reflects the country's contradictions, as well as the official lack of interest in the social role of art.

For some artists the present is a time to turn inward so as to explore identity and more personal dramas and to investigate sexual and gender politics and roles. Many retain their faith in the transcendental potentialities of art as reconstructor of spiritual aspirations and restorer of human dignity. Others choose to remain activists, not only in the political sense, but also in the way in which they engage in and with communities in order to use their creativity as an agent for social change and transformation. This is a situation that Greenberg could not have imagined.

But what difference can art and art institutions make in the face of the HIV/AIDS pandemic? Globally, AIDS has killed some of the great creative talents of our time and it has been a subject for artistic action and reflection for more than a decade. At the South African National Gallery (Sang), which now forms part of Iziko Museums of Cape Town, we have had exhibitions and programmes on HIV/AIDS since June 1993 when we displayed the second memorial quilt that was produced in Cape Town by the AIDS Support and Education Trust (ASET). The Sang was the first public building to be 'wrapped' with a gigantic red ribbon on International AIDS Day, 1996, by Wola Nani (Embrace) in Cape Town. It took until 1999 before Parliament could be 'wrapped'.

The first international photographic exhibition, 'Positive Lives: Responses to HIV', was hosted at the Sang in 1995. Initiated by Network Photographers in 1993, it explored the complex individual and social responses to HIV/AIDS in Britain, with a special section by Gideon Mendel, a South African photographer living in London, dealing with the situation in South Africa. Sponsorship by Levi Strauss & Company, the Terrence Higgins Trust (founded in 1983), Old Mutual and the AIDS Foundation of South Africa enabled us to run extensive education programmes for schools and to create a duplicate edition of Mendel's South African photographs. These have been shown from Oudtshoorn in the Western Cape to Dakar, Senegal.

'Positive Lives' comprises a unique and growing collection of photographs – as it travels the world new works and new stories are added. On International AIDS Day, 1, December 2001, Zackie Achmat, Chairperson of the Treatment Action Campaign (TAC) opened a different 'Positive Lives' exhibition at the Sang. In a powerful, emotional speech he added his voice to the struggle of the Sang to convince the South African public and the authorities that a work of art not only has the power and capacity to speak for itself, but also to speak to and for individuals and society. Education is the key to building and changing attitudes and perceptions and to alleviating ignorance. Far-reaching education programmes, workshops, film screenings, an excellent brochure and the presence of HIV-positive people as volunteer guides at the gallery formed part of the exhibition. This also prepared the way for Gideon Mendel's project.[2]

The heart of 'Positive Lives' was occupied by 'A Broken Landscape', Mendel's photo-journalistic study of AIDS in Africa. For him the status of the national art museum and its location near the South African Parliament offered a remarkable opportunity to create a radical, stimulating and newsworthy project. For three months the Liberman Room at the Sang provided a focus for the battle against AIDS, the central authority in particular and leadership in general. It became, in the words of the artist, a 'live documentary space', an evolving series of works created by Mendel in collaboration with TAC and people participating in an anti-retroviral programme in Khayelitsha, a township near Cape Town. An open letter sent to President Thabo Mbeki became part of the display, but there was no reply.

The key concept of Mendel's installation was that people living with HIV or AIDS could be intimately involved in the creation of an exhibition rather than being passively depicted as victims. The end result was an unorthodox and groundbreaking social art project. The artist created a positive activist environment in the national art museum on the doorstep of Parliament. The launch of the project on 16, February 2002 was an exciting and moving experience. Together we broke new ground in our shared vision – and commitment – to making a difference, to offering solutions in a crisis.

The central installation comprised four parts, the vibrant colour creating a striking contrast with the back and white work on the surrounding walls. Each part was developed collaboratively, drawing individuals living with HIV or AIDS and their organizations into the process of deciding how they wanted to be represented, and what they wished to say. The four components were:

The frame series

'Self-portraits' of people living with HIV or AIDS, shown alongside their testimonies. Participants got a blank frame on the wall that they could fill as they wished. They could choose to display objects or parts of their own bodies.

Memory boxes

Across Africa there are projects where HIV-positive women are making boxes and filling them with objects and photographs by which they wish their children to remember them. In Cape Town the Art and Society Research Unit is using these boxes as a form of art therapy. Each week, during the show, the unit invited women from Cape Town's poorest communities to the gallery to share their boxes, big and small, with the public.

The notice board

This included new photographs about HIV/AIDS taken by Mendel in the course of the exhibition. Displayed as enlarged contact sheets, they changed frequently and were shown alongside oral testimonies, community flyers, viewers' comments and newspaper clippings.

A website for a global audience

Photographs and material gathered were added daily to the website, and feedback was welcomed to contribute to interactive creative input.

The closing ceremony on Saturday 13, April and the launch of Gideon Mendel's (2001) book, *A Broken Landscape: HIV and AIDS in Africa*, was another extraordinary and memorable event. Organized by the *Mail and Guardian* newspaper and TAC, it had all the energy and power of a political rally during the apartheid years (indeed TAC has its roots in the anti-apartheid movement and the organizers are accustomed to mass mobilization and strategies that strike chords in society). There were songs, announcements and testimonies interspersed with 'Viva!' and 'Amandla! Awethu!'[3] In the course of his hard-hitting and inspiring closing speech Edwin Cameron, a judge of the Supreme Court of Appeal, convinced me that Greenberg's words do not fully apply to South Africa in 2002. The quality of art is at least to some extent linked to the well-being of our citizens. And so is the national art museum. I quote from his speech:

> This exhibition has been a remarkable event. Its presence here represents a major commitment by the South African National Gallery to

people living with HIV and AIDS. The work on display itself shows deep commitment.

What does it mean to say that an artist (or an art gallery) 'shows commitment'? It means that he or she brings not only an *engagement* to the subject of the display, but an *involvement* in it that transcends mere observation or representation. This is plain from Gideon Mendel's *A Broken Landscape*. The photographer has shown an imaginative and respectful engagement with his topic. But he has done infinitely more than that. He has aligned himself unmistakably with the reality that confronts his subjects and those around them.

His depiction of that reality is astonishing in its power, in its graphic truth, in its respectful distance and in its searing intimacy.

He places before us images that shock us with their force and closeness. The reason is that he has involved himself with the extremity of his subjects' struggle, who are at the very edge of life. He shows us the inexpressible complexity, the terrible simplicity, and the dignity of that state.

In achieving this, neither the artist nor his exhibition has been static. As events have moved, he has included them – the court battle about the provision of antiretroviral medication to pregnant mothers, the claim to life of those who for the first time are now gaining access to longer-term drug therapy.

In all of this the artist is depicting a truth. But his work also makes a call to action. The exhibition challenges those who view it to take a position on the lives and the deaths of those it represents. That call to action echoes the most urgent current question in our national life.

Judge Cameron went on to outline the nature of the crisis of HIV/AIDS in South Africa. On the one hand it is a crisis of illness and death on a scale globally that is worse than anything the world has known for more than 600 years; on the other hand, it is one of leadership and management and a crisis of truth-telling. He regards this as the third crisis in AIDS – a crisis 'engendered by those in our country who deny the facts about AIDS'. They deny that the new and different patterns of disease and dying are the result of a virus and they deny that the destruction of the human body by the virus can be completely contained by carefully administered and properly monitored antiretroviral medications. The deniers attack those speaking the truth about HIV/AIDS as agents of an apparatus engaged in 'a massive political-commercial campaign to promote antiretroviral drugs' and accuse them of wanting 'to medicalise poverty and underdevelopment'.[4] The facts about HIV/AIDS are depicted as a plot against Africans because they are black. In Judge Cameron's view 'this denial of AIDS represents the ultimate relic of apartheid's racially imposed consciousness, and the deniers achieve the ultimate victory of the apartheid mindset'. As a result the national response to the pandemic has been paralysed and confusion reigns. People are shamed into silence and their energies and determination sapped, while suffering increases, but more than that, the denial 'is a profound insult to those South Africans who are living with and dying from the effects of the virus. They deny us the dignity of our suffering. They deny us the dignity of our struggle for life against the workings of a viral agent.' Judge Cameron ended his speech with a rallying call to action:

> But, as we have seen today, from the terrible grief of those affected by the virus a terrible determination arises: a determination to defeat untruth and misrepresentation and distortion, and to assert hope. That is the ultimate significance of the unforgettable images of this exhibition: that untruth and inaction are the greatest crimes of all. Let us take an angry inspiration, and deep determination, from that.

Two of Mendel's works from this project form part of the exhibition 'Artists for AIDS'. Unlike Mendel, few visual artists in South Africa had confronted HIV/AIDS until they were invited to participate in the project that I curated for Bristol-Myers Squibb (BMS) and the Harvard AIDS Institute in 2000. Together with Chris Howard, then Corporate Associate of the BMS Secure the Future Programme, I commissioned thirty-one artists from five southern African countries – Botswana, Lesotho, Namibia, South Africa and Swaziland – to tackle the subject of HIV/AIDS. The participants surpassed all our expectations and the superb collection – ArtWorks for AIDS – was shown in Durban at the XIII International AIDS Conference. It then travelled to Washington, DC, Brussels and Boston where an auction took place on 30 November 2000. Proceeds from the sale benefited community care and health research in the countries involved in the project.

I met Kyle Kauffman at the auction and some time later he invited me to collaborate on 'Artists for AIDS' with him and Jeremy Fowler of the Davis Museum and Cultural Centre at Wellesley College. I accepted with enthusiasm. I was enormously grateful to have another opportunity of engaging some of South Africa's foremost visual artists to identify with and focus on the subject of HIV/AIDS. Informed by the Bristol-Myers

Squibb and Harvard AIDS Institute project, we selected the artists – ten from South Africa and one from Botswana. Their work is very different, but they have one thing in common. They remain convinced that the creative act can and must engage more than itself. The guidelines for the project were simple: each artist would receive an amount of money for a two-dimensional work, no larger than one metre by one metre and would provide biographical information as well as a brief statement on the work. All the artists accepted the invitation and David Goldblatt generously donated his photograph.

The guidelines may have been straightforward, but the demands were not. Again I was asking artists to aestheticize a complicated and increasingly political and controversial public issue. And the challenges are greater and more penetrating than the immediate situation in South Africa. HIV/AIDS has forced a wider discussion of varied sexual practices. It has detonated and compelled changes in sexual behaviour and conventions (for example, condom use and male privilege in demanding sex), and demanded a reassessment of our private and public views, consciousness and taboos. AIDS as disease-metaphor was identified and articulated by Susan Sontag as early as 1988. It has stirred deeply contested beliefs and issues around homosexuality, sexual liberty, the body, religion and the repression and marginalization of the Other, those who are seen as different, and those who are regarded as victims.

Artist Hentie van der Merwe (1995) has the following to say:

> I think that the AIDS epidemic is one of the main concerns for a need of a new way of thinking and living. AIDS then becomes, not the unfortunate and fatal disease that is threatening human existence, but part of our post-modern condition which requires a whole new mindset and the way we perceive time and relate to each other as human beings.

According to Reverend Gideon Byamugisha (2001, p. 199) of Kampala, Uganda:

> AIDS isn't just a disease. It is a symptom of something deeper which has gone wrong within the global family. It reveals our broken relationships, between individuals, communities and nations. It exposes how we treat and support each other, and where we are silent. It shows us flaws in the way we educate each other, and the way we look at each other as communities, races, nations, classes, sexes, and between age groups. AIDS insists that it is time for us to sit down and

address all the things we have been quiet about – sexuality, poverty, and the way we handle our relationships from the family level to the global level.

The HIV/AIDS illness as metaphor has highlighted social inequities and the binary opposites of rich and poor, black and white, first and third worlds in a terrifying way. And it has given rise to or resurrected myths and practices that are unimaginable, from having intercourse with virgins as a cure to using goats for sexual relief and viral firewalling by teenagers in Mamvuka, a village situated in Limpopo Province in South Africa. In a South African Broadcasting Corporation (SABC) interview, one of the young men said: 'We know about AIDS and we are very afraid of it. That is why we have sex with these goats. Goats don't have AIDS. We boys discussed AIDS and how people in our village are dying. We agreed to stop sleeping with women and settle for goats' (Kirby, 2002).

'Artists for AIDS' merges private and public experiences and embraces the social and activist domains; it transcends perceived and constructed boundaries with regard to race, class, creed, gender and sexual orientation. Participants have created thoughtful, beautiful, poignant, moving, hard-hitting and powerful works of art. They have concretized their ideas and conceptions in many different ways – narrative and allegorical, abstract, didactic, subtle and enigmatic. They have done so in a variety of media – photography, painting, college, embroidery, silicon sand, carboniferous material and latex. Their written statements reveal their feelings and intentions.

Karel Nel (Figure 6.1) has created two non-figurative works of great transcendental beauty and meaning. He notes, 'The long and extended format in *Life's Tide* and *Permian Dust* alludes to the notion of duration or a time line. The works explore recurrent themes within my work: the enigma of life and death, of energy and the void and of life's traces left in matter, no matter how small and insignificant these events may seem in the scheme of things. Within this context, AIDS focuses life expectancy and the concomitant questions around the traces we leave behind consciously or inadvertently.' The surface textures are exquisite and they enhance the black and red shapes that have a powerful associative impact.

At first glance Andries Botha's piece, *Rupture* (Figure 6.2), also appears abstract. Closer viewing, however, shows that he has drawn and painted on paper, densely working the surface to resemble skin – the skin of a body that is bruised and battered. By adding human hair and enclosing it all in latex he emphasizes both the appearance of skin and the notion of rupture, decline and disintegration. According to Botha, 'Skin represents the fragile physical membrane that mediates body, humanity and identity. Its tenuous veil negotiates our relationships with the physical and emotional world. It also provides the necessary illusions of permanence, endurance and inviolability.'

Lien Botha has used the jet-ink method to create *Book of Gloves: the Obstetrician* (Figure 6.3), a colour photograph on canvas. The plain whiteness of the background against which the red gloves are isolated creates an image that is simultaneously clinical and bloody. '*Book of Gloves* is a continuing series of glove images, alluding to the notion of the book of life or *identikit*. The glove, while concealing the fingerprint, becomes a second skin, which in the most minimal language codifies the identity of its human residue: ornithologist, volplanist, florist, chemist, and etcetera. This confirms my interest in cloth/fabric and its ability to protect, conceal or reveal aspects of the human condition.'

Red is the colour of blood in Botswana artist Neo Matome's mixed media work *Ties that Bind* (Figure 6.4). Matome explains that, 'The work is essentially about the complex relationship between cultural values, and social and economic pressures as they affect individuals and their ability to make prudent choices about their lifestyles.' In spite of the constant stream of information about HIV/AIDS and its attendant risks, teenage girls and young women are still victims of unplanned pregnancies, which have far reaching implications where the spread of HIV is concerned. In Botswana women are considered to be the group most at risk of being infected.

In this artwork, culture is symbolized by the cowrie shell. The purpose of the cowrie is to question the role of culture and norms within the context of the HIV threat. There is also reference to veins and the dual role blood plays – that of the life giver and life taker. The red blood cells that contain collaged images of nets symbolize HIV/AIDS infection and potential health complications. The abstracted image of a flower, on the other hand, highlights the beauty and fragility of life. The staring eye of a child and the foetus-like forms refer to the youth and the monumental threat they face from the HIV pandemic. The title of the work highlights the inextricable link that exists between our choices and circumstances.

The red ribbon associated with HIV/AIDS takes on new meanings in Penelope Siopis' cibachrome photograph *Baby in Red* (Figure 6.5). This image forms part of a series of photographs in which the artist bound a baby in an AIDS ribbon. The ribbon contains and threatens. The baby is both mummy and newborn, cold and warm, dead and alive. This is a generic baby; she or he may provoke more general questions about AIDS: 'I wanted to emphatically connect the "universal" AIDS ribbon to the body of a baby so that the ribbon becomes less symbol, motif, logo than a representation of flesh and blood.' And it reminds us that wearing the red ribbon can be empty rhetoric if action is missing.

Other figurative works pay homage to individuals who have died of AIDS or who are particularly vulnerable to the virus. David Goldblatt's colour digital print (Figure 6.6) presents us with an image of a beautiful African family in a domestic environment – a Madonna, complete with halo, and her children. Until we read the title: *Victoria Cobokana, housekeeper, in her employer's dining room with her son Sifiso and daughter Onica, Johannesburg June 1999. Victoria died of AIDS 13 December 1999, Sifiso died of AIDS 12 January 2000, Onica died of AIDS in May 2000.* The physical symptoms of an invisible microbe's presence are completely absent, deceiving us into thinking that Victoria Cobokana and her family are healthy.

In sharp contrast is Sue Williamson's portrait of Benjamin Borrageiro, who also died of AIDS (Figure 6.7). Williamson's work on HIV and AIDS started in response to the Bristol-Myers Squibb and Harvard AIDS Institute project, but it did not stop there. Williamson is interested in what people experiencing a situation have to say and the language they use to express their feelings. She started interviewing women who are HIV positive, particularly those who have had the courage to disclose their condition. She realized that a different approach was required in the display of the work, that the gallery environment was not enough. Working with a graffiti artist, she selected suitable outdoor sites to make public the words of the women, the essence having been distilled from the interviews. The person's name was added in vinyl lettering below the text, the statement becoming a quotation rather than just graffiti. Photographs of the walls with a portrait of the individual who made the statement comprised a series of works 'Breaking the Silence'.

The first message was that of AIDS activist Busi Maqungo – the work that was auctioned in Boston in November 2000. Williamson worked with Mitchells Plain graffiti artist Falko to depict Busi's message next to a railway bridge that already contained graffiti of the Sexy Boys gang: 'It should be taken as a crime if someone doesn't wear a condom and he makes you go to bed.'

Benjamin was the third in the series, shown at the Goodman Gallery in Johannesburg in April 2002 under the title *From the Inside: Benjy.* 'Benjy lived in Observatory, and was brought up very close to the bridge in the Gardens, a Cape Town suburb, that bears his statement: "I'm sick of Mbeki saying HIV doesn't cause AIDS." The photograph was taken about three weeks before Benjy died in November 2000, and shows Benjy provocatively thrusting his leg out of his bed to show just how wasted he was. His remains on the bridge, though since then someone attempted to paint out the name "Mbeki" in black paint.'[5] In 2001 Williamson started working in Johannesburg and, with the assistance of a team from the Department of Fine Art at the University of the Witwatersrand, put up twelve messages on walls around the city.

A crackdown on graffiti in Cape Town prompted Williamson to inscribe a message by André Steyn on a vinyl couch: 'People with HIV/AIDS should be treated just like anyone else . . . this is a new millennium.' She intended the couch for the VIP lounge of the 2002 North Sea Jazz Festival, but the organizers regarded it as offensive and inappropriate. In protest to this muffling action, the couch was set up outside Parliament and photographed (Maart, 2002, p. ii).

Sam Nhlengethwa's *Miner* (Figure 6.8) is a generic portrait through which the artist wishes to focus on a particular aspect of the pandemic: 'The mining theme I chose was inspired by the situation in the mines in South Africa. The mines are some of the places where the rate of HIV/AIDS infections is high. This is as a result of the migrant labour system. Miners from rural areas and neighbouring countries, being away from their families, get involved in other relationships for the better part of their adult working life in urban areas. Prostitutes' business is booming around the mines. Since most of the miners are semi-literate it is very important that HIV/AIDS and other campaigns about sexually transmitted diseases reach them in different formats. It is equally important to remove the stigma around AIDS and dispel the many and varied myths about it.' In a country where a large percentage of the population is illiterate, images, music and plays become important tools in preventing the spread of the virus. Through the sensitive and yet dramatic use of paint, collage and *chiaroscuro* Nhlengethwa has created a poignant and moving portrait of a miner.

Senzeni Marasela offers a different kind of portrait. Dedicated to Gugu Dlamini, she has delicately embroidered five handkerchiefs with thread and beads. Redolent of intimacy and domesticity, *The Invisible Martyr* (Figure 6.9) symbolizes the life and death of a woman who, according to Kay Wright, 'became an accidental symbol for the invisibility of African people living with HIV and AIDS'.[6] Marasela tells us, 'The death of Gugu Dlamini on 12 September 1998 by stoning, is an example of how extreme the consequences of revealing your HIV status can be in our society. Many after her death were forced into silence and live with

6.1 Karel Nel (b.1955, Pietermaritzburg, KwaZulu-Natal, South Africa). *Life's Tide* (red) and *Permian Dust* (black), 2002. Mixed media, 10x100x1.5 cm.

6.2 Andries Botha (b. 1952, Durban, KwaZulu-Natal, South Africa). *Rupture*, 2001. Mixed media, 100x100 cm.

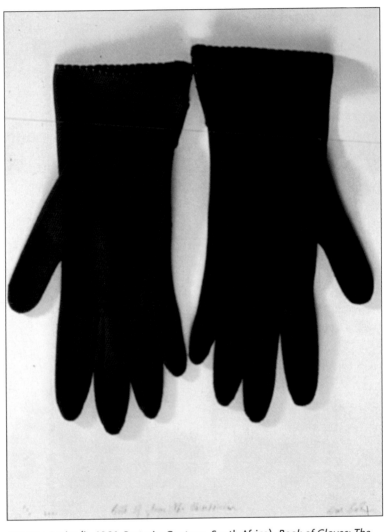

6.3 Lien Botha (b. 1961, Pretoria, Gauteng, South Africa). *Book of Gloves: The Obstetrician*, 2001. Ink jet print on canvas, 45x35 cm.

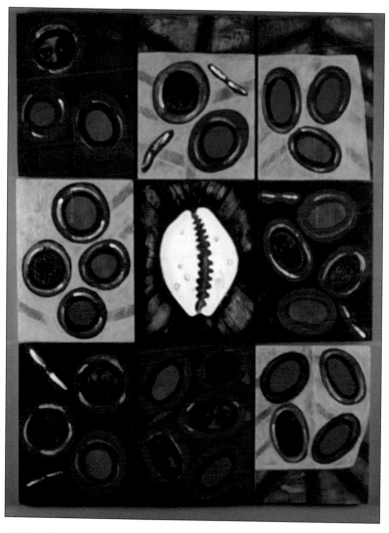

6.4 Neo Matome (b. 1967, Johannesburg, Gauteng, South Africa). *Ties that Bind*, 2001. Mixed media, 40x30x2.5 cm.

6.5 Penelope Siopis (b. 1953, Vryburg, North West, South Africa). *Baby in red*, 2000. Cibachrome photograph, 100x80 cm.

6.6 David Goldblatt (b. 1930, Randfontein, Gauteng, South Africa). *Victoria Cobokana, housekeeper, in her employer's dining room with her son Sifiso and daughter Onica, Johannesburg June 1999. Victoria died of AIDS 13 December 1999, Sifiso died of AIDS 12 January 2000, Onica died of AIDS in May 2000, 1999.* Digital print, 59x59 cm.

6.7 Sue Williamson (b. 1941, Lichfield, United Kingdom). *From the Inside: Benjy*, 2000. Digital print, 90x200 cm.

6.8 Sam Nhlengethwa (b. 1955, Payneville Springs, Gauteng, South Africa). *Miner*, 2001. Oil/Collage on canvas, 60x68 cm.

6.9 Senzeni Marasela (b. 1977, Boksburg, Gauteng, South Africa). *The Invisible Martyr*, 2001. Mixed media, 28x28 cm.

6.10 Clive van den Berg (b. 1956, Kitwe, Zambia). *Love's Ballast I*, 2000/2001. Acrylic on board, 50x37 cm.

guilt and shame. Very little is known about the life of Gugu Dlamini. She dared to think that she could, through herself, show the reality of this dreadful virus. Dlamini perished at the hands of those she thought she could help. HIV continues to spread. This is POSITIVELY FRIGHT-ENING.' Things have changed, but for an individual to declare his or her HIV or AIDS status publicly remains a brave and admirable act.

Fear and the threat that the pandemic poses to love and relationships find moving expression in Clive van den Berg's *Love's Ballast, I* (Figure 6.10). 'Much of my recent work has been concerned with imaging the love between men. I became aware of AIDS as a threat to love early in the eighties. Then we knew little of the workings of the virus and each act of love carried with it not only the taboos of church, parents, peers and state, but a new set of dangers, amorphous, deadly and seemingly retributive. Twenty years on I have known and admired many who have died. As I make love now in the more secure present tense I honour those men. They are often in my thoughts as I experience pleasure and enact in and on skin the proof of my being. They are dead, yes and their death haunts me and haunts me most powerfully in the act of love. The ballast of pleasure is memory and it is that, perhaps new geography of love, that I am picturing.' The muted tones and colouring and the subtle, minimalist imagery and articulation of the surface, hauntingly evoke the artist's experiences and emotions.

In conclusion I must return to Greenberg's statement. The quality and power of contemporary South African art is only to some extent revealed in the exhibition 'Artists for AIDS'. It is a vast and complex field and if I consider it, as I have tried to do in this paper, in the face of the overwhelming problems we face in our society, I have to concede that we have a long way to go before it could reflect the well-being of the majority of our people. The art works in this exhibition, and in others, show that a medical condition has become a social condition; a pandemic has become the most serious social problem facing the African continent in general and South Africa in particular. Every single one of us is required to respond, to take responsibility, to think and to act in a meaningful way.

The pendulum may be swinging from figuration and installation to painting and abstraction and for all we know Greenberg's writings may soon be reinvoked to justify art that is separated from and immune to the conditions and demands of society. For now, we can decide not to choose between life and happiness on the one hand and art on the other; we can have both. I believe that this modest project has succeeded in harnessing the creative energies of some prodigious talents for

HIV/AIDS and has revealed a new face of artistic activism in South Africa. By contributing to the debate and to a better understanding of and caring for those who are infected and affected by the virus, we are making South Africa a better place. And we are doing so through the power and truth of the images, and the messages that they so eloquently and memorably convey.

Postscript. In his keynote address at the conference, delivered on Friday, 19 April 2002, Professor Jeffrey Sachs announced a statement by the South African cabinet, made two days before, that promised a leadership role in fighting the pandemic in partnership with those at the front line. While welcoming it, I publicly expressed scepticism and a desire to see results before rejoicing. The continued denialism, the failure at the level of leadership and the continuing rows between government and AIDS activists mean that we find ourselves in the same place as we were a year ago. South Africa is still an international AIDS pariah, while hundreds of people die every day.

Notes

1 Greenberg's words were recorded in a radio broadcast for the United States Information Service. Accone does not give the date of the broadcast.
2 I would like to acknowledge the sponsors: Network Photographers, Levi Strauss & Company, the Terrence Higgins Trust, the City of Cape Town and Iziko Museums of Cape Town; and the organizations with whom the Sang and Gideon Mendel worked: Treatment Action Campaign, Beautiful Gate, National Association of People Living with AIDS (NAPWA), Triangle Clinic, Positive Muslims, Wola Nani, Networking AIDS Community of South Africa (NACOSA), Caring Network, Rape Crisis, Family and Marriage Society of South Africa (FAMSA), Nazareth House.
3 *Amandla* means 'power'; *Awethu* means 'to us', 'to the people'. The slogan means 'the power is ours'.
4 From Hlongwane (2000).
5 Approximately a year later the city of Cape Town has painted out the entire piece.
6 Quoted by the artist in her statement; source not given.

References

Accone, D. (2002), 'Why S and T Beats A and C', *ACEmail*, www.at.artslink.co.za.
Beresford, B. (2002), 'Radio Host Modise Cleared of Sedition', *Mail & Guardian*, 5 April p. 2.

Byamugisha, Rev. G. (2001), 'Afterword', in Gideon Mendel, *A Broken Landscape: HIV & AIDS in Africa* (London: Network Photographers).

Hlongwane, C. (2000), 'Caravans, Cats, Geese, Foot and Mouth and Statistics – HIV/AIDS and the Struggle for the Humanisation of the African', African National Congress document distributed in April 2002.

Kirby, R. (2002), 'Goatesque behavior in Mamvuka', *Mail & Guardian*, 28 March–4 April, pp. 21–2.

Maart, B. (2002), 'Turning Inside Out', Friday supplement of the *Mail & Guardian*, 12–18 April.

Mendel, G. (2001), *A Broken Landscape: HIV and AIDS in Africa* (London: Network Photographers).

Sontag, S. (1988), *AIDS and its Metaphors* (New York: Farrar, Strauss and Giroux).

Van der Merwe, H. (1995), 'Love, Friendship, Sex', *Review Noire*, 19, p. 14.

7

From Policy to Practice:
the Anthropology of Condom Use

Claudia C. Bermudes Ribiero Da Cruz

Introduction

In October 1992, nearly 450 people representing the widest possible range of organizations attended the launching conference of the National AIDS Co-ordinating Committee of South Africa. In June 1994, a draft AIDS strategy was formulated which culminated in the publication of a comprehensive and detailed National AIDS Plan (Schneider and Stein 1997, p. 4). This plan called for the provision of free condoms and STD treatment services. In 1995, 98 million condoms were distributed nationally to all provinces in South Africa (Operational Plan Report, 1999).

The provision of free condoms was achieved via government clinics, community health centres, hospitals and non-conventional outlets, such as night clubs and taxi ranks. Despite the vast quantity of condoms that have been distributed, relatively little information is available on the actual use, disuse, misuse or abuse of these condoms. It is well known that condoms are 'freely' available to young people in South Africa, but what is less known are the challenges young people face in terms of procuring condoms, negotiating condom use and general condom use practices. Since HIV is spreading most rapidly among young people between the ages 15 and 30, with young women most at risk, an effective HIV/AIDS prevention programme must understand and address these challenges.

The goal of this chapter is to gain a clearer understanding of the knowledge, attitudes and beliefs underlying condom use and disuse among South African youth. Material for the study was drawn over a period of eight months beginning in the middle of 1998. Fieldwork sites included a community health clinic in the southern suburb of Cape

Town and a government clinic in the high-density area of Kimberley, called Galeshewe. Information was obtained through qualitative and quantitative research methods, including focus group discussions, participant observation and in-depth follow-up interviews through the use of a detailed questionnaire. Individuals making use of clinic facilities and procuring condoms were approached to participate in the study. Questionnaires elicited demographic information relating to age, educational backgrounds, employment status, number of sexual partners and the like. The qualitative aspects, which formed the bulk of this research, explored some of the reasoning behind knowledge, attitudes and behaviour related to condom use.

Basic survey responses

Interviews were conducted on 82 participants ranging in age from 14 to 27 years. Almost 60 per cent of the group was female. The participants' mean age was 22.5 years. A majority had completed standard 8 (grade 10). At the time of interviews, 74 per cent of the participants were in a relationship (non-cohabiting and cohabiting) and another 24 per cent were married. Forty per cent of the participants were employed with jobs ranging from manual, part-time work to teaching professions. The majority of participants held low-paid and unstable work. About one-quarter of the sample was made up of students and some 35 per cent were unemployed.

In response to questions relating to condom use, 86 per cent of respondents indicated it was *not* difficult to procure condoms from the clinic. For those who indicated difficulty, they often commented that condoms were 'freely available' but that this did not automatically translate into 'easy to obtain'. Often issues relating to privacy and confidentiality had an impact on this perception.

Among women who responded positively to the question 'have you ever used condoms', 48 per cent said that they used condoms as a contraceptive, 21 per cent used them for protection against STDs (including HIV/AIDS), and 31 per cent used them as both a contraceptive and barrier method of protection from STDs. Sixty-nine per cent of women said that the reasons for ever using condoms were a direct result of the intervention of a health worker, as a temporary protection against STDs and/or for the unreliable periods of their normal contraceptive (the pill or the injection). Men participants said that they used condoms primarily for protection against STDs and as a 'double protection' against pregnancy.

In response to where informants had first learned about HIV/AIDS and STDs, there were a variety of responses. Over 80 per cent said that they had gathered the bulk of their information from the media (which included radio, television and newspapers). Some representative responses follow:

'I first heard about these diseases at school and from the television' (19-year-old male student);

'I heard about it in an AIDS awareness workshop' (27-year-old unemployed man);

'We first learned about it at school with magazines and we found out that the disease is real and not a government propaganda. We also learned how to protect ourselves' (21-year-old student);

'I first learned about it from a friend who caught "drop" [an STD]. He told me that he got it from a girlfriend he did not know very well and he told me to protect myself by using condoms' (19-year-old male student);

'I learned about them in Johannesburg from newspapers and the clinics. They said that people sell their bodies and then they die from these diseases. I understood that it only attacked prostitutes and women who have many boyfriends' (27-year-old female).

In response to a question on whether the knowledge of HIV/AIDS and STDs had changed the way participants thought about sex, some of the responses included:

'Yes, I keep only one partner and always use a condom' (19-year-old male student);

'Yes, therefore I realise the importance of using condoms because I know my husband can bring diseases home' (22-year-old married woman);

'No, I always believed in one partner' (21-year-old female);

'Yes, I do not sleep around anymore' (21-year-old male);

'Yes, I meet different girlfriends so I must try and be safer' (23-year-old male);

'No, because I always protect me at all time' (21-year-old male);

'Yes, I now always use a condom with my spare because I am scared of catching diseases' (24-year-old male);

'No, because I always use a condom so I can still go around as much as I wish' (27-year-old male);

'I never discuss these things with my boyfriend as I do not believe these diseases exist. But I do want to use condoms, but he refuses so we sleep without one' (20-year-old female student);

'No, because I know that there are pills available to cure it and this is why I have not changed my behavior' (19-year-old male student).

These responses highlight some of the differences in knowledge about and behaviour towards the risks of transmitting HIV/AIDS. In response to who initiates condom use within the relationship the following responses were elicited:

'I tell her to use a condom to protect us and she agrees' (19-year-old male);

'We negotiate condom use within our relationship' (21-year-old male);

'I initiate condom use as I don't want the ladies to fall pregnant' (22-year-old male);

'I always decide to use a condom. If a girl asks me to have sex I tell her I am a man and use condoms. All my girlfriends, except my original, understand. My original is on the injection' (20-year-old male);

'I decided to use them as I do not trust my husband. I think that he has other women and has sex with them without my knowledge' (23-year-old married woman).

In response to the question, 'why do you or your partner not like to use condoms', the following responses were obtained:

'My boyfriend does not like to use condoms as he says that it does not feel the same. He says that it is like eating a sweet with a wrapper on it' (22-year-old female);

'I do not like to use condoms with my wife as we trust each other and so I do not believe it is necessary' (27-year-old married man);

'My boyfriend complains that the condoms are not pleasurable and that they are too tight for him. We both feel that we do not need to use them because we trust each other' (24-year-old woman);

'We believe that to use condoms within our relationship is like saying that we do not trust each other. We have tried to use them because my wife was unprotected by her contraceptive for a while, but we both did not enjoy them' (26-year-old man);

'We always use a condom and I am on the pill, because we want to make sure we are "double" protected against pregnancy' (18-year-old woman);

'Condoms are crucial for my business. They represent a boundary between work and play and they are the only way we have to protect ourselves from HIV and STDs. I always use a condom with my clients, but never with my boyfriend' (27-year-old female sex worker);

'Condoms are unnecessary. I do not like them as they do not feel like a man is really having sex' (28-year-old male).

These responses show that there is more than one reason attributed to condom use (protection against STDs and HIV as well as protection against pregnancy), and that condom use or disuse is not tied solely to physical barriers but also to symbolic barriers of emotional closeness or distance.

Challenges and constraints facing intervention strategies

One of the challenges confronting HIV prevention, unsafe sexual behaviour and STD treatment is finding ways to offer health services to youth and to better equip them with appropriate preventative information. Besides issues of physical accessibility, including distance from clinics, high transport costs and inappropriate clinic hours, young people also face other impediments to actual clinic use.

Many South African youth are sexually active according to the Health Systems Development Unit (HSDU, 1998), but many of those who face problems of HIV/STD infection fail to consult a healthcare worker. Part of the problem is due to a lack of reproductive health knowledge among young people, as often the information they have is unreliable or inaccurate. Based on statistics gathered from the response of participants at the Galeshewe clinic, over 72 per cent said that neither a nurse nor anyone else working at the clinic had ever shown them how to use a condom properly.

Young people also experience significant problems in accessing reproductive health services. They often have extremely negative perceptions of the health services which acts as a barrier to their use (HSDU, 1998, p. 3). Specific issues include:

- Confidentiality/privacy issues;
- Poor relations between health worker and patients;
- Fears of asking for contraceptives and being found out.

Confidentiality/privacy

This study, like many others, found that many young people fear going to clinics to speak about sensitive issues related to reproductive health, HIV/AIDS and STDs because they fear that their problems will not be kept confidential. The manner in which the Galeshewe and, to some extent, the Wynberg clinic were laid out was not conducive to privacy. In Galeshewe, condom distribution points were often an issue of contention for many of the participants. It was found that many of the participants felt embarrassed and fearful of obtaining condoms from existing distribution points. This particular clinic only had two points of distribution. One could procure condoms from the contraceptive nurse or from the dispensary jar, which was situated in the main waiting room and did not offer any privacy from those waiting for their clinic appointments. There was no jar or box of condoms anywhere in the clinic that offered potential procurers an opportunity to obtain condoms without interaction with a health worker. As a result many participants voiced their reluctance to coming alone to the clinic to procure condoms and tended to procure in a group of three or more. Due to the privacy offered by our interview office, young people would often ask us during their follow-up interviews to fetch more condoms for them. When questioned about this reluctance to obtain condoms at the clinic, one of the participants replied, 'I sometimes feel shy to fetch more condoms at the dispensary because the people sitting there seem to be looking at me in a funny way.' And another indicated, 'I have to come back to the clinic often because the sisters do not like it if I take a lot of condoms at a time.'

Many young clients felt uncomfortable asking for condoms as they said that the 'old people waiting to see the sisters watched them and seemed to judge them'. This lack of privacy meant that young men would often wait to procure condoms from the local 'Spaza's' or night clubs in an attempt to keep some anonymity.

According to a government study (HSDU, 1998, p. 6), in many community clinics there is insufficient space to guarantee privacy. As a consequence, it is easy for conversations between nurses and their clients to be overheard. Abdool Karim et al. (1992, p. 361) found that a lack of privacy could inhibit youth in relation to health workers. This same study found that although private rooms were available in most permanent clinics, students wanting to procure condoms usually were not taken into them. In the Galeshewe clinic, only young women seeing a contraceptive nurse or partners seeing STD nurses were able to obtain condoms within the privacy of a consultation room.

Poor relations between health workers and patients

A majority of participants (72 per cent) agreed with the statement, 'Clinic staff were generally friendly.' But many of these same young people later went on to say that they had sometimes encountered hostility from health workers. Many participants felt that the relationship they formed with healthcare workers was both inadequate and wanting. Some young people perceived nurses as being hostile and judgmental towards them and, as a result, often avoid going to clinics.

Conversations with various participants contradicted the high statistic showing that young people find the staff friendly and helpful. Some of the young girls interviewed on condom use practices complained that the sisters were 'unfriendly and unhelpful', and that they would, 'scold them for sleeping around'. They said that often they felt scared to come to the clinic for a pregnancy test as they thought that the nurses would judge them and pass comment on their sexual practices.

Another young woman, who had a sexually transmitted disease, came to our office crying because she said that the sister would not treat her unless she brought her boyfriend. Although this is part of the new policy on STD treatment, this particular girl felt that the nurse was 'short–tempered and impatient with her and not understanding of her problems'. Some participants also complained that some healthcare workers 'discussed their private and confidential problems loud enough for the elders in the waiting room to hear'. One 20-year-old man pointed out that he did not feel comfortable seeing a healthcare worker in this particular clinic because of this perceived lack of privacy:

> My friends and I do not come to this clinic to get treated for STDs as the nurses are unfriendly and ask all sorts of questions of us if we come here. Sometimes they also embarrass us by speaking very loudly at the entrance of their offices so that all those people in the waiting room can hear our problems. When we need advice for STDs, or 'drop' treatment we go to the clinic in town where no one knows us.

Young women also complained that it was too embarrassing to ask for condoms and as a result their partners were relied upon to bring the condoms into the relationship. One or two participants wanted to procure condoms, but felt that if they were seen taking condoms at the clinic they would be labelled 'cheap or those kind of women', with the consequence that few young women procured condoms from their local clinics.

Often adolescents are afraid of asking clinic staff for contraceptive advice, especially when the client is very young. According to Wood et al. (1997, p. 3), teenagers seeking contraceptives without parental permission were frequently a source of conflict between staff and clients. Based on conversations held with young women in Wynberg and Galeshewe, it was found that these same conflicts were often a source of frustration for young clients. Some healthcare workers believe that it is their responsibility to discourage young people from being sexually active. One particularly young participant, a 16-year-old girl, indicated that some of the nurses treated young girls who seek contraceptive advice with contempt:

In some clinics I get strange looks because I am so young. The nurses make me feel as if I am too young to be sexually active; they are abrupt and sometimes not that helpful. I believe that no one but myself can look after my body, so I simply ignore them. I still come and get my injection and condoms regularly. The problem is that I have many friends that feel too intimidated to come to the clinic and as a result they often practice unsafe sex. I think that they believe we are too young and should not be having sex, but I know lots of girls my age who are regularly having sex.

This attitude towards young people who are sexually active only serves to isolate young people from obtaining contraceptives and barrier methods necessary to protect them from contracting HIV/AIDS or STDs. In a study carried out in the Northern Province, teenagers said that nurses would not provide the method (contraception) until they had asked whether they had told their mothers, and had lectured them that they were far too young to be sexually active and must 'stop going around with men' (Wood et al., 1997, p. 27). Teenagers who refused to answer these questions reportedly were scolded. Such 'scolding' provoked emotions of shame, unhappiness and fear in the teenagers and many stopped using contraceptives as a result.

Fears of asking for contraceptives and of being found out

Some younger participants in Galeshewe and Wynberg complained that they found it hard to procure condoms and contraceptives because of the attitude of health workers towards their age. One 15-year-old girl said that often the health workers were reluctant to issue condoms to her and would ask 'funny questions about my relationships'. In another case, a 17-year-old girl complained that not only did some of the health workers pass judgement on her requests for a pregnancy test, but they also discussed her situation in front of other patients that were known to her. This type of behaviour seems tied to the conflict health workers have between their professional and moral role in society. It may also be because in a close-knit community, health workers often know the parents of these young clients and might fear the anger of the parents (Wood et al., 1997, p. 4).

In Galeshewe in particular, the fear of being found out seemed to be a problem with some of the males coming not only to procure condoms but also to see a health worker in connection with a sexually transmitted disease. In this high-density area, health workers very often were known to their clients outside the professional sphere. A few participants knew the nurses from church or in other social contexts, and quite a few even knew the health workers by first names.

The effects of a close-knit community on the relationship formed between client and health worker has obvious implications. To add to this, the presence of other clients in the clinic known to these participants made anonymity virtually impossible. This often resulted in young clients looking for healthcare in other clinics away from their area of residence. In particular, young men said that they avoided seeing a health worker in Galeshewe if they suspected a sexually transmitted disease out of a fear of being stigmatized by the other clients or even the health workers. They no doubt also fear that their medical problems will reach the ears of their parents. Perceptions of a lack of anonymity and professionalism only serve to push away the young person most in need of contraception or barrier protection.

The nurse has an important role to play. She acts as a counsellor and decision-maker. She must guard against value bias rooted in her own cultural or religious background (Kunene, 1995, p. 49). Some nurses have been known to resist giving teenagers contraceptives because they believe it encourages pre-marital sexual relationships (Wood et al., 1997). This has been found in more than one study in South Africa, where health workers regard moral guidance of young people and discouragement of sexual activity as part of their social role. Often health workers struggle to put their professional ethics above their moral ones and in so doing do not fulfil their role as health professionals (Kunene, 1995, p. 48).

Gender as a barrier to safer sexual practices

Although the promotion of condom use by various intervention programmes aims to empower people with a means of protection against HIV/AIDS and STDs, often the simple access to free condoms does not automatically translate to consistent use. Many programmes promote the use of the male condom, based on a 'knowledge leads to action' model. The condom is seen as a protective device to be introduced into the sexual act at the 'right' moment (Wood and Jewkes, 1997, p. 39). This implies that the individual is an independent person who can make decisions regardless of the opinions and behaviour of others, and of the wider social context. This ignores the realities of power dynamics, not least of which are gender inequities, which structure heterosexual relations (Campbell, 1995, p. 207).

In South Africa, besides the biological factors contributing to women's increased vulnerability to HIV, vulnerability is compounded by the context of women's lives within a patriarchal society. Male dominance pervades every aspect of women's lives including family, social, religious, legal and institutional link, and influences their ability to be assertive and to protect themselves (Abdool Karim, 1998, p. 19). Women, especially black women, often find themselves in relationships where they have little power and are unable to negotiate safer sexual practices with their partners. In cases of extreme poverty, lack of education and the ingrained belief that women should be subordinate to men lead to sexual interactions that are often dominated and controlled by men. These factors, worrying in themselves, often translate into issues of violence and coerciveness in sexual relationships. Especially in black communities it is common for young women to be forced into sexual intercourse by boyfriends who believe it to be their right (Richter, 1997; Varga and Makubalo, 1996, pp. 33–4). Young women, who find themselves in sexual relationships, are often unable to control the nature and safety of their sexual encounters with their partners.

In this study, women's attitudes towards condom use tended to support assumptions about the relevance of cultural factors when negotiating condom use with sexual partners. The younger women in the sample (from 14 to 19 years of age) tended to be far more assertive and suggested that they had a sense of empowerment where issues of safer sex were concerned. These issues included protection from unplanned pregnancies, sexually transmitted diseases and HIV. Issues pertaining to male partners who had multiple sex partners did not seem to be as well negotiated. A few of the women, who found themselves in new relationships, or who were single at the time of research, suggested that they felt confident and assertive enough to negotiate condom use with new partners. Quite a few commented that condom use within a sexual relationship was symbolic of a very new relationship and that the importance placed on condom use declined with increased time within a relationship. But even in this young age group there were many young women who felt unable to suggest condom use with their partners for fear of being labelled 'loose' and 'forward'. Very often these women said that they were aware of the dangers of unprotected sex with a new partner, or with a partner who had other girlfriends, but were afraid to discuss issues relating to safer sex practices for fear of rejection.

Women who found themselves in stable relationships seem to have a different attitude towards condom use that was often related to perceived issues of trust and love. Some of the women who had regular partners were often aware that their partner had other girlfriends but seemed to accept this as a cultural norm. Based on the findings of this study, stable relationships were the primary motivation for the disuse of condoms with a regular partner. The danger in this practice is evident in South Africa. Today, it is mainly monogamous women who are being infected with HIV (Abdool Karim, 1998, p. 19). Male condom use within a regular relationship is rare and influenced by issues of love and trust. The pattern shown in this particular sample suggests that women perceive condom use as a negative experience for men and many seem reluctant to push the issue with their primary partners, fearful that it will result in conflict or embarrassment.

A few of the women who found themselves in a relationship where it was known to them that their partner had sexual relations with other women indicated that they would like their partner to use condoms. However, like the attitudes of women in other studies who found themselves in similar situations, these participants did not believe that they had the right to insist on condom use (Abdool Karim et al., 1994, p. 6).

Women who are older, married or involved in a long-term relationship seemed to fit in with the traditional idea that women should be submissive and dependent on their primary partner. Some commented on their primary partners having affairs and pointed out that they did not trust their partners but were resigned to the fact and simply accepted this behaviour. Many participants indicated that some form of barrier protection with new sexual partners was crucial today, but becomes unimportant once they have established long-term relationships. Some participants pointed out that steady relationships symbolized faithfulness and trust with those involved and thus condom disuse symbolized a step towards true commitment. From discussions with participants, including both women and men, it became apparent that stable relationships and marriage were primary motivations for the lack of condom use.

Many women do not use condoms within their relationship due to reasons associated with trust and love, but still knew that they were at risk of HIV/AIDS and STDs from their primary partners. Four of the women interviewed found out that their partners were being unfaithful as a result of being infected with a sexually transmitted disease. Numerous others simply suspected their partners were being unfaithful. One woman's story was particularly disturbing. Despite being reinfected on various occasions, this woman was still unable to negotiate regular condom use with her partner:

> Yes, I am using condoms right now, but usually I am on the injection as a regular form of contraception. My partner does not like condoms. He says that they do not feel the same and that we should not use them as we are in a long-term relationship. He says that he likes 'flesh on flesh' and that condoms are for those who are not in serious relationships. This is the second time I come to STD clinic as I have become infected with some diseases. I do not have other partners, but I know he does because he brings these diseases home. He does not come to the clinic with me to get treated, maybe he goes elsewhere for treatment, but when I become infected is the only time he will use condoms with me. The nurse here gave me medication and condoms and told me to use them while I am on treatment. My partner is only willing to use condoms during this period and only because he does not want to catch the disease again. After I am cured he again will not allow condom use in our sexual relationship.

This scenario illustrates how some women have little room for negotiating safer sexual practices and how their perception of the situation is one of resignation. Reasons for lack of negotiation abilities are directly related to many black women's unequal access to power. According to Ramphele (1993, p. 70), the cornerstone of traditional control of women by men among Africans in most parts of South Africa is the system of *lobola* (bride-wealth), which is used to secure control of the reproductive power of women. Ramphele points out that unwillingness to change is not a reflection of lack of gender consciousness, so much as a deliberate decision not to upset well-tested and established social structures.

This particular case shows how a lack of negotiating power might be influenced by the partner's view of the relationship in terms of ownership. Some partners seem to consider women as property and often fall back on tradition to justify their needs and wants. As a social worker in van der Vliet's 1991 study on tradition points out 'the man is so selfish and arrogant that he will go along with change when it suits him and will resist change and hide behind tradition when he cannot defend a particular practice' (van der Vliet, 1991, p. 223).

In other situations women find themselves not only in relationships where they are powerless in terms of their reproductive rights, but this powerlessness is often tied up with the violent and coercive nature of their sexual relationships. One woman, who took part in this study with some initial reluctance, broke down in tears in her follow-up interview:

> I met my partner three years ago when I came from Johannesburg for a visit to my family who live in Kimberly. We met at Club 2000 and within five days he made me have sex with him and quit my job in Johannesburg. I did not want to have sex with him but he forced me. One night he came to my house and demanded that I stay away from work and that I have sex with him. I said no and went to spend the night with my friend across the road. That night he came to that house and started knocking on the door. My friend went to open it and he told my friend to go buy him some beer. My friend said no it is late and we are sleeping. He ran into the house and started shouting and throwing saucers around and when he got hold of me he threw me down too. Then he dragged me outside and stabbed me. He had taken a knife from my friend's house and stabbed me because I did not want to go with him to his house. My friend went to call the police at a friend's place but my boyfriend told me that I must come with him or he is not finished with me. I went, because I was scared he was going to do something. We are now together three years and he does hit me, but especially if he is drunk. I only ever refused to have sex with him that first time . . . when he is drunk he acts violent. When he starts to get violent with me I run away. I was so many times at the police station, but they told us to stay together. He often hits me when he is drunk. When he is drunk he is like someone who is unhappy. He just wants to fight and he touches other girls, as he likes. Sometimes he touches my friends in front of me and if I complain he threatens to hit me. So I keep quiet.

Not unlike the study carried out by Varga and Makubalo (1996, p. 33), where the majority of girls interviewed stated that they were usually unsuccessful in refusing sex with their partners, this example demonstrates that any attempt at refusal resulted in physical abuse. Sexual coercion among black women is not unusual. Wood et al. (1997, p. 42), in a study carried out in Khayelitsha among young teenagers, have shown that in most cases men were reported to use violent strategies from the start of the relationship, forcibly initiating partners who often had no awareness about what the sex act involved.

It also has been noted in numerous studies carried out in the South Africa context that males seem to have an 'unnatural' control over female sexuality and that in many black communities it is expected and accepted that men will dominate heterosexual relationships. There is a belief, put forward by men but unchallenged by women, that romantic relationships must necessarily involve full penetrative sex when the male partner wants it (Eaton et al., 1999, p. 7). As a result, young women, if they want to have a partner or boyfriend, are often unable to have any real control over their sexual behaviour.

Another participant in this study had come to the clinic to see a nurse in connection with a sexually transmitted disease. She said that she was faithful to her partner so she believed that he must have other sexual partners. She commented that within their relationship no discussion relating to contraceptives had ever taken place and that she was now using condoms, with his permission, only because the nurse had told her to do so.

> My partner said to me that if I ever mentioned pregnancy or contraceptives with him he will throw me out of the house. So I never talk about these things with him. We have never talked about HIV/AIDS and I do not even know if I have experienced these STDs before . . . I found out that he had one because he told me that he had a sore on his penis and I told him to go to the clinic. He came back and told me that the doctor wanted to see both of us together. I asked him if he had other girlfriends because I was not infected but he was, but he said no. I know he has others. I want to use a condom always now because I won't know when he is clear of that.

Given the coercion and violence that appears to take place within this participant's sexual relationship, it seems highly unlikely that she will be in any position to negotiate regular and consistent condom use with her partner. The threat of violence or rejection effectively means that she might be unable to insist on the use of condoms or to demand fidelity from her partner (Meyer-Weitz et al., 1998; Varga and Makubalo, 1996, p. 42). Despite having information related to safer sex as well as freely available condoms, this particular woman, like many others in the same situation, will still be unable to protect herself within a sexual context. This is one of the main reasons that heterosexual women in South Africa are at high risk from HIV infections.

Relationship dynamics: condom use and multiple sex partners

The majority of South Africa's young people start their sexual activity in their mid-teens. According to Eaton et al. (1999), the national average age is 15 years for girls and 14 years for boys, though there is great variability around these figures. Sexual risk-taking among young people has been well documented and includes high levels of sexual activity (especially among young men), a tendency towards multiple partnering and nonuse or inconsistent use of condoms (Hein, 1989; Moore and Rosenthal, 1991; Rollins, 1989; Lerner and Spanier, 1980; and Sorenson, 1973 as cited in Macphail, 1999, p. 3). Such behaviour obviously has implications for risks of HIV infection and for contracting any sexually transmitted diseases.

This study finds striking differences in the sexual behaviour of young men and women. Although both seem equally knowledgeable about various aspects of HIV/AIDS, the men seem more aware of the types of sexually transmitted diseases one could contract. Male interpretations of what constitutes safe sexual encounters also seem skewed in favour of condom use without a drop in the number of sexual partners, rather than towards fidelity and one partner. Women, in contrast, know that condoms would protect them but also felt that a monogamous relationship would offer even greater protection from HIV infection than condom use alone. Women in this study tend to favour monogamous relationships and no woman mentioned having more than one partner at the time of interview.

Stable relationships and trust

Various women who were asked if they used condoms within their relationships reported that they did not need to do so as they were presently in a monogamous and stable relationship. Condom use to these women symbolized a lack of trust and love. Condoms were only used in cases where their regular form of contraceptive was unreliable. Other women felt that although they would be willing to use condoms within their relationship, their partners were not as keen to do so. Condom use seems symbolic of 'distance and barriers' and, according to Meyer-Weitz et al. (1998, p. 49), implies a lack of love or care between partners. Other women said that they did not like condoms and that they were for the use of 'those kind of women'. Besides associating condoms with sex workers, some of the women said that they were only used by 'loose or cheap girls who had many partners' and that because they did not behave in this manner themselves, they saw no need to use them. Some adolescents appear to justify their nonuse of condoms with the belief that they are unnecessary because their current relationship is monogamous and promises to be long term (Akande, 1997, p. 330).

Based on conversations and interviews held with women in this study, trust is the yardstick for deciding when it is safe to start using another form of contraceptive instead of condoms. Trust, as defined by the participants, is a 'feeling of belonging to' and the knowledge that one is now in a stable relationship. Social norms internalized by young women encourage them to adopt elements of trust and assumed monogamy into relatively new relationships so that the relationship can be viewed as permanent and therefore sexually justified (McPhail, 1999, p. 6). There also seems to be a clear correlation between length of time within a relationship and condom use.

The yardstick, which decides condom use within a relationship, is based purely on subjective measures. According to one young woman, 'When we first start a relationship with a new guy we insist on condom use as we do not know each other well yet. However, after a few months or so you start feeling as if you trust the guy and then you stop using condoms.'

Another young woman indicated, 'When one stops using a condom within a new relationship one knows that the relationship is now serious and that you really love one another.'

And a somewhat older woman commented, 'I do not believe in using condoms if I am in long-term relationship and if one trusts and knows their partner. Condoms are for those who are not in serious relationships and for those who have many sexual partners.'

There seems to be a clear trend between condom use and the type of relationship men and women find themselves in. Many women in steady relationships voiced reluctance at regular condom use within the relationship. They believed that to suggest condom use to their partners – or if their partners were to suggest it – might imply mistrust and lack of true commitment. They felt that trust and 'knowing' their primary partner was a good enough indicator of when to stop using condoms. As an indication of the trust in relationships, partners tend to terminate condom use and in this way expose themselves to greater risk of both HIV and STD infection (Holland et al., 1990; as cited in McPhail, 1999, p. 6).

Women who took part in one focus group were specifically asked about issues of risk. Most of the participants felt that casual relationships posed a higher risk to the contraction of HIV/AIDS and sexually transmitted diseases. They felt that the nature of this particular sexual encounter constituted a high-risk practice because one did not know the sexual history of the partner in question. Most of the participants felt that individuals involved in casual relationships would be at higher risk of HIV infection because they had multiple – and often casual – sex partners. However, a few of the women disagreed with this theory. They thought that there were more dangers associated with long-term relationships where condom use was not the prescribed norm. Within these relationships, it might be common for one or both of the partners to have 'spares' (casual girlfriends or boyfriends) and due to lack of condom use within the stable relationship the 'original' partner might be in more danger of contracting HIV/AIDS or sexually transmitted diseases. The majority of women interviewed in this study, nevertheless, still felt that they fell within a low risk group for the contraction of HIV/AIDS because they found themselves in stable relationships.

Originals and spares

According to answers to questions on number of sexual partners, 59 per cent of male participants had more than one sexual partner and, of these, 22 per cent had three or more sexual partners at the time the interviews occurred. This information was supplied without coyness or embarrassment; often these numbers were offered with pride. Men would describe in great detail how they pursued their original girlfriends (original signifying long-term partner or 'true love'). In contrast, little detail was offered on how men met their spares (casual sexual partners). The men also appear to construct a clear definition around what constitutes an original and a spare. Original girlfriends are the women these men feel are their true girlfriends. These relationships symbolize love, trust, romance and emotional involvement. Most of the men said that they had waited at least a few months to have sexual relations with these girlfriends. A clear ritual of romancing was often voiced with intense detail whereas spares only offered a physical outlet. When these same men described the process that led to the meeting of spares the scenario was often strikingly different. One participant described how he met his other girlfriends, 'Spares are easy to meet. We just go to the tavern and buy some of the girls drinks. I have a saying that goes like this: Two beers and panties down!'

Other male participants said that they met spares in the same manner they met their original girlfriends. The only difference was the length of time one waited to have sex with them. As a rule, it was acceptable to wait a longer period to initiate a sexual relationship with an original than with a spare. More importantly, an obvious difference in the manner in which these young men construct the two relationships is through the perceived need to use a condom with all other partners but their original girlfriend.

'I have a long term, original girlfriend. I have been seeing her for two years and we met at a school play. I pursued her for a few months and then we became partners. I love my girlfriend and trust her, but I also have three 'spares'. I met them at the tavern. It is easy to meet these girls there. I have never discussed HIV/AIDS and diseases with these spares as I always wear a condom with them. I have spoken to my original about it though, and I told her not to have other boyfriends because of diseases. She [the original] is not willing to use condoms with me – she was angry when I once suggested using a condom with her. I have spoken about contraception with my original and about pregnancy, but not with my spares, because I always use condoms with them. I am safe from pregnancy with my original as she uses contraception' (19-year-old male);

'I have many partners, but only one original. I always use condoms with the others but not with my girlfriend who is on the injection and I trust her' (20-year-old male);

'I have two girlfriends and I always struggle to make the one use a condom' (16-year-old male);

'Yes, I now always use a condom with my spare because I am scared of catching diseases. I only do not use them with my original as I trust her' (21-year-old male).

By contrast, an older participant said, 'I am always travelling and I have many women wherever I go. I am not scared of AIDS or HIV because I know that it can be cured. I only use condoms when the sister says that I have "drop", but otherwise I do not believe it necessary. There are "doctors" who can cure AIDS by cleaning your blood, so I am not worried.'

These responses indicate that among this group of black men multiple partners are seen as acceptable and even desirable, though not safe. Risk-taking may even be part of the 'game'. Other studies support this finding. Meyer-Weitz et al. (1998), Wood and Jewkes (1997) and Wood and Jewkes (1998) report that young black South African men commonly claim that it is 'natural' for them to seek casual sex outside their steady relationships – and that their girlfriends or wives cannot challenge this attitude. Although black women also have concurrent partnerships (though none admit to it in this study), a double standard operates in many communities. Men openly claim the prerogative of having outside relationships, while expecting their partners to be monogamous. Women sometimes support this double standard. They agree that it is inappropriate for women to have many partners, and accept the notion that men's sexual urges are uncontrollable (Eaton et al., 1999).

An 18-year-old male explained how the construction of different types of relationships took place:

> I have two girlfriends. I met my first girlfriend on the street and asked her if I could talk to her. She seemed to like my approach so she became my girlfriend. With the first girlfriend, she wanted to wait six months to have sex with me, but I told her that I loved her and so we only waited one month before we had sex. The second girlfriend I met at a school play. We had sex after a week of seeing each other. The second girl knows about my first girlfriend, but the first does not know about the second one. I have never discussed HIV/AIDS with either of them, as I am more worried about pregnancies. I always use a condom, though sometimes I do not use one with my original as we have been together for over a year. I am the one who brings the condom to the relationship and I do so because I need to be protected from unplanned pregnancies.

Multiple concurrent partnering seems accompanied by selective condom use. A high value is placed on condom use with casual sex partners. A majority of men in this study said that they were willing to use condoms regularly with their spares but that they would not be eager to do so with their stable partners. Due to the nature of casual relationships, which to most seem tied to physical needs in the absence of emotional involvement (though some would argue that they have emotional bonds with their spares), the introduction of condoms does not seem inappropriate.

The introduction of condoms into what is perceived of as a stable and long-term relationship might be seen as suggestive of distrust and infidelity. This, perhaps, is the reason that some women might be opposed to the use of condoms within their relationships. To accept condom use with their stable partner might be symbolic of the acceptance that one's partner is being unfaithful. To resist condom use a woman might be asserting her position as an original girlfriend or denying that her partner is involved in multiple partnering. This, of course, assumes that a woman has the power necessary to negotiate condom use or disuse within a relationship. In the majority of cases where a woman's partner dictates the nature of the sexual encounter, a woman may simply be forced to accept the decisions made for her. Ideas surrounding trust coupled with issues pertaining to empowerment, place women in stable relationships in an extremely vulnerable situation with respect to HIV/AIDS.

If women who are in long-term relationships are at risk, how about the women who are 'spares'? This study is unable to offer much insight into these women for the simple reason that all the women taking part said that they either were in a monogamous relationship or that they were single, that is, not currently involved with any man. If the women believed that they were all original girlfriends or partners, then who are the spares that make up the 'other' within these multiple partnering scenarios?

Some of the women interviewed might have been party to a multiple partnering relationship where they may not have been the original, but thought they were. Although the men interviewed suggested that they used condoms with their spares, some did mention that they often did not use them with all their spares. Another scenario might be that with time a spare might become an original, and as a result a multiple partnering relationship might be made up of more than one original. The existence of more than one original within a multiple partnering relationship effectively means that the male is discontinuing condom use with more than one partner. Alternatively, some young men may exaggerate the number of partners they have, while some young women may under-report their partners. This would be consistent with social stereotypes that approve of male sexual experience while disapproving of female sexual activity. Most of these explanations for 'missing' spares further suggest risky behaviour and increased vulnerability to HIV/AIDS among young South African men and women.

Conclusion

This study finds that AIDS knowledge is good among young people and that some individuals, particularly males, choose to make use of condoms in specific contexts. This study has also shown that intervention strategies cannot simply assume that knowledge and condom availability will lead to overall safer sexual practices. Wider social and cultural factors have to be taken into consideration if meaningful change in behaviour is to occur. Intervention has to encompass more than just pure education; young people's behaviour is not governed simply by what they know. Knowing something is dangerous does not necessarily mean that young people, especially young women, are empowered enough to act upon this knowledge. Intervention strategies must take into account social norms, existing peer pressures, and the socio-economic and cultural taboos that play a crucial role in shaping the knowledge that individuals chose to internalize.

To ensure high levels of condom procurement, healthcare provision and accessibility of condoms needs to be as user friendly as possible. In the two government clinics observed in this study, the percentage of young people who were offered instructions by healthcare professionals on how to use a condom properly was strikingly low. Although condoms are free and 'available' to all, their availability is hampered by certain constraints, including embarrassment, a lack of privacy and limits relating to number of condoms that one is allowed to procure at any one time. Although no participant complained of ever being refused condoms, many mentioned that they found it embarrassing that almost all procurements involved interactions with a healthcare worker and often in a public space. Young people frequently found that the clinic staff had negative attitudes towards young people who are sexually active and quite a few young men objected to staff members' critical comments in connection with sexually transmitted diseases services. Some healthcare workers struggle to put their professional ethics above their moral ones and this acts as a further barrier to the provision of adequate healthcare, especially care directed at HIV/AIDS and STDs.

It also was observed that clinic staff fail to encourage regular condom use among young people. This places all clients, especially young women, at greater risk. Family planning staff tend to focus on the prevention of pregnancy and not the prevention of HIV/AIDS. Since condoms are not as reliable as other contraceptives, staff may inadvertently discourage condom use. Among women participants in this study, the 24 per cent who ever used condoms (whether regularly or irregularly) said that in almost all cases condom use had been a result of health worker intervention for periods of the year when their contraceptives did not offer enough protection or as a result of STD treatment. Healthcare workers need to capitalize on opportunities to offer young people more than the easiest or most reliable contraceptive for prevention of pregnancy. It is imperative that young people are provided with accurate and reliable reproductive knowledge as well as information on HIV/AIDS prevention.

The availability of free condoms in government clinics and the provision of sexually transmitted diseases services do not necessarily translate into regular and consistent condom use practices among young people, despite high levels of awareness. Attitudes towards HIV/AIDS prevention and condom use are complex. To understand the forces that shape these attitudes one needs to look at the social and cultural constructions that inform these attitudes. Attitudes towards condom use found in this study appear directly related to the individual's perception of risk but these perceptions do not necessarily translate into condom use. Despite having misgivings about their partners' promiscuity, young women often were unable to act upon these perceptions.

According to the young men in this study, condom use is a 'norm' and acceptable with casual sex partners or 'spares'. To many of the male participants, condom use within a stable relationship is not as acceptable due to negative connotations associated with condom use. Lack of pleasure and closeness with their partners were some of the negative feedbacks associated with condom use with regular partners. Other negative stereotypes included symbolic associations with a lack of trust, love or feelings within the relationship.

Young women, who voiced their willingness to use condoms within a stable, long-term relationship, illustrate that it is wrong to assume that behaviour change lies solely with the individual. In order for a young woman to insist on condom use she will have to reach agreement with her partner. Although this argument applies to both sexes, it is harder for negotiation to take place for women who find themselves in disempowered positions. For young women, the lack of negotiating powers and an inability to discuss sexual matters due to existing cultural norms, do nothing to facilitate the conversion of knowledge into safer sexual behaviour practices.

In many ways, young women's attitudes towards condom use are much more positive than their male counterparts. Quite a few of the young women, most of them in relationships, felt that condom use within a stable relationship would be a positive step towards protecting themselves from HIV/AIDS and sexually transmitted disease. Others felt that condom use was inappropriate within a stable relationship due to its suggestion of promiscuity. In these cases, as an indication of the trust in the relationship, partners tend to terminate condom use and in this way expose themselves to greater risk of both HIV and STD infection.

Responses gathered from males in this study highlight the selective nature of condom use within relationships. Where men perceive the relationship to be purely physical and casual in nature, the introduction of condoms does not seem inappropriate and is encouraged by male peers. Condom use within the context of promiscuity is seen in a positive light. Many of the slogans preaching for the protection of individuals from HIV/AIDS and STDs reinforce this perception. They create the impression that if you cannot have a single partner, use condoms with your multiple partners and you will be 'safe'. The male interpretation of what constitutes safe sexual practices includes condom use with multiple partnering relationships rather than a drop in the number of sexual partners.

The problem with such selective condom use does not appear to lie in a lack of knowledge regarding protection but rather with the manner in which individuals selectively internalize this information. Many of the black men in this study were able to appropriate practices, such as condom use, because they offered no resistance to usual social practices. Condom use is viewed in a positive light in the context of casual sex and is easily incorporated into existing multi-partner practices. It was hard to ascertain the levels of regular condom use within these relationships, but it was obvious that there is regular disuse with original or long-term partners. This has implications for the safety of partners involved in long-term relationships. By dissociating themselves from a casual relationship and attempting to give the relationship a sense of permanency through the disuse of condoms, individuals place themselves at higher risk for the contraction of HIV and STDs. In certain cases, casual sex partners may be involved in lower risk sexual practices than those who find themselves in stable relationships.

The women in this study who find themselves in long-term relationships and wished to use condoms often do not do so because of the perceived negative connotations and stigmas associated with condoms. In some cases women do not insist on condom use within a relationship because of the fear of rejection or anger at their suggestions.

Despite the small age gap between the youngest and oldest women in the sample, there was some evidence of differences in the way in which condom use was constructed. Younger women (14 to 23 years of age) showed a more positive attitude towards both negotiation and assertiveness in dealing with condom use matters than did their relatively older counterparts.

This study suggests an emerging pattern in condom use. There is a correlation between time within a relationship and drop in condom use levels. The older women, who do not believe in condom use within their stable relationship, feel that trust is an appropriate yardstick for deciding when to discontinue condom use. For many of these women, condom use is symbolic of a new or casual relationship, and discontinuing condom use within a relationship is symbolic of permanence and of commitment. Many women feel that having a meaningful, loving and long-term relationship necessarily involves the disuse of condoms. The use and disuse of condoms within relationships seems tied up with the stages of a woman's life. Despite starting off a relationship with the protection of condoms, she invariably decides or agrees to terminate their use with both time and the perceived stability of the relationship. This is problematic in itself, but more problematic is that young people tend to have many of these preconceptions in their search for the partner who may become their life-long mate. Intervention strategies need to focus on ways to promote continued condom use within a perceived monogamous or permanent relationship. There is a need to promote and encourage the practice of condom use within relationships that have passed the stage where trust becomes the deciding factor for condom disuse. Very few young women – only one out of five surveyed – said that they regularly used condoms out of their own perceived need to protect themselves against HIV/AIDS. Halting the spread of HIV/AIDS requires more women and men to make similar choices to protect themselves.

References

Akande, A. (1997), 'Black South African Adolescents' Attitudes Towards AIDS Precautions', *School of Psychology International*, 18: 325–41.

Campbell, C. (1995), 'Male Gender Roles and Sexuality: Implications for Women's AIDS Risk and Prevention', *Social Science and Medicine*, 41: 197–210.

Eaton, L. and Dr A. Flisher, and C. Cruz and V. Mathambo (1999), Unpublished report on the State of Health of Youth in South Africa, commissioned by the South African Youth Commission.

Health Systems Development Unit (1998), 'Adolescent Sexuality and Reproductive Health in the Northern Province Johannesburg', Department of Community Health, University of the Witwatersrand.

Karim, Q. Abdool (1998), 'Women and AIDS: the Imperative for a Gendered Prognosis and Prevention Policy', *Agenda*, 39: 15–25.

Karim, Q. Abdool, S. S. Abdool Karim and E. Preston-White (1992), 'Teenagers Seeking Condoms at Family Planning Services. Part II: a Provider's Perspective', *South African Medical Journal*, 82: 360–62.

Karim, S. S. Abdool, Q. Abdool Karim and E. Preston-White (1992), 'Reasons for Lack of Condom Use among High School Students', *South African Medical Journal*, 82: 107–10.

Karim, Q. Abdool, N. Morar, N. Zuma, Z. Stein and E. Preston-White (1994), 'Women and AIDS in Natal/KwaZulu: Determinants of the adoption of HIV-Protective Behavior', *Urbanisation and Health Newsletter*, 20: 3–9.

Kunene, P. J. (1995), 'Teenagers' Knowledge of Human Sexuality and their Views on Teenage Pregnancies', *Curationis*, 18: 48–52.

McPhail, C. (1999), 'Adolescents and HIV in Developing Countries: New Research Direction', unpublished document. Epidemiological Research Unit, Johannesburg.

Meyer-Weitz, A., P. Reddy, W. Weijts, B. van den Borne and G. Kok (1998), 'The Socio-cultural Contexts of Sexually Transmitted Diseases in South Africa: Implications for Health Education Programmes', *AIDS Care*, 10, Supplement: S39–S55. Operational Plan Report (1999/2000), Government Publications.

Ramphele, M. (1993), *A Bed Called Home: Life in the Migrant Labour Hostels of Cape Town* (Cape Town: David Philips): 70.

Richter, L. and L. Kuhn, 'Knowledge, Attitude, Belief and Practice' (KAPB) Surveys', in J. M. Katzenellenbogen, G. Joubert and S. S. Abdool Karim (eds) (1997), *Epidemiology: a Manual for South Africa* (Cape Town: Oxford University Press).

Schneider, H. and J. Stein (1997), 'From Policy on Paper to Action on the Ground: Contextual Issues Affecting Implementation of the National AIDS Plan in South Africa' (briefing document produced by the MRC).

Van der Vliet, V. (1991), 'Traditional Husbands, Modern Wives? Constructing Marriages in a South African Township', in *Tradition and Transition in Southern Africa*, ed. A. D. Spiegel and P. A. MacAllister (Johannesburg: Witwatersrand University Press).

Varga, C. and L. Makubalo (1996) 'Sexual Non-negotiation', *Agenda*, 28: 31–8.

Wood, K. and R. Jewkes (1997), 'Violence, Rape, and Sexual Coercion: Everyday Love in a South African Township', *Gender and Development*, 5: 41–6.

Wood, K. and R. Jewkes (1998), 'Love is a Dangerous Thing: Micro-dynamics of Violence in Sexual Relationships of Young People in Umtata' (Pretoria: Centre for Epidemiological research in South Africa – Women's Health).

Wood, K. R. Jewkes and F. Maforah (1997), 'The Violence Connection in Reproductive Health: Teenage Accounts of Sexual Relationships in Khayelitsha', *Urbanisation and Health Newsletter*, 34, 21–4.

Wood, K. J. Maepa and R. Jewkes (1997), 'Adolescent Sex and Contraceptive Experiences: Perspectives of Teenagers and Clinic Nurses in the Northern Province' (Pretoria: Centre for Epidemiological Research in South Africa – Women's Health).

8
The Role of Tertiary Institutions in the HIV/AIDS Epidemic

Cal Volks

Introduction

The scourge of HIV/AIDS has affected all aspects of South African society. For the university-aged population, a number of factors have contributed to making the crisis particularly acute. This chapter highlights specific challenges faced by tertiary institutions in South Africa. In addition, a number of programmes developed specifically at the University of Cape Town that directly target university-age students are discussed.

The consulting firm ABT Associates estimated that the rate of HIV infection among the South African undergraduate population in 2000 was 22 per cent and that by 2005 it would be 33 per cent (SAUVCA, 2001, p. 4). The magnitude of these estimates is worrying, but it is difficult to know the actual HIV prevalence among students, as the only sure way would be to undertake comprehensive testing. In South Africa, as in most countries, compulsory testing is widely viewed as unethical. In the current climate of denial and stigmatization, insufficient numbers of students are volunteering for HIV testing at higher education clinics that provide voluntary counselling and testing. Thus it remains difficult to obtain an adequate or unbiased sample.

Some higher education institutions have completed HIV testing surveys with small groups of students. In 1998, the University of Durban Westville student health clinic administered a voluntary saliva test and survey to students who visited the clinic over a set period. Out of 337 students tested, 86 of them (23 per cent) were found to be HIV positive. Among female students under 25 years of age, 24 per cent were HIV positive and in the group of female students over 25 years of age, 29 per cent were positive. There was a somewhat different pattern for male students. Among male students under 25 years who were tested, 10.5 per cent were HIV positive compared to males students over 25 years of age of whom 23 per cent were.[1]

It is problematic to extrapolate the findings from this study to students at other South African institutions, or for that matter even to the entire student body of the University of Durban Westville. This study was conducted on a sample of students who were attendees of the student health clinic, representing an already unwell population group. Nevertheless, even among such a narrowly defined group, HIV prevalence is quite high and is the same order of magnitude as predicted for the higher education sector as whole in the ABT study and in the South African government's antenatal clinic surveys.

Background of HIV/AIDS and tertiary institutions

HIV/AIDS has had and will continue to have a considerable impact on higher education institutions in South Africa. Since they are the structures that produce our future leaders and educated workforce, as well as producing the research that guides industries and government, the importance of higher education institutions in the fight against HIV/AIDS is incalculable.

It is only recently that higher education institutions, as a sector, have begun to put HIV/AIDS programmes in place. Martin and Alexander (2001, p. 7), in their essay on HIV/AIDS in South Africa's higher education institutions, comment: 'As with many other institutions, until very recently the universities and technikons responded at tortoise-like speed, if, that is, they moved at all . . . The University of Cape Town adopted a policy in 1993 that focused on the rights and responsibilities of staff and students, raised awareness and implemented education and support programs. But this is a special case. With the partial exception of the University of Stellenbosch, which introduced a more limited policy at the same time, [South African] universities did not respond until 1999.'

In 1999, the World Bank sponsored an HIV/AIDS impact study of five universities in Africa, including one in South Africa. Commenting on these impact studies Michael Kelly (2001, p. vii) of the University of Zambia comments, 'The most striking feature of the university response to HIV/AIDS is what can only be described as the awe-inspiring silence that surrounds the disease at institutional, academic and personal levels . . . Both individuals and institutions conduct themselves as if the disease did not exist.'

Why has there been such a stunning silence from higher education institutions in South Africa? Two reason often put forward are: (1) the general funding crisis experienced by many higher education institutions due, in part, to the inability of many students to pay their tuition and fees; and (2) the lack of senior university management leadership on the issue of HIV/AIDS.

Mary Crewe (2000, p. 11), the Director of the Centre for the Study of AIDS at the University of Pretoria, noted, 'It may be that, like business, despite the projections and the warnings, [universities] did not until very recently imagine that AIDS was an issue that they needed to take seriously. There are still many people in universities who believe that the sexual behaviour of their students, their colleagues and possibly even themselves is not relevant to the university role in preparing the next generation of lawyers, teachers, doctors, scientists, farmers and priests.'

Before exploring the specific response of higher education institutions to HIV/AIDS, it is important to place this response in the overall context of the HIV/AIDS pandemic in South Africa. Scientists and social scientists are beginning to understand that there are several complex and interrelated reasons why HIV/AIDS has spread in South Africa, including: lack of access to healthcare and education; disrupted family and communal life caused by apartheid; low status of women in relationships; resistance to using condoms; and established epidemics of STDs (Sunter and Whiteside, 2000, pp. 59–67). HIV/AIDS is spreading rapidly among university-age youth because these people are generally at an experimental, developmental stage of life, and because social norms have in the past frowned on the discussion of sexual matters, including sex education.

South Africa also is enveloped by a climate of denial and stigma around HIV/AIDS. In a recent survey of South African youth by the NGO, Lovelife, it was found that despite the high prevalence of HIV infection, only 0.5 per cent of the sample believed that there is someone infected with HIV in his or her broader family. In a survey of attitudes to HIV/AIDS conducted at the University of Venda, 8 per cent of youth sampled said that they still do not believe in the existence of HIV/AIDS, while 61 per cent maintained that AIDS was not on the increase (Kenyon et al., 2001, p. 165).

The stigmatization of the disease results in very few people being open about their HIV status. This was demonstrated in a survey in 2001 of 726 patients, conducted at two sites in KwaZulu-Natal by Pawinski and Laloo (2001), which found that 65 per cent and 92 per cent respectively of HIV-positive patients had not told anyone of their HIV status, owing to the stigma (Kenyon et al., 2001, p. 165).

In South Africa, widespread violence against women and children has contributed to the rate at which HIV is spreading. Suzanne Leclerc-Madlala (2002, p. 2), an anthropologist from the University of Natal who is an expert in the field of HIV and AIDS and gender socialization, commented recently that: 'SA has the highest rape statistics in the world of any country not at war; that SA has the highest reported cases of child abuse, most especially sexual abuse of girls (for example Calls to Childline – a help-line for abused children – now number 5000 per month (whereas in 1997 it was 350 per month)); and South Africa has now gained the reputation of being the Baby Rape Capital of the World.'

She further states: 'A very destructive force is driving this epidemic, and that force has much to do with the irresponsible, aggressive, and indeed, criminal ways in which men are enacting their sexuality and proving their manhood . . . Local studies consistently point out that as far as sexual negotiations go – there are basically no negotiations taking place at all . . . Women report (and complain about) a bare minimum or utter lack of foreplay by their partners . . . Studies show that for a large percentage of women, their first sexual experience was a forced, coerced experience. For many, they know nothing but coerced sex. They report sex as unpleasant, leaving them with much regret and a deep sense of ambivalence' (Leclerc-Madlala, 2002, p. 2).

Leclerc-Madlala finds that among youth there are deeply entrenched ideas about manhood associated with an ability to control women, and that very often this is expressed through a man's control over the sexual encounter. 'A woman is expected to show "respect" by being demure, submissive and obliging to her partner. A man believes he can command or extract "respect" by a display of dominance and violence. "If you hit a woman, she will respect you" is a not uncommon view of young men' (Leclerc-Madlala, 2002, p. 3).

HIV/AIDS education in secondary schools

Against this general background it makes sense to turn briefly to HIV/AIDS education in secondary schools in order to understand the level of awareness that first-years have acquired prior to enrolling in higher education institutions. The National Education Policy Act of 1996 sought to introduce life skills programmes, including HIV/AIDS, into schools. The goals of the three-year national integrated plan for life skills education were to establish a life skills programme in all secondary schools by 2001 and a life skills programme in 65 percent of primary schools by 2002 (Rutenberg et al., 2001, p. 6).

Rutenberg et al. (2001, p. 6) report on an evaluation study of school life skills programmes conducted in 1998 in KwaZulu-Natal. At that stage, there were a number of setbacks in the rollout of the life skills programme including delays in government funding, poor development of materials and unqualified trainers. Anecdotal evidence suggests that the life skills programmes remain uneven and ad hoc in quality and comprehensiveness both across and within schools. Despite the proposed life skills programmes in secondary schools, many students still arrive at higher education institutions having received little or low quality life skills education.

HIV/AIDS programmes at South African higher education institutions

Not until almost the turn of the millennium did the majority of South African higher education institutions begin to look seriously at the problem of HIV/AIDS. Some global and national developments affected the response of higher education institutions. The Association of Commonwealth Universities (ACU) held a conference, HIV/AIDS and Tertiary Education Institutions, at the end of 1999. This was followed in 2000 by an ACU-administered survey to assess what systems were in place to address HIV/AIDS at tertiary education institutions. In 1999, the World Bank AIDS Campaign Team for Africa funded the previously mentioned impact studies at five different universities in Africa and in October 2000 the South African Universities Vice Chancellors Association (SAUVCA) completed a more detailed survey of HIV/AIDS activities underway at universities in South Africa.

Key points in the findings of the SAUVCA study as reported in Chetty (2001, pp. 64–5) included:

- Responses from the twenty-one universities surveyed were uneven and ad hoc;
- The political climate surrounding HIV/AIDS was detrimental to the universities' efforts;
- Universities which had committed leadership from those in the higher levels of management, tended to have a more coordinated and effective response to HIV and AIDS;
- Many institutions focused too heavily on policy to the exclusion of implementation;
- Many interventions operated in a once-off manner or defined HIV and AIDS solely as a health issue and often responsibility for

coordinating a response was delegated to a person or department which also had many existing responsibilities;

- Networks and partnerships had been poorly developed and maintained and many institutions were working in isolation;
- Various issues, including rape, needed to be addressed more effectively;
- More focus was needed on the output of HIV/AIDS research at higher education institutions. Monitoring and evaluation of programmes needed to be increased;
- Most institutions lacked financial, human, material and intellectual resources in order to handle this epidemic effectively.

Following the survey, SAUVCA submitted a funding proposal to the UK Department for International Development (DFID) requesting individual grants for each university to address HIV/AIDS management, teaching, research and outreach. The grants were approved and ranged from R150 000 to R350 000 ($15 000 to $35 000) per institution.

In April 2002, three and a half months following the announcement of these awards, a rapid and somewhat informal assessment of the change in HIV/AIDS related services among South African universities since the beginning of 1999 was conducted.[2] Seventeen universities were contacted and it was clear that there had been an increase in services provided.

Prior to 1999 only five of the seventeen universities had an HIV/AIDS policy, but as of April 2002 representatives of sixteen institutions said they were developing and/or finalizing HIV/AIDS policies. Previously, only two universities had a dedicated HIV/AIDS budget. The April 2002 appraisal found that fifteen of the seventeen institutions had created a dedicated HIV/AIDS budget. Only five of the seventeen universities contacted had staff education programmes prior to 1999. The numbers by early 2002 had grown to nine out of seventeen institutions. Several universities discussed plans for peer education programmes, integration of HIV/AIDS in the formal academic curriculum and involvement in outreach projects.

The evidence suggests that the majority of the increase in services had been very recent, coinciding with the SAUVCA/DFID grants. The deafening silence from tertiary institutions in the 1990s may not only have been a crisis of leadership, but also one of resources.

In 2003, the African Association of Universities (AAU) started an HIV/AIDS project to assist higher education institutions in Africa to put HIV/AIDS policies in place, develop education and support programmes and enable networking among HIV/AIDS programmes at universities in the different regions. South African higher education institutions can only benefit from this initiative.

HIV/AIDS and the University of Cape Town

The possible impact of HIV/AIDS on tertiary institutions is manifold and includes effects on student academic performance and social development, management of student health, management of staff health and benefits, staff education, staff absenteeism due to illness and funeral attendance, and staff replacement costs.

At the University of Cape Town (UCT) there is a holistic and integrated planned response to the HIV/AIDS crisis. Recent activities include commissioning a study on projected rates of infection among students and staff; making HIV/AIDS one of the top three priority themes for UCT; involving senior management in HIV/AIDS policy development and the management of HIV and AIDS; changing the academic curriculum to include relevant HIV/AIDS material both at the undergraduate and at the postgraduate level (including the development of a specialized masters programme in HIV/AIDS); developing a peer prevention and treatment education programme; providing HIV/AIDS education workshops for staff and students on innovative HIV/AIDS related topics; holding HIV/AIDS social awareness events; allowing students to develop their own HIV prevention and support media; distributing condoms; establishing a clinical response including pre- and post-HIV testing and counselling as well as ongoing counselling and referrals for treatment; engaging in community outreach (for example, education workshops for schools and other youth groups); seeking higher education sector collaboration; and increasing HIV/AIDS research across departments and faculties.

The University of Cape Town has a number of specific HIV/AIDS projects that it supports and oversees, providing wholly or partially subsidized funds and/or office space and other benefits. These include the HIV/AIDS Unit, which works on the prevention, education and support of staff and students within and outside the formal academic curriculum and on outreach education in schools in the surrounding area. The AIDS Society and Research Unit is involved in various research projects and also promotes and funds HIV/AIDS research in the humanities, social sciences and commerce faculties and houses the Memory Box project, which utilizes narrative and art therapy to work with people living with HIV. There also are a variety of health sciences HIV/AIDS research projects including the infectious disease unit's research on

ARV treatment, the department of medical microbiology's work on developing an AIDS vaccine, the actuarial science department's efforts on AIDS infection rates and modelling of the impact of the disease on society, and the Children's Institute's HIV/AIDS projects geared towards assisting children and those who make decisions about and care for them.

The University of Cape Town is sometimes viewed as having started an HIV/AIDS programme early because of its relatively privileged financial position, but it was due even more to the dedication and commitment of a small group of staff and students who wanted to prevent the spread of HIV, to support people who were infected and to empower youth to respond to the disease appropriately. Funding had to be raised at a time when people thought the predictions of future rates of HIV were exaggerated, and there were several months when the programme continued without certainty of its future. It was not just a question of resources, but also one of leadership.

University of Cape Town HIV/AIDS Unit

The vision of the HIV/AIDS Unit is to have no further students or staff infected with HIV. The Unit also supports a UCT Community which responds to the epidemic in an integrated and holistic way, with compassion and responsible behaviour, and a supportive environment for people living with HIV/AIDS.

The programmes are based on regional and global successes in HIV/AIDS education including employing a multifaceted approach; influencing individual knowledge, attitudes and perceptions through education workshops and media; using education models that recognize contextual factors involved with the spread of HIV; teaching people both information as well as skills to act on that information (including the practice of communication and/or negotiation skills); focusing on specific behavioural goals (for example, increasing correct condom use, condom negotiating skills, and encouraging HIV testing); setting up a supportive environment; involving the target audience in developing education; and using peer education.

The programmes also are based on current research on HIV/AIDS and youth. In a review of research on South African youth concerning knowledge of HIV/AIDS, the authors found that most youth showed variable knowledge about the illness itself, including awareness of modes of transmission, the presence of an asymptomatic phase, etc.). The study found that many South African youth do not know the basic facts, that knowledge is often superficial, and that the important facts often are mixed with fiction (Eaton et al., 2001, pp. 7–8). Ross and Levine (2002) coordinated a study among tertiary education students in 2001. In their study, third-year social anthropology students interviewed roughly 500 students. It is difficult to obtain quantitative information from this study as most students asked peers a range of different questions. There were few students who had been tested for HIV and many believed that their education protected them from contracting HIV. Still, many reported having unsafe sex despite knowing about HIV and at the same time many said they were tired of hearing about HIV/AIDS. Condoms were negatively associated with trust and were more often used in sexual encounters that are considered 'on the side', and less permanent. Some thought women less able to negotiate condom use due to cultural constructions of subordination (Ross and Levine, 2002, pp. 13–14).

Participants' comments that they perceive themselves, as educated students, as invulnerable to HIV infection may be as a result of 'othering' the disease or perceiving others who are different in some way as being more susceptible to HIV transmission. Helene Joffee in her book *Risk and the Other* summarizes: 'people control anxiety evoked by danger by forming social representations which alleviate the worry by portraying others, rather than the self, as the targets of danger' (1999, p. 2). It is not uncommon in an HIV/AIDS education workshop to find members of a particular racial group attributing blame for the spread of HIV to another race group.

In another HIV behaviour and attitude study conducted among young people at five different sites in South Africa, Kelly (2000, p. 5) found a high level of perceived vulnerability to HIV infection. Sixty per cent of the youth surveyed who had a boyfriend/girlfriend had discussed the risks of AIDS with a partner; 70 per cent of the 71 per cent of youth who had sexual intercourse used a condom; and 52 per cent of youth who had sex before, but were not currently living with a partner, reported using a condom in the previous sexual encounter.

In yet another behaviour study, conducted over the course of 1999 and 2000 in KwaZulu-Natal, about 3000 young people were interviewed. In this study, the majority of participants disagreed that condoms denote mistrust, are unnecessary in serious relationships, are difficult to carry because they show intention of having sex, cause females to lose the respect of their partners, or are embarrassing to request or buy. Half of young people surveyed, who had a partner in the past year, used a condom the last time they had sex (Rutenberg et al.,

2001, p. 34). The variation in responses in these research findings suggests the need for a wide variety of approaches to respond to a wide range of behaviour.

Activities of the University of Cape Town HIV/AIDS Unit

One of the goals that permeates the work at the HIV/AIDS Unit at UCT is to ensure that young people engage with this pandemic on a theoretical and on an experiential level, and that they express their responses to it. In order to effectively address the wide range of issues dealt with at the unit, it is of critical importance that young people are involved at every level of the programme. Many institutions and organizations have moved away from prescribing educational programmes from the top down and increasingly have raised the role of participants' in the planning of programmes. Ensuring the active involvement of people affected by the programme has been critical for the Unit's success.

The field of health promotion has focused interventions to promote public health that move away from simplistic, individually based strategies towards those that support healthy lifestyles through social and environmental change. Paulo Freire, a Brazilian educational philosopher, stresses the need for education that encourages individuals to become conscious of the political realities of their situation and to take collective action. He suggests that participation fosters reflection on the determination of social influence that affects people. With direct participation, students can obtain a deeper understanding of their role in a situation and find a way of altering it (Toroyan et al., 1995, p. 6).

Since 1994, the UCT HIV/AIDS programme has facilitated student-developed peer-led workshops, media and events in an attempt to shift Western Cape youth culture to one of compassion and action in response to the spread of HIV, and away from discrimination against people living with HIV. In doing this we try to get people to question why there is denial, stigma and discrimination, what factors reinforce such behaviour, and what this says about society.

In 1994, the Student's HIV and AIDS Resistance Programme (SHARP) was started at UCT to train students to facilitate workshops and to develop a new group of leaders in the field of HIV/AIDS. 'Sharpies', as student members of SHARP are known, are trained as workshop facilitators on a variety of HIV/AIDS issues. Topics covered include: basic HIV/AIDS information; sex, choices and relationships; gender and HIV; human rights and HIV/AIDS; living positively with HIV; treatment literacy; and supporting someone with HIV. The facilitators are not trained to dictate a response to HIV/AIDS, but rather to get participants to reflect, ask questions, and have enough information to make informed decisions.

A key HIV/AIDS Unit project is the development by students of their own awareness and support media for distribution on campus including posters, pamphlets and newsletters. Media depicting young people (and using their language and phrases) have the ability to provoke responses, influence and alter social norms among young people. By depicting role models who exhibit the desired behaviour, posters encourage students to incorporate those values into their culture. Involving members of a target group in developing health messages enhances the likelihood that the messages are culturally appropriate, credible, pertinent and ultimately successful. The various forms of media developed for students and by students are shared with other tertiary education institutions in the Western Cape. In addition to developing posters and newsletters, students host a weekly radio programme on UCT Radio, using a talk-show format with phone-ins to discuss various HIV/AIDS issues. Beyond these advances, we are also developing an interactive question and answer section on our website so that students can ask questions about HIV and AIDS while remaining anonymous so that fear of stigmatization does not prevent them from acquiring knowledge.

The Unit also has been developing photocomics in an attempt to prevent the spread of HIV. Photocomics are used around the world for entertainment and for educational purposes. They can reflect situations that are culturally appropriate and pertinent while, most importantly, connecting with university-age students on a level other media may not. By depicting real people and places, the medium lends itself to the depiction of realistic situations, common social experiences, and the exploration of emotional responses to an issue. The photocomics closely resemble life and are integral to the identification process by which these comics are believed to work (Toroyan et al., 1995, p. 5).

According to Lucy Clarke, 'stories allow us to confront issues, rather than simply receive messages . . . Fotonovelas frequently present romantic, heart-wrenching stories, so readers are not disturbed when they find family planning issues coming up in familiar tales of unwanted pregnancy or financially overburdened families. Because sequential art can explore the relationship between cause and effect, it is possible to see the consequences of the characters' actions . . . By working together to produce materials based on sequential art, groups can share in participatory learning. This process allows them to actively develop skills and understanding of an issue' (Clarke, 1994, pp. 3–5).

The HIV/AIDS Unit sees a crucial role for the university in working with the various communities surrounding it in the struggle to prevent HIV and to support people living with it. Our education programmes have been offered beyond the university and we have held workshops for various community groups, including the Western Cape Society of Traditional Healers, and for thousands of secondary school pupils in areas surrounding Cape Town. We also have trained a number of individuals at other universities and technikons.

Workshops have not only provided people with information and thought-provoking questions, but have included experiential and expressive components incorporating aspects of drama, art and narrative therapy, encompassing the work of Paulo Freire and of Augusto Boal, including the latter's work on the Theatre of the Oppressed. Participants have been encouraged to take scenes from their life where they felt disempowered by a situation and get other participants to play various roles and act out a scene from their lives. In this model, participants come up with creative solutions as to how they would like to change the situation. Each workshop takes on a different tone, a different life, and ultimately explores a different path in the HIV/AIDS pandemic. Some participants just want the information, others respond to the decision-making workshops, others have eye-opening experiences in the gender and HIV workshop, and others enjoy expressing themselves and reflecting on this political, passionate and all-consuming pandemic and what it has done to South Africans as a people.

In addition to raising individual awareness, the Unit also facilitates events and festivals to increase broader social responses on campus to HIV/AIDS issues. These have included workshops for students on writing songs and poetry, and designing posters and graffiti around various themes. Other events have included candlelight days where we commemorate people who have died, give strength to those living with HIV, and renew all of our commitment to this struggle. Another project involved creating quilts in which participants were encouraged to paint their responses to the pandemic and the various pieces were sewn together and displayed in public spaces where others can write their responses to the quilt display. These events have taken place on campus and at youth centres in townships in various communities as part of our commitment to comprehensive interventions not only on campus, but also in the greater Cape Town area.

Beyond these events, broad HIV/AIDS awareness events are planned at different times during the year. An orientation week party campaign was introduced in response to research that suggested that students were engaging in risk-taking behaviour such as unplanned, unsafe sex at parties during orientation week. The campaign ensures that condoms are handed out on arrival and departure from the party; that there are posters up in the toilets; and that the DJs are educated to broadcast safer sex messages during the course of the evening. All first-year students are provided with HIV/AIDS workshops in the faculty orientation meetings prior to the parties taking place.

The Unit also runs a treatment literacy education project to train peer educators to teach people about living positively with HIV. This includes education about nutrition, treatment options and how to live positively from a physical, emotional, mental and spiritual perspective.

Evaluation at all levels is seen as integral to the programme, from the design of an intervention through post-intervention follow up, rather than as something that is conducted solely after an intervention. The Unit conducts ongoing internal research to assess whether the programmes are having an impact by increasing knowledge, changing behaviour, and reshaping attitudes. Evaluation procedures look at both process and outcome evaluation.

Conclusion

The Western Cape was the first province to set up a collaborative partnership between tertiary institutions in 2000 and we have a strong network that meets on a monthly basis. In the Western Cape, the University of the Western Cape, Peninsula Technikon, Western Cape College of Nursing, Cape Technikon, and the University of Stellenbosch are strong allies in the struggle against HIV and AIDS.

As a way of illustrating the challenges that we still face at institutions such as UCT, I can relay a conversation I overheard recently. A senior staff member at UCT (not involved in management) recently suggested to one of my colleagues that he believes that the rates of HIV at higher education institutions are lower than was previously thought and that perhaps we should downscale and lower the budget of the HIV/AIDS Unit. If it is the case that HIV rates are lower than expected, all the more reason to keep AIDS units at universities open to ensure that HIV infection rates stay low. Furthermore, HIV/AIDS units are not just there to encourage students to protect themselves, but also to ensure that we send graduates out into society equipped to address this epidemic on a personal, professional and intellectual basis, and to play a role in addressing HIV/AIDS in the communities in which they live, work and serve. This comment represents the denial of the pandemic and furthermore it represents the denial of the crucial role that higher education institutions can play in changing the course of the human tragedy that is HIV/AIDS.

Notes

1 Personal communication with University of Durban Westville Head of Department for Student Health, Dr Rana, March 2001.
2 For assistance in this rapid appraisal conducted at the University of Cape Town, I am indebted to Mandy Govender, Nontsasa Nako, Nonela Bunga and Emma Durden.

References

Chetty, D. (2001), 'HIV/AIDS and South African Universities: Current Issues and Future Challenges', in M. J. Kelley, *Challenging the Challenger: Understanding and Expanding the Responses of Universities in Africa to HIV/AIDS* (Washington: Working Group on Higher Education, Association for the Development of Education in Africa, World Bank.)

Clarke, L. (1994), 'Comics and Fotonovelas for Health Promotion', *Learning for Health*, 5: 3–6.

Crewe, M. (2000), 'A University Response to HIV/AIDS', *AIDS Analysis Africa*, 10 (5): 11–12.

Eaton, L., Flisher, A. J. and Aaro, L. E. (2001), *Unsafe Sexual Behavior in South African Youth* (Cape Town: Department of Psychiatry and Mental Health, University of Cape Town).

Joffe, H. (1999), *Risk and the Other* (Cambridge: Cambridge University Press).

Kelly, K. (2000), *Communicating for Action: a Contextual Evaluation of Youth Responses to HIV/AIDS* (Pretoria: HIV/AIDS and STD Directorate, Department of Health).

Kelly, M. J. (2001), *Challenging the Challenger: Understanding and Expanding the Responses of Universities in Africa to HIV/AIDS* (Lusaka: Association for the Development of Education in Africa, Working Group on Higher Education, World Bank).

Kenyon, C., Heywood, M. and Conway, S. (2001), *Mainstreaming HIV/AIDS Progress and Challenges in South Africa's HIV/AIDS Campaign* (Durban: Health Systems Trust Annual Health Review).

Leclerc-Madlala, S. (2002), 'And the Word was made Flesh: Gender Power and Socialization for Sexual Communication', paper written for the conference 'Getting the Word Out: Spreading the Message to Youth on their Own Terms', hosted by the Centre for the Book, Cape Town, 22–23 March.

Martin, L. and Alexander, P. (2001), 'Responses to HIV/AIDS in South Africa's Tertiary Institutions: Policy, Practice and Shortcoming' (Rand Afrikaans University Centre for Sociological Research: unpublished paper).

Ross, F. and Levine, S. (2002), 'Perceptions of and Attitudes to HIV/AIDS amongst Young Adults at UCT (University of Cape Town: unpublished paper).

Rutenberg, N., Kehus-Alons, C., Brown, L., Macintyre, K., Dallimore, A. and Kaufman, C. (2001), 'Transition to Adulthood in the Context of AIDS in South Africa' (Report of Wave 1, Horizons).

SAUVCA (South African Universities Vice Chancellors Association) (2001), *South African Universities and HIV/AIDS: Developing a Sector-wide Response to the Epidemic* (Gauteng: ABT Associates).

Sunter, C. and Whiteside, A. (2000), *AIDS: the Challenge for South Africa* (Tafelberg: Human and Rousseau).

Toroyan, T. and Reddy, P. 'Learner Produced Phoctocomics for Health Promotion in South Africa' (unpublished report).

9
Afterword: Challenges and Lessons

Challenges: David L. Lindauer

The chapters presented in this volume permit us to identify some of the challenges in addressing the HIV/AIDS pandemic. These challenges exist at three levels: the level of the individual, of government and of the international community.

Every twenty-four hours it is estimated that over 2000 South Africans will be infected with the HI virus.[1] Of course, we do not know who these individuals are. Even they are unaware of what has happened to them. But we do know most will be young adults, with women outnumbering men. Some will be newborn children or infants. In each case, some individual made an irreversible decision.

The primary challenge on an individual level is to take responsibility for safe sex and to reduce behaviour that increases the risk of catching or transmitting HIV/AIDS. Claudia Cruz's paper highlights the risky behaviour that remains prevalent among young adults in South Africa. She emphasizes that education, in a narrow sense, is not enough to change behaviour. South Africans between the ages of 15 and 25 years, generally, have good information about HIV/AIDS. They know the disease is sexually transmitted and that condoms significantly reduce the likelihood of infection. But knowledge alone is insufficient. Attitudes must also change. Healthcare providers must relate differently to their clients, especially younger ones. More importantly, there must be changes in how sexual partners relate to each other. Prevention is the only long-term solution to controlling HIV/AIDS and, absent a vaccine, prevention in large measure remains a matter of individual behaviour and individual responsibility.

But there is more to the challenge at an individual level. There also is the challenge of activism. From Marilyn Martin we learn that artists can play a leading role as social activists. From Cal Volks we learn how for students at the University of Capetown activism is essential to raising awareness, to changing behaviour and to producing a political response to the pandemic. Another challenge for individuals is the challenge of hope. Xoliswa Sithole, a South African film-maker, has produced a documentary, *Shouting Silent*, about mothers, daughters and AIDS. It portrays individuals, no matter how desperate their situation, as not solely filled with despair. Some are, but for others, including some of the daughters who now are AIDS orphans, there is hope amidst the despair. Similarly, among the HIV-positive women who are part of the Memory Box project mentioned by Cal Volks, many think of the future. In essence, many say, 'Maybe I don't have that many years to live but I have next week, next month and maybe the week and month after that to live. I have children. I have family. I have friends. I have hope for their future.' Hope remains an individual challenge.

At the level of government the first challenge is to end the denial. We are focusing on South Africa but it could be Ghana. It could be China or India. It could be Russia. This pandemic is not over. It is going to be much more than an African phenomenon in the decades ahead. Ending the denial is the first challenge for government. Howard Phillips describes an all too familiar pattern of government response to epidemics: denial, fear and scapegoating. These responses will not resolve any epidemic. Ending the denial is a necessary first step but obviously it is far from a sufficient government response to HIV/AIDS.

Governments must mobilize resources, both human and financial, to address AIDS. Some countries have responded to HIV/AIDS better than others. In Africa, Senegal and Uganda have used public policy to reduce HIV prevalence rates. In a telling graphic, Kyle Kauffman compares the time trend in HIV infections in South Africa, Uganda and Senegal. In the early 1990s rates in South Africa and Senegal were virtually identical, with adult prevalence rates hovering in the low single digits. The Senegalese government responded, committing substantial resources and mounting an aggressive prevention programme. Today, adult prevalence rates in Senegal remain under 2 per cent, essentially the same as they were a decade ago. South Africa's government did not respond. Adult prevalence rates exploded and today are reported at close to 25 per cent. The challenge facing governments is apparent in these comparisons of national experiences.

But the challenge to mobilize resources is not a straightforward and technical matter. The underlying challenge is one of setting priorities and exercising political will. Virginia van der Vliet's paper makes clear the systemic nature of South Africa's political failure in addressing the pandemic. The Mbeki administration, rightly, is criticized for its actions and inactions in addressing HIV/AIDS. But the failure to respond has deeper political roots. The legacy of apartheid and the challenges of the democratic transition both played a role. The greatest weakness, perhaps, of Nelson Mandela's presidency was an unwillingness, as Virginia van der Vliet puts it, '[to] personally lead South Africa's AIDS crusade'. Today, Nelson Mandela is attempting to correct this mistake as he speaks out on HIV/AIDS. Virginia van der Vliet offers explanations for South Africa's historic lack of political will in confronting HIV/AIDS. But today, especially with the advance and maturation of the epidemic, these same explanations increasingly sound like excuses. Government must meet the challenge to act.

What is the challenge for the international community? The first is to be informed. Deborah Cotton, a medical doctor and an infectious disease specialist, describes infectious diseases as some of the world's greatest terrorists. They strike randomly. They strike the innocent. It is not clear what their objectives are. Deborah Cotton has said that the most devious terrorist mind could never conceive of a virus like AIDS – its stealth and the treachery it exacts on the human body. If the news on the HIV/AIDS pandemic was not bad enough news, it may be just the beginning. Deborah Cotton identifies a horde of other infectious diseases which are on the horizon which could be as horrific as AIDS.[2] If this is true, then it is essential that the rich nations keep these issues on the agenda.

In addition to being informed, the second challenge for the international community is to care. It is too easy for those of us living in the 'North' to forget about the pandemic. Most of us are not immediately affected. Few of us know people with HIV/AIDS. We probably have not lost colleagues, friends or family members to this disease. Attending AIDS funerals is not a regular part of our lives. Our challenge is to care and not to forget.

As Jeffrey and Sonia Sachs' work passionately argues, it is not enough for the international community to care and to keep HIV/AIDS on the agenda. The international community must also transfer some of its enormous wealth to this fight. Jeffrey Sachs estimates that 25 billion dollars a year could save eight million lives annually. We must meet this challenge not only because it is in our self-interest, but because it is our moral and humanitarian obligation.

Lessons: Diana Chapman Walsh

The contributors to this volume represent a range of disciplines, from anthropology, economics, political science and other social science perspectives, to education and the humanities. Before coming to Wellesley College as president, my own field was public health, an interdisciplinary enterprise that has as its central concerns the study and control of transmissible disease, the improvement of the physical and social environment in which disease takes root, and the organization, financing and delivery of interventions to prevent and treat illness and to promote and protect health. Through the course of history, and as disease patterns have evolved, the relative weight of these various concerns has shifted back and forth, but they are interrelated and have always been embedded in a concept of community life.

Progress in public health involves a constant interplay between the pursuit of the scientific origins of disease, on the one hand, and, on the other, the organization of political, economic, social and cultural arrangements necessary for effective preventive action and control. In his sweeping history of public health from the Greco-Roman era to the 1950s, George Rosen (1958) demonstrates how uneven progress has often been, how slow communities have been to take up collective responsibility for epidemic disease, how inadequate funding and administrative structures invariably are, and how dependent all progress has been on underlying ideologies about the balance of social and personal responsibility.

What we know now with utter clarity – even when we fail to act upon it – is that society itself produces preventable risks to health (Amick et al., 1995). All the investments in medical technology and research, and all the efforts to educate and mobilize individuals to take charge of their health, will always be inadequate if they fail to take account of a broader social context. The social construction of knowledge about health, subtle mechanisms of social control, and the differential distribution of resources and power are fundamental factors affecting the physical well-being of populations (Walsh et al., 1995). The AIDS pandemic in Africa illustrates this reality on a global scale.

Albert Camus ends his 1947 novel, *The Plague*, with a statement by his hero, Jean Tarrou, that sums up the struggle in which public health is always engaged: 'All I maintain is that on this earth there are pestilences and there are victims.' Tarrou concludes with resignation: 'and it is up to us so far as possible, not to join forces with the pestilences' (Camus, 1991, pp. 253–4).

The haunting message from Jeffrey and Sonia Sachs, who, like Tarrou, have been desperately trying to slow the spread of this new plague, is that in our indifference and our failure to act forcefully against HIV/AIDS, we 'rich nations' have in effect joined forces with the pestilences. This volume enters into the growing chorus of urgent warnings from many quarters that it is past time for the rich nations to throw their considerable weight against the pestilences that are spreading around the globe. The chapters in this volume point to five lessons we should bear in mind as we take up a challenge we must not ignore.

The first lesson is that we are all in this together. Our global interdependence is accelerating rapidly and with it our shared susceptibility to the spread of new contagion and to new environmental risks to health. Developments in travel, communications technology, media coverage, and the creation of world markets are moving capital, labour and cultural expression around the globe with unprecedented speed and mobility. No longer is it possible to conceive of erecting barriers to contain the spread of contagion or exposure to risk. Managing future epidemics is going to require a degree of global cooperation that has yet to be imagined, much less initiated.

When the modern public health movement took root in mid-nineteenth-century Europe, the reformers were able to impress upon the elites that the investment in sanitary improvements would benefit the society at large. This argument evolved in three major strands, each more practical or instrumental than purely humanitarian. First, it became evident that, as a British Poor Law Commission concluded in 1838, 'the expenditures necessary to the adoption and maintenance of measures of prevention would ultimately amount to less than the cost of the disease now constantly engendered' (Rosen, 1958, p. 211). Allowing infectious disease to spread and decimate the working poor, in short, would stall the industrial revolution and create unacceptable economic losses for the whole community. Second, as cholera spread in the 1830s in the squalid conditions of the crowded factory towns, it became evident that the disease was not going to be contained within the lower classes. 'Without being his brother's keeper, anyone who valued his life felt it eminently desirable not to have virulent diseases and the conditions that fostered them too close at hand' (Rosen, 1958, p. 208). Third, the reformers held out 'the specter of a proletarian uprising, casting an ominous shadow on the middle class mind [which] acted as a persuasive argument toward some degree of reform' (Rosen, 1958, p. 219).

This last point is captured chillingly in a powerful Langston Hughes poem that Xoliswa Sithole cites as partial inspiration for *Shouting Silent*, her heartbreaking film on the devastating impact of HIV/AIDS on the children of South Africa. The Hughes poem (Hughes, 1951, p. 75), written well before the advent of AIDS, reminds us of the high cost of our self-absorption and indifference to the suffering of others that we fool ourselves into believing we can safely ignore.

> What happens to a dream deferred?
> Does it dry up
> Like a raisin in the sun?
> Or fester like a sore –
> And then run?
> Does it stink like rotten meat?
> Or crust and sugar over –
> like a syrupy sweet?
> Maybe it just sags
> like a heavy load.
> Or does it explode?

We are all in this life together, that is lesson one.

The second lesson in this collection, paradoxically, is that we are not all in this together, not in the simplistic sense that our interests and sensibilities are or can ever be in full synchrony. If we delude ourselves into thinking that globalization will eventually produce a boundary-less and homogeneous world community, we will not be successful in slowing the spread of HIV/AIDS. The collaboration and cooperation that will be needed to address the pandemic will have to be built on an appreciation of differences: profound and fundamental differences in health-related beliefs and practices, in the history of economic and social development, in the structures of political systems and their responsiveness to local community needs.

The third lesson is that uncertainty is inescapable. As a conscious, and admirable, strategy to hold the rich countries to account for our unwillingness to look this epidemic squarely in the eye, Jeffrey Sachs deliberately reduces the problem to its simplest terms – a lack of money. Tens of millions of people are too poor to stay alive. Sachs knows that complexity is often our excuse for leaving problems to the experts and looking the other way. This tendency was brought out in a thoughtful essay, 'An Agenda for the 21st Century' (Kidder, 1989), in which the *Christian Science Monitor*'s Rushworth M. Kidder interviewed twenty-two thought leaders about challenges they saw for the new century. The late Norman Cousins, noted author and editor, listed four problems that require a collective response (the proliferation of weapons of mass destruction, environmental degradation, world hunger and world poverty), and added that these are not new problems but that 'they exist nowadays, in a "form so heightened that people don't want to think about them". The No. 1 problem in the world is not the presence of all this destructive weaponry. That's the No. 2 problem. The No. 1 problem is the inability to recognize the No. 2 problem' (Kidder, 1989, p. 39). And so it is with AIDS.

Jeffrey Sachs tells us that we must not look away, that there are things we can do, that we face a fairly simple choice. We can attack this epidemic with resources that can be assembled and that can have an impact or we can look the other way and allow the epidemic to win. As simple as that choice is, we know that there are not and will not be simple answers. The idea that we are going to find *solutions* is itself misleading. In this sense the AIDS crisis resembles global terrorism. A bitter lesson Americans had to learn after the attacks on 11 September 2001, and a lesson we are still learning, is that we are not going to root out terrorism and destroy it permanently, as much as we might wish that were a possibility. There is no turning the clock back. Instead, we are going to have to find a way to live with terrorism without allowing it to destroy our humanity and the values that make life worth living, just as people with AIDS are learning to live with their disease when they have access to basic life-saving medications.

The AIDS epidemic, like global terrorism, means that those of us who were born in the rich nations have been much less safe than we imagined we were. We were living in a bubble. Nothing that we do is going to rid the world of these threats, not the best of intelligence, not the best of scientific research, not the best international cooperation or cultural understanding. We talk about mobilizing against AIDS, as though preparing for a war but it is no more a winnable war than is the war on drugs or the war on cancer. Neither of these 'wars' is going to be won or lost once and for all any more than a war against epidemic disease will be won. We can discover vaccines that are effective against specific pathogens, but others will emerge because the health of populations is embedded in social practices that constantly change. There was a time not so long ago when the belief was taking root that infectious diseases were largely under control because of the growing therapeutic effectiveness of antibiotic agents. And yet during the 'antibiotic era' of the past seventy years 'pathogenic bacteria have developed relentlessly with clinically significant resistances to one class of antibiotic after another' (Walsh, 2003). It is hubris to think that we can win a war against uncertainty, illness and danger.

The fourth important lesson is that time is of the essence – a message that virtually every contributor to this volume emphasizes. In just a decade AIDS progressed in South Africa from a tragic illness affecting relatively few people to an epidemic of historic proportions. Howard Phillips draws an important distinction between this epidemic and South Africa's experience with the Spanish influenza in 1918, a six-week rampage. HIV/AIDS has moved much slower than that, creating the illusion of more time to mount a response. But the rapidity with which this pandemic has established itself in South Africa cries out for immediate action. There is not a moment to waste.

The fifth and final lesson is that this epidemic demands of each one of us that we focus on what truly matters, on what our responsibilities are as citizens of a world community. The epidemic confronts us with our mortality and that awareness can be a stimulus to ask ourselves fundamental questions about the ultimate meaning of our lives. There is no more powerful teacher about what matters than facing death. Just as individuals who learn that they have the AIDS virus have no choice but to re-examine and reorder their personal priorities, societies facing a world pandemic will ultimately have to come to terms with the fragility of human life. The voices from South Africa are summoning the rest of the world to wake up from our state of somnolence, to re-examine our priorities and to think afresh about what it means to live a healthy life in the broadest possible sense.

Notes

1 The estimate of over 2000 new infections per day is based on the ASSA2000 AIDS and Demographic model of the Actuarial Society of South Africa (2003). The South African estimate compares to a worldwide estimates of 14,000 people – 12,000 adults and 2000 children – becoming infected with HIV every day (Lamptey et al., 2002, p. 3).
2 From remarks made by Deborah Cotton at a presentation at Wellesley College, 11 April 2002.

References

Actuarial Society of South Africa (2003), http://www.assa.org.za/downloads/aids/summarystats.htm#NATIONAL.
Amick, B., Levine, S., Tarlov, A. and Walsh, D. (eds) (1995), *Society and Health* (New York: Oxford University Press).

Camus, A. (1991), *The Plague*, translated by Stuart Gilbert (New York: Vintage International Edition, Random House).

Hughes, L. (1951), *Montage of a Dream Deferred* (New York: Holt).

Kidder, R. (1989), *An Agenda for the 21st Century* (Cambridge: MIT Press).

Lamptey, P., Wigley, M., Carr, D. and Collymore, Y. (2002), 'Facing the HIV/AIDS Pandemic', Population Reference Bureau, *Population Bulletin*, 57 (3).

Rosen, G. (1958), *A History of Public Health* (New York: MD Publications).

Walsh, C. (2003), *Antibiotics: Actions, Origins, Resistance* (Washington, DC: ASM Press).

Walsh, D., Sorenson, G. and Leonard, L. (1995), 'Gender, Health, and Cigarette Smoking', in Amick, B., Levine, S., Tarlov, A. and Walsh, D. (eds), *Society and Health* (New York: Oxford University Press).

Index

185